Essays in INTERPERSONAL DYNAMICS

The Dorsey Series in Psychology

Consulting Editor   WENDELL E. JEFFREY

University of California, Los Angeles

Essays in
INTERPERSONAL
DYNAMICS

WARREN BENNIS
Author, lecturer, and
immediate past President, University of Cincinnati

JOHN VAN MAANEN
Massachusetts Institute of Technology

EDGAR H. SCHEIN
Massachusetts Institute of Technology

FRED I. STEELE
Development Research Associates

1979

THE DORSEY PRESS   Homewood, Illinois   60430
IRWIN-DORSEY LIMITED   Georgetown, Ontario   L7G 4B3

ISBN 0-256-02231-3
Library of Congress Catalog Card No. 78–70011

Printed in the United States of America

1 2 3 4 5 6 7 8 9 0 ML 6 5 4 3 2 1 0 9

Preface

Fifteen years ago the book entitled *Interpersonal Dynamics* appeared. During the decade and a half since, two revisions came out, in 1968 and 1973. In planning this new textbook we decided that, despite our satisfaction and our readers' apparent satisfaction with the other three volumes, it was high time to undertake a more thorough evaluation of these preceding volumes than we ever had and to see what changes suggested themselves as a result of our critical review.

We then looked at the patterns and themes (some of them not altogether visible at the time of their publication) of the three previous editions. We analyzed whether our format of a long, theoretical essay followed by a section of readings made the best sense. We questioned our criteria for the selection of readings, after which we examined the readings to see if they conformed to those criteria. We explored what might have been "neglected variables" or overlooked but important aspects of interpersonal relations. We attempted to survey new and fresh developments that might be included in this book. We weighed the assumptions and the "decision rules" that guided us in putting together the previous three volumes. We questioned the principles we had used to organize them. And we concluded with a certain amount of "derring-do" that both pleased and scared us to suspend disbelief, and even if we *had* achieved something important in the past, not to worry if we came up with a new textbook that had virtually no correspondence between it and its three ancestors.

No one ever said that self-examination is any guarantee of objectivity; nor would we. And, rest assured, dear reader, there are many correspondences and continuities between this and our earlier editions. At the same time, our review has led by all accounts, to the most significant changes in format and substance that we've ever considered, let alone implemented. Time and reader feedback, alone, will tell us how successful we've been in creating a more useful introduction to this complex and fascinating field.

It is still clear, however, that even here we have barely scratched the surface of this "strange territory" we call interpersonal dynamics. Just as one swallow does not make a summer, one book of essays does not make a "field," or even the frontier of one.

To some extent, though, we hope we succeed in inching forward in our pursuit of the boundaries, strategic variables, and substance of *interpersonal dynamics*. And, more importantly, we hope we succeed in illuminating and creating better understandings of *your life in others*.

January 1979   **Warren Bennis**
                                                                 Aspen, Colorado

Contents

Introduction

by JOHN VAN MAANEN and WARREN BENNIS

Our experience with others represents the domain of interpersonal dynamics. It is here in the buzzing, blooming social realm of our lives that our sense of selfhood, our sense of good and evil, and, more generally, our patterns of thought and action are shaped, maintained, and altered. It is in this sphere too that the perennial problems of human existence—like the meaning of life and death, misery and happiness, fortune and misfortune—are continually confronted. Our experience with others not only reflects such historical and existential themes, but it creates and recreates them for us throughout our lifetimes. Let us look more closely at this deceptively simple point, for it is a central one in this book.

Imagine, for example, we have in our possession some sort of time machine that allows us to travel backward for centuries or even eons. Undertaking such a journey to partake in conversation with the natives of whatever region of time we decide to enter would surely reveal some very special truths to us about the nature of our so-called modern world. We would, no doubt, discover that when it came to matters such as space flight, world geography, or the neutron bomb, the natives would be predictably and understandably behind in their knowledge of such things. But, when our dialogue turned to consider such things as the nature of friendship, authority, success, tragedy, or moral rights and wrongs, we would discover that speaking to the natives was essentially no different from speaking with our contemporaries. These most pressing yet altogether human concerns have no final solutions and they will always present a challenge to our thinking and feeling. In short, we are no more or less preoccupied with seeking answers to these existential problems than were our ancestors. And, if we were to suspend our own beliefs for a moment, we would also discover that our explanations for these riddles are no more rational than those of our long-since-departed counterparts, for there are no criteria upon which rationality in these matters can comfortably rest.

As was true in times past, however, our journey would allow us to see that we do not face these existential problems alone. For most of us, the interpersonal circles of which we are a part help us develop explanations for the riddles of existence, sharpen our understandings of human strivings, and, when necessary, provide us with remedies to follow when our world seems to go astray. Like our ancestors, in place of the unknowable we substitute a belief in some symbolic but shared universe within which we can feel reasonably at home. That this universe arises from and is changed by interpersonal relationships is perhaps the single most important idea we wish to get across to the readers of this book.

THE PROBLEMATIC PERSPECTIVE

We argue throughout the following chapters that feelings such as love, hate, honor, envy, pride, anger, elation, warmth, shame, and sorrow are fundamental, not peripheral, to the understanding of interpersonal dynamics. As we all seem to know rather matter of factly, our lives and our dreams are unavoidably connected to these complex feelings which are sometimes conflicting, often fleeting, and always changing. This argument is so obvious, so patently true, that the reader may find it somewhat ridiculous that we have even bothered to make a point of it here. But, we hope too that the reader will also appreciate and recognize how ridiculous it has been for social scientists, in all of their many studies of social life, to have rarely mentioned this human truth except to sweep it under the proverbial rug as a fact of life perhaps too personal to be of generalized value, or as a fact of life too unsuited for study in the scientific manner.

As the materials presented in this book document, we take such reasoning to be false. Social scientists cannot, by decree, neatly and conveniently amputate human feelings from the study of social life. They are simply too omnipresent, too crucial for the student of human affairs to sidestep. It is, of course, far easier to merely state this than it is to correct for such oversight since there are several very real and present epistemological dilemmas to be confronted when trying to understand interpersonal dynamics as they occur in everyday life. While we have hardly "solved" these dilemmas here, we have in the course of putting together this volume come to at least better understand them. In particular, we have faced five rather central, interrelated, and largely unavoidable problems in coming to terms with our subject matter.

First, there is the danger that in the process of examining and communicating an understanding of interpersonal relations, an analyst will distort, if not mutilate beyond recognition, the object of his or her concern. Can friendship or love, for example, be understood by use of a seven-point scale? Can people be put in a laboratory and then have the presumed elements of their relationship systematically varied by a technician in order that a better understanding of interpersonal dealings will eventually emerge? We think not, for interpersonal relationships are natural phenomena, they are inherently symbolic and dramatic affairs and their analysis cannot be conducted by a computer or a technician. While there is much that a computer or a technician can do, neither can calculate for us the significance or meaning of a relationship for the people that comprise it. We have tried therefore to emphasize the intangible or qualitative aspects of interpersonal dynamics in this volume and, as such, concentrate far more upon the various forms and functions of interpersonal relationships than upon their frequencies and distributions.

Second, there is the problem that what is crucial to interpersonal dynamics may well be so rooted in our common experiences and so fundamental a part of our everyday lives that we cannot make it explicit. If, for example, some of the functions served by interpersonal relationships are largely unintended or unconscious, they will obviously be quite difficult to identify and analyze. As the old proverb goes: "It is hardly a fish that can discover water." We are also presented here with something of a paradox because the very concepts and categories we employ in our analysis are also a part of the interpersonal domain we are trying to describe. Like all others who have also approached this problem, we have no real solutions. We have only a faith in the results of our common and lengthy endeavors to capture and record some of the elusive qualities of interpersonal dynamics. Thus, in this matter, the reader must ultimately be the judge as to whether or not our treatment of the topic justifies our faith.

Third, and perhaps more troubling, is the fact that even if we are able to at least partially resolve the above problems, an element of nihilism unavoidably creeps into the picture. Consider the organizing theme of this book: *The functions of interpersonal relationships.* If these functions are to continue to be accomplished routinely in our day-to-day lives, they must also remain largely taken for granted by people since once these functions (and the many forms they take) become known, explicit, and subject to discourse, they may well begin to lose a good deal of their efficacy. For example, when we gather on a Sunday to pray as members of a church congregation, we do not say: "Let us pray in order to enhance the moral distinctiveness of our religious community" or "Let us pray in order to consolidate the moral bonds that unite us." Certainly our motives for prayer are likely to be mixed, varied, individual, and most often will have little to do with the functions served by prayer for a group or other collective unit as revealed by an examination of interpersonal behavior. This is perhaps one good reason why students of social life are often viewed with suspicion and why they are sometimes seen as dangerous to an existing order. Yet, against this nihilistic danger, we would argue that interpersonal dynamics are manipulated as often as not by powerful individuals and groups within a society for their own benefit, and unless we begin to comprehend the various functions served by the diverse forms of interpersonal dynamics, we run the risk of being exploited by others without our knowledge or consent. It is the case too that by making salient some of the forms and functions of interpersonal dynamics, the powerful can even further their hold over the powerless. This is, of course, a very general problem and concerns the uses of virtually any science, natural or social. Yet, despite our concern and our hope that a deeper understanding of interpersonal dynamics will, in the end, help us all out, these dangers remain, and the discriminating reader cannot fail to notice their presence lurking in the background of virtually every essay in this book.

Fourth, examining interpersonal dynamics inevitably points to the impossibility of separating the knowing subject from the objects of knowing. This is a crucial issue, for we believe it axiomatic that in the social world the subject and object are highly interdependent, and the "truth" of any study in this sphere depends in part upon some form of introspection on the part of the analyst. Of course, the mere mention of introspection as a basis of knowledge suggests that solipsism is a possible outcome. While, in the coming essays, we present some reasoned arguments against the fear that introspection always leads to solipsism, we can also argue here that our own year-long experience at putting this volume together itself offers some tangible evidence to partially reduce this fear. Consider the fact that the four authors of this book represent a fairly wide range of social backgrounds and past experiences, a broad distribution of ages, a diversity of political attachments and loyalties, and a variety of other differences. Some of us are good friends, others of us have barely met. Importantly, we have sometimes disagreed on what we were doing or on how we were doing it, and there have been some very real feelings involved in these disputes. These matters are not incidental to the point here, for it is also visibly apparent that we were able somehow to learn from our differences and to put them to work in completing our joint project. Thus, when it is suggested that introspection always deteriorates into solipsism, we must reject this point of view, for our own experience at putting forth this book denies the inevitability of such a process. Though it is perhaps true that all thought is essentially introspective, it is not the case that all thought must necessarily remain at that level. Again, as our own efforts tell us, we have been able to share with and to learn from one another so that our individual thoughts and feelings have been in some ways collectively and productively fused.

Fifth and finally, there is the danger that by emphasizing as we do in this book the creative ways in which people handle their interpersonal relationships, we would also exaggerate the extent to which people are free from social constraint. While we firmly believe that internally we all develop an autonomous self that more or less acts upon the world, we also just as firmly believe that we live within a social and cultural reality which confronts us externally. Consider, for example, marriage. Most of us are quite convinced that we are free to choose our partner in marriage and that we marry for love. To a large extent, such beliefs are entirely justified because we certainly seem to behave in just this fashion. But it is also true that we nearly always wind up married to our social equals. This does not imply of course that we are all dwarfed by a massive reality that is both out of sight and out of mind. It does imply however that our relationships with others are dialectic ones and that as students of interpersonal dynamics we must be continually watchful lest we overdetermine certain sources of human action.

By listing these five problems, we have tried very briefly to depict some of the pervasive epistemic difficulties we have faced in developing the perspective on interpersonal dynamics that is laid out in this book. These problems stem from the very nature of our reflexive subject matter and, therefore, do not yield to easy definitional solutions. In the final analysis these problems are actually dilemmas that can be approached but not solved, for there is no verifiably correct method to examine interpersonal dynamics. What we have attempted to do in this book then, is to properly respect the intractable way in which we all struggle to achieve something of a personal identity in the world and yet still respond to those shared and ever-present problems of our life with others.

Let us now return for a moment to where we began and again consider those questions that surround the human condition, for it can be argued that it is the very "irresolvable-ness" of these questions that literally forces us to forge links with others. Modern people, no less than ancient people, need answers to the questions surrounding the meaning of life and death, fortune and misfortune, misery and happiness. As a case in point, it is not merely a hollow ritual when the cantor at a Jewish burial ceremony dramatically pauses before the open grave and poses the question: "From where did you come and where are you going?" These are crucial matters indeed, and without some available answers at hand most of us would be lost, unable to find our bearings in the world, and perhaps overcome with feelings of fear and foreboding. Yet, as we shall demonstrate in this book, the answers we discover to such problems are necessarily interpersonal constructions which are marked by their open-endedness, their partial rationality, and their embeddedness within the social circles which espouse them. From this standpoint, there is absolutely no evidence that the advance of science or enlightenment has reduced or even changed the role interpersonal dynamics plays upon our coming to know the world. People come to terms with the basic but irresolvable facts of their existence only by use of the interpersonal pathways they discover to share their thoughts and feelings with others. And, as we argue in the essays to follow, how such sharing takes place is ultimately what interpersonal dynamics are all about.

THE APPROACH

As mentioned in the Preface, this book has a history—a fifteen-year, three-edition history to be exact. This history and the approach to understanding interpersonal relations that it embodies have not been abandoned in this edition. We have taken this opportunity to deepen our approach by including new material as well as judiciously editing, culling, and deleting old material. It is, however, not a revisionist textbook in any sense. Perhaps the most convenient way of making this point and of also introducing our approach to interpersonal dynamics is to note, first, what we have preserved from the previous editions in this book—the constants, so to speak—and what we have decided to change.

The Constants

1. Our value commitments have undergone virtually no change. The same desire to publish a book of essays on that class of human problems caused by incompetent interpersonal relations remains—as do, unfortunately, the problems. In the 1963 edition, we wrote

> When it comes to human problems, we have been notoriously incompetent. One would think, judging from the report of history, that we simply cannot progress; that unlike knowledge about physical phenomena, human knowledge is not cumulative, that parents cannot teach their children nor learn from their own parents. On the very day we are writing this preface, railroads threaten a national strike, war simmers in Viet Nam, and racial tensions imperil the schools. Last year's newspapers would have carried almost identical news, with other place-names.

Only the place-names change it seems, and not all of them. In the 1973 edition, Northern Ireland was cited as a point of explosive conflict and it remains so today. Today, the morning's papers carry news about severe problems in southern Africa, residual bitterness from the coal strike, tax revolts, and no especial relief from the racial tensions that continue to plague this country's schools.

We are still immobilized by conflict, the "little murders" inflicted routinely on people, the erosion of decency and unity, both of which are best caught lighting the world's skies in the drama of nation-state warfare. But, also, we are immobilized by equally destructive (though less visible) conflict at every level of human intercourse: in small groups, in marriages, in friendships, between lovers and siblings, between teachers and students, between workers and bosses. And, unless the protagonists are famous enough to be reported in gossip columns or *People* magazine, the tensions go unnoticed, only to be registered anonymously in the divorce rates, homicides, gang wars, or often in the more banal way "civilized" people cope with their existential groaning: poison pen letters, unproductive relationships, battered women and children, prejudices, practical "jokes," destructive fantasies, unstable careers, ulcerative colitis, "frayed" nerves, weekend bashes at a health farm, tennis clinic, or "growth" center, tranquilizers, sleeping pills, and, most of all, a general feeling that life wasn't supposed to be this way, that there just must be something better.

So while the place-names have changed and we still, as citizens, express our moral outrage, we feel, as scientists, that it is even more obligatory now to explore and illuminate the class of problems that we identified in 1963. We believe that the truth behind a statement in the Preface to the first edition holds more weight today than ever before: "The unusual challenge lies in the fact that we do not practice as much as we know, and do not know as much as we could."

Fifteen years ago we believed—again, more so today—that if we can help to deepen the understanding of human relationships, then it might be possible to improve not only their quality, but that progress, even if a sliver, would have a secondary effect on institutional and possibly societal arrangements.

Another value in practice was an intellectual *and* academic one. To paraphrase Pope, we were committed to the tenet that the proper study of man is man-in-relation-to-man. Pope's unwitting sexist phrasing should not divert us (at least for now). Our 15-year-old goal was to make the idea of the scientific study of interpersonal relations more central to the conventional paradigm of social psychology. Perhaps, about this goal, we can feel some solid sense of achievement, though not complete.

While progress has been made on the academic front, the same cannot be said about our most pragmatic goal: the promotion of better interpersonal relations.

Life is with people, we said 15 years ago, and we can repeat that felicious phrase with the same amounts of enthusiasm and apprehension today. We listen to the following advice more closely now as a basis for this volume:

> Now listen carefully. You in others—this is what you are, this is what your consciousness has breathed, and lived on, and enjoyed throughout your life, your soul, your immortality—your life in others."

This brief excerpt from Boris Pasternak's *Dr. Zhivago* still manages to integrate our moral, scientific, and pragmatic concerns.

2. Another constant has to do with the users of this book. It's difficult to detect any significant differences between our 1963 version and the present one in this regard. We have always tried to reach a broad audience

of readers: the psychology major, graduate and undergraduate, the non-major with a subsidiary interest in human problems, the student of a profession who, like it or not, needs far more interpersonal awareness and competence than presently seems to be possessed by practitioners of virtually any profession—for their clients' sakes if for no other reason. We still put a claim on these publics and we certainly want not to neglect the general, interested layperson. In fact, the more of the latter who come into contact with this book, the better. We feel an obligation to communicate to a general public, an obligation we take even more seriously with this volume. And, finally, we believe that this book has much utility for the scholar, professor, and advanced student in the social sciences.

Since the first edition, our hopes have largely been confirmed. The book *has* been used by a wide range of readers and for diverse purposes: as a text or ancilliary text, for courses in personality, interpersonal theory, and introductory social psychology; as a supplemental reading in the broad area of human relations; and for the education of the professions: social work, business, medicine, nursing, education, and engineering. It seems as if only schools of law and journalism have shown no demonstrable interest, a comment perhaps on those two fields about which the less said, the better.

3. Not only have our purposes and readership remained constant, so have our views of the academic status of interpersonal dynamics. Consequently, our approach to it has remained virtually unaltered. The field as we saw it in 1963, 1968, 1973, and today can still be characterized as a "strange field": loosely organized, interdisciplinary, and interstitial, that is, tangent to or on the frontier of the behavioral sciences. It is a field without fixed boundaries or stable definitions. An analogy may help to bring it into better focus. We can compare it to a "foreign" territory, claimed by all because of its strategic importance, explored by only a few adventurers, and understood fully by none. It is not a "no-man's" land, however. It is everyman's land. And this means that long before social scientists invaded this domain, the poets, troubadours, essayists, lyricists, and novelists were tilling its rich soil. In fact, the "humanists" have long claimed this territory for their own and have looked askance at the social scientists, referring to them as poachers or *arrivistes,* depending on their mood and style.

Those social scientists who do forage around in these uncharted lands not only receive abuse at the hands of the humanists, but also from their colleagues. Quite often, they will be harshly attacked for losing their "scientific" bent; others, more subtly, say that they are "too dense" or, that they create a private language, bordering on neologism. Even if their work is recognized, they are considered, at best, soldiers of fortune who should return to the fold; at worst, fugitives.

Our analogy helps to brings into focus a number of points we can make about the current status of research and theory in the field of interpersonal dynamics.

A. There is as yet no single, comprehensive theory of interpersonal relations. Sociology, social psychology, and psychiatry have offered important insights to the understanding of its phenomena, but the area has resisted successful theoretical comprehension.

B. Because it is a complex and subtle field, it tends to be treated in a discursive, exploratory way. This is not as true now as it was 15 years ago, but the generalization is still valid nevertheless.

C. The third thing implied in our analogy is that despite its relevance to the behavioral sciences, it has been treated only tangentially in those fields. In social psychology, for example, we would expect it to play a fundamental role. This does not seem to be the case. Social psychologists have been more interested in the group or in the individual than in interpersonal relationships. The field of psychiatry also has not yielded the expected results with respect to interpersonal theory. It has been dominated by a neurobiophysiological philosophy of people, a reliance on the instincts, and a silence regarding people's interactional behavior. Anthropology and sociology fare no better, though a branch of sociology, known as the "symbolic interaction" school, has made crucial contributions to interpersonal theory. More about this later on. In summary, *the scientific study of interpersonal relations still lags behind other, less crucial areas of social research.*

D. Fourth, we can say that where disciplines *have* contributed to the understanding of interpersonal relations, where they have enriched its theoretical or research base, they have been "marginal" or *avant garde* or perhaps sturdy iconoclasts. This is rather a blunt statement, one which undoubtedly requires qualification. Nevertheless, as we examined the main theoretical influences that shaped our own interests, it appeared to be true.

E. In the earlier essays of this volume, we relied on four major theoretical strands which, we wrote, "shaped our thinking, have dominated this book, and appear to provide the basic structure of the field of interpersonal relations." We summarized these influences as (1) symbolic interactionism, (2) interpersonal theory, (3) object relations, and (4) existentialism.

While all of these influences remain, some have emerged as more dominant and others as less so. In addition, another theoretical emphasis, ignored for the most part in the previous books, takes, along with symbolic interactionism, a more dominant role in this book.

All of which signals us to turn to the "flip side" of continuity.

The Changes

1. *Theoretical Influences.* Without question, the work of the symbolic interactionists remains a pervasive influence. And, though the background comes out of the pioneer work of Mead, Baldwin, Cooley, James, and Dewey, we find that the work of sociologist Erving Goffman has become

one of the most dominant threads in the still dense and emerging tapestry of symbolic interactionist theory.

Similarly, psychoanalytic theory, existentialism, Sullivanian theory, "object relations," and "ego psychology," while all alive and well, resemble the "abominable snowman" in this edition: the foottracks are everywhere to be seen, but the beast is nowhere to be found. In other words, the footnotes may have disappeared but the influences continue.

While we're on the topic of theoretical influences, it is fair to say that we have become more eclectic, a tendency which probably parallels the development of the field of interpersonal dynamics. Can we call Carl Rogers an existentialist? Certainly, but he's far more than that. How about Rollo May or Abraham Maslow or virtually every other seminal thinker in the field? The answer: Certainly, but mere categorizing can and has become a dangerous exercise of imprisoning theoretical contributors and their contributions in absurd ways which only serves to block a view of reality, not illuminate it.

The one major theoretical addition—and a long overdue one at that—is introduced by John Van Maanen. In his two essays, he relies extensively upon phenomenological thought. This approach gives the volume an epistemological and philosophical framework heretofore absent and so pivotal if progress toward the development of a more integrated framework for the scientific study of interpersonal dynamics is to be made.

2. Mentioning Van Maanen's essays and our increased emphasis on a phenomenological approach brings us to what has to be the most dramatic, though not necessarily the most important, single change: our new format. Users of previous editions will notice that this volume (a) contains essays only and no readings; (b) is paperback, not cloth; and (c) includes a new author while excluding an original contributor. We consider each of these three changes now.

a. and b. For some time now, many of our readers have urged us to consider two separate books, that the essays should stand by themselves in a single volume and that the same would hold true for the readings. After long deliberations among ourselves as well as discussions with our publishers, we decided to try it. This book, therefore, contains only essays. And, in order to make the book even more available, we suggested and the publisher agreed to publish it in paperback.

We think this format makes more sense than continuing in the old way. We hope you do too. We know its going to be more economical for you— and undoubtedly, more convenient. We hope it succeeds as well in its central educational mission.

c. John Van Maanen has taken the bulk of the responsibility and leadership for this volume. His two essays bring to bear on our thinking the newest and most integrative framework we've been able to establish to date. This is no acknowledgment; it is a fact from which we have all profited. David Berlew has been unable to contribute to this volume which is why his name isn't among those listed as authors.

3. The organization of these essays follows almost exactly the organizing framework used for our previous three volumes. We decided that Van Maanen's work, consisting of the following two chapters, provides the single best intellectual-theoretical armature—a complicated and demanding *opening* to the field of interpersonal dynamics—we could possibly come up with. His work is a natural beginning, compatible with as well as augmenting the original design of the book.

The rest of the essays fall into place as responses to the elemental question: Why do people come together? Or: Why do people engage in and involve others in interpersonal relationships? This question—the basis of our organizing principle—was grounded on the assumption that all interpersonal relationships are oriented toward some primary goal, some *raison d'etre* whose presence is necessary for the relationship to exist and whose absence would deter its existence or seriously undermine it. Obviously, a relationship exists for more than one purpose, but we assume, for clarity's sake as well as theoretical guidance, a primary and salient reason for its formation.

Our essays flow from this *raison d'etre*. The first two, again, are Van Maanen's theoretical essay—"On the Understanding of Interpersonal Relations" (Chapter 2) and "The Self, the Situation, and the Rules of Interpersonal Relations" (Chapter 3). Both chapters include, incidentally, a concern for the material discussed by David Berlew in earlier editions that dealt with interpersonal aspects of "self-confirmation"—those activities that help a person define (or, at least, gain some knowledge of) "Who am I?," "Who are we?," and "What is that?"

Chapter 4 is entitled "Emotional Expressions in Interpersonal Relationships." It deals with the relationship that is formed for the purpose of fulfilling *itself*, such as love, marriage, or friendship. The main transaction in the relationship is "feelings." It deals with the expressive-emotional aspects of interaction and with love, hate, ambivalence, and alienation.

Chapter 5 is entitled "Personal Change through Interpersonal Relationships." It deals with relationships that are formed for the purpose of *change* or *influence*, that is, relationships where one or both parties come together to create a change in each other or the relationship. The change may entail anything from acquiring new behaviors to personal growth; the change may be planned and institutionalized or spontaneous. This is a broad topic, encompassing many theoretical positions and many types of change. It covers, for example, such diverse matters as psychotherapy and "brainwashing," seduction and persuasion, indoctrination and socialization. The antecedents and consequences of interpersonal change and the processes which guide them are all topics treated in this chapter written by Edgar H. Schein.

Chapter 6 is entitled "The Instrumental Relationship." It covers those relationships that are formed in order to produce or create some goal or task, outside of the relationship itself, such as a conductor and his or her violin section, a boss and his or her workers, two collaborators on a research project. These are all examples of an instrumental relationship. How the nature and quality of the interpersonal relationship affect and relate to the task is the central concern of this chapter written by Fred I. Steele.

To express feelings, to establish social realities—to confirm, to change and influence, and to work and create are the main reasons for inter-personal relationships. These four primary factors provide the organizing structure and the content for the first five chapters.

Chapter 7 is entitled "Towards Better Interpersonal Relationships." Like Chapter 4, it is written by Warren Bennis. This chapter tries to make explicit the values, ideals, and ethics of the preceding sections. In addition, this chapter attempts two other things: the creation of an ideal interpersonal relationship based on normative criteria. Given that ideal, certain social and personal conditions as well as competences necessary to realize that ideal state are proposed. In short, Chapter 7 is concerned with a vision of what an ideal human relationship would be like and the most effective ways to approach that state.

We have tried to show our practical concern in Chapter 7 by focusing exclusively on *improving* interpersonal relationships. But action, alas, does not flow ineluctably from diagnosis. As Aristotle said over two thousand years ago: "In practical matters the end is not mere speculative knowledge of what is to be done, but rather the doing of it. It is not enough to know about Virtue, then, but we must endeavor to possess it, and to use it, or to take any other steps that may make us good."

The knowledge available in this book may indeed sound like "eternal verities," too abstract, too remote from an experiential basis for either emotional resonance or guides to action. In any case, the practical steps that "make us good," to use Aristotle's words, are ultimately up to the reader. We can only suggest some ideas, some truths, and some possible options that may be helpful.

On the Understanding of Interpersonal Relations[1]

by JOHN VAN MAANEN

*If ideas disappoint me, give me no pleasure, it is because
I offer them my approval too easily, seeing how they
solicit it, are only made for that. Ideas seek my approval,
demand it, and it is only too easy for me to offer it; this
offering, this consent, produces no pleasure in me but
rather a kind of queasiness, a nausea. On the other hand,
objects, landscapes, events, individuals of the external
world give me much pleasure. They win my trust. For
the simple reason that they don't need it. Their concrete
presence and evidence, their density, their three
dimensions, their palpable undeniable aspect, their
existence—much more certain than my own, their way of
implying: "This doesn't get invented (it gets discovered)";
their way of expressing: "This is beautiful because I
wouldn't have invented it, I couldn't have"—all this is
my sole justification for existence, or more precisely,* my
pretext; *and* the variety of things is what really constructs
me. *What I mean is this: their variety constructs me,
permits me to exist even in silence, like the locus around
which they exist. But in relation to only one of these
things, with regard to each one in particular,* if I consider
no more than one, *I disappear; it annihilates me. And
if it is only my pretext, my justification for existence, if
indeed I must exist, if my existence begins with it, then
that will only be, can only be, through some creation
of mine about it.*

FRANCIS PONGE, *The Voice of Things* (1972)

---

[1] This chapter was written specifically for this volume.

I. INTRODUCTION

The Phenomenological Mandate

This essay introduces several ideas fundamental to understanding how we attempt and most often succeed in making sense of the world around us. Yet, as prose poet Francis Ponge rather poignantly suggests, ideas in and of themselves can lead to a sort of nausea, since the truth certain ideas lay claim to can always be overturned by new and contradictory ideas. Like the twin notions of understanding and knowledge, ideas cannot be directly observed. They have no essential properties, no acquired capital, no solid ground upon which their figure stands out. In a sense, ideas remain forever like the waves on an ocean, always in motion and flux. Indeed, in the so-called modern world, many ideas seem so unsettled that there often appears to be nothing at all we can count on including, at the abyss, no ultimate truth to rely upon for an explanation of the whys and hows of our lives.

Is there any way out of such an ambiguous existence? Certainly on a day-to-day basis most of us do not directly confront such an existential nightmare. When we look around, we see people doing things, we see creatures acting with what seems to be a sublime intelligence, and we see objects of both natural and unnatural splendor. Such worldly subjects of our glances exist because we exist, because through some creation on our part, we are able to render the things of the world meaningful beyond their mere physical functioning. In short, we are keenly aware of the presence of objects, others, and ourselves in the world because of the verbal and non-verbal world of signs or language. Without language and the ideas made possible through its use, the world would be stubbornly closed to us. Thus, running parallel to the course of the evolution of the physical world is its counterpart, the evolution of meaning.

The recognition of such a state of affairs represents a phenomenological manifesto of sorts, since it suggests that understanding the world is dependent upon the medium of understanding itself. Moreover, there is an effective principle embedded within this manifesto. As the world changes, so does its meaning, and as meanings change, so does the world. Ideas then are doomed to periodically ebb and flow, to rise and fall. This point was made well by George Orwell when he noted that it is the fate of any given bit of human knowledge of the world to begin as heresy and end as superstition. While we may become weighted down by particular grandiose ideas for centuries at a time, we must know deep within us that the objects of the world cannot be fully contained by such ideas, for these objects also have an essence of their own. They are free to become beautiful or ugly, active or passive, virtuous or wicked, heroes or derelicts. From this standpoint, objects not only represent a particular form, they are capable, through the ideas they engender, of changing, inspiring, impoverishing, or otherwise altering the captured form itself. Of course, as the forms change, so does our understanding of what the forms mean. And so on.

The following material is presented in a fashion that attempts to give voice to certain forms of the world. This approach suggests that understanding such things as interpersonal relations is less a matter of observing them per se than it is of installing oneself within the hearts of others and trying to grapple with the world as they do. This is very much like the good novelist who attempts to give voice to a character by sinking deeply into the character's consciousness and then portraying the world as seen by the character, not by the novelist. All this is to say that the conceptual matters we deal with in this essay go well beyond a mere description of a world kept at bay by the writer's pen. The world we examine here has a voice, and if we listen closely to it there is much to learn.

The Organization of This Essay

If we take seriously this phenomenological mandate, understanding interpersonal relations as either a spectator or a participant is dependent upon the way in which we come to understand the world at large. At a most general level, this understanding of the world is keyed to three tightly interconnected aspects of social life. The first aspect is experience itself, that concrete part of life that more or less washes over us in an unending flow. The second aspect is the mental or cognitive part of our life. As such, it represents our ability to both cull and call out from experience certain meanings which enable us, for the most part, to make practical sense of the world. The third aspect of social life is action or behavior, the guided doings of people going about their everyday lives. The interconnections between these three aspects are rather obvious. For example, to make sense of an experienced event in the world requires the cognitive skill to recognize and catalog the event as an instance of something. To take action in regard to the event requires that one have in mind some ideas about what the action will bring forth. And, to take action implies that a changed experiential and cognitive world will be produced since action is a part of this world.

Figure 1 depicts this most basic idea. As shown, the three elements of this scheme can be visualized as a series of boxes within boxes. The outermost box represents experience, some of which is captured and made meaningful by cognition. The innermost box is action, and it is embedded within cognition because action is always but a subset of the cognitive possibilities. This scheme implies that not only do we selectively perceive the world around us, we behave selectively within this perceived world.

This essay examines the process by which interpersonal experiences are shaped into certain cognitive views of the world. The essay that follows, "The Self, the Situation, and the Rules of Interpersonal Relations," examines the process by which action in interpersonal situations flows from

FIGURE 1

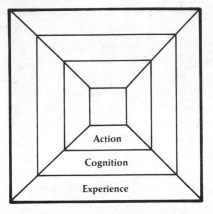

cognition. In both essays, however, a perspective on interpersonal relations is mapped out. This perspective places great emphasis upon the socially acquired and shared knowledge we use to organize, interpret, and account for our own behavior and the behavior of others. How we come to directly experience, cognitively assess, and act upon such knowledge in specific interpersonal domains is, therefore, the central and enduring question pursued in these two essays.

The material presented below begins in Part II by considering the general problem of how meaning is organized in everyday life. In this section, certain premises inherent in the use of a cultural approach to understanding the social world are presented. Part III builds upon the definitional matters covered in Part II and presents some of the basic human capacities or skills required to both create and sustain a sense of meaning in the world. In brief, this section examines the universal building blocks which underpin and make possible interpersonal relations. These building blocks are essentially cognitive abilities which allow us to interpret the behavior of others and ourselves within a world characterized increasingly by the nagging, continual, and altogether troublesome presence of doubt, ambiguity, and risk. Finally, Part IV delves into the manner in which these capacities are put to work by individuals in their common and routine life. The construction of social reality is approached in this section, and stress is placed upon the contingent, negotiated, and, at best, tentative character of one's conceptual grasp on reality.

Summarily, the aims of this essay are difficult ones. The materials to be presented are tied to much important philosophical, anthropological, sociological, and psychological work.[2] What I attempt here, then, is merely

---

[2] A sampling of some of the more important work that has guided the development of this essay would include: from philosophy, Maurice Merleau-Ponty, *The Structure*

to familiarize the reader with a few of the more crucial grounding concepts necessary to appreciate interpersonal relations as the touchstone of our understanding of the world around us. In a sense, all knowledge starts and ends in our interpersonal dealings with one another. Yet, as we shall see, the problem of studying interpersonal relations is a most tricky and paradoxical affairs because in the process of conducting our investigations, we must make use of the very skills we wish to study. Jean Paul Sartre put this matter well with his cogent remark: "The thing which differentiates every inquiry about man from other types of rigorous questions is precisely the privileged fact that reality is ourselves and understanding is not a quality coming to human reality from the outside, it is its characteristic way of existing."[3]

II. THE SOCIAL ORGANIZATION OF MEANING

To many people, the sight of a smartly uniformed police officer going about daily rounds calls forth feelings of well-being, security, and perhaps pride in the community. To others, this same sight may provoke feelings of fear, forewarning, and a sense that things do not bode well for the community. An outstretched hand attached to the arm of a stranger represents, under most conditions, merely warm and friendly intentions, but under special conditions, this same gesture from a stranger may represent a veiled threat behind which stands menace and danger. Teenagers gathered together in a city streetcorner may appear to a passerby as simply students waiting for a bus, or they may appear as gang members hatching yet another plot against the civil order. In all of these cases, different versions of reality are both available and plausible. The one selected depends, of course, upon the eye of the beholder. How we come to select a certain version of reality from among a set of what may appear to be clashing versions is central to understanding interpersonal relations.

---

of Behavior (Boston: Beacon Press, 1963) and Alfred Schutz, Collected Papers: The Problem of Social Reality (The Hague: Martinus Nijhoff, 1971); from sociology, Peter Berger and Thomas Luckman, The Social Construction of Reality (Garden City, N.Y.: Doubleday, 1966) and Jack D. Douglas, ed., Understanding Everyday Life (Chicago: Aldine Publishing Co., 1966); from anthropology, James P. Spradley, ed., Culture and Cognition (San Francisco: Chandler Publishing Co., 1972) and Stephen A. Tyler, ed., Cognitive Anthropology (New York: Holt, Rinehart & Winston, 1969); and from psychology, Erwin Straus, Phenomenological Psychology (New York: Basic Books, 1966) and George A. Kelly, The Psychology of Personal Constructs (New York: W. W. Norton & Co., Inc., 1955). The unifying theme across this substantial body of work is captured well by Alfred Schutz's remark: "Every social science sets as its primary goal the greatest possible clarification of what is thought about the social world by those living in it." (Schutz, Social Reality, p. 8.)

[3] Jean Paul Sartre, The Emotions: Outlines of a Theory (New York: Philosophical Library, 1948), pp. 12–13.

Meaning in Everyday Life

At the outset, it is vital to recognize that the objects, facts, events, and relationships seemingly present in the everyday world have no meaning apart from what an observer chooses to give them. The raw empirical world is essentially absurd. We do not, of course, experience the world as absurd because we have learned that behind certain appearances stand certain meanings that are more or less useful for our purposes given the always particular circumstances in which we find ourselves. This is what is meant when it is said that the world we live in is a symbolic one. The police officer, the outstretched hand, the youngsters on the corner are made meaningful to an observer only in terms of what such perceptual events symbolize or signal to the observer about something else such as friendship or danger.[4]

It is true too, that behind any symbol stands another symbol which may point to still other symbolic matter of our concern. The hand extended in greeting perhaps points to friendship which may point to a debt or obligation we have in the past failed to honor which points to our potentially damaged self-image which may point to even other signs of our current situation. This makes for a potentially difficult existence, since the objects, facts, events, and relationships in the world are not self-defining. A yardstick, for example, does not announce that it is one yard long, it takes an observer to first decree that a particular distance shall be called a yard. Indeed, it is our ability to define meanings out of the swarm and tangle of the experienced world that enables us to fix certain definitions for our immediate situation and, hence, possess some sense over what is occurring in the world.[5]

From this view of the world as potentially devoid of meaning, as absurd, come several key assumptions necessary to the understanding of interpersonal relations. *First,* all human behavior or action is based upon some sort of belief, accurate or faulty, about what is going on in the immediate situation, as well as what it is one wants to accomplish by a given action

---

[4] It is important to recognize that the meaning of a symbol, signal, or sign arises by interpreting the thoughts and actions of others. Symbols depend on the existence of others and are therefore social in origin and in use. For a good introduction to these matters, see, Herbert Blumer, *Symbolic Interactionism* (Englewood Cliffs, N.J.: Prentice-Hall, Inc., 1971).

[5] As noted in the introduction of this essay, language is closely related to any definitional concern about the world. Language, in a sense, is a primary generator of reality since it enables us to transmit our knowledge and understanding from generation to generation, from group to group, and from person to person such that others do not have to rely entirely upon their own experiences in order to act in the world. To put it most strongly, language determines our patterns of thought, behavior, and feeling and thereby exerts great influence upon our social structure. For perhaps the finest introduction to the study of language, see, Roger Brown, *Words and Things* (New York: The Free Press, 1968).

within that situation. Unlike iron filings which are mindlessly drawn to the pull of a magnet, human behavior is both interpretive and purposeful. We respond to the meanings that certain things have for us, not to the things themselves. *Second,* events, objects, persons, facts, relationships, and so forth exist for us only insofar as they are conceived in our minds. The locus of interpersonal relations is in the individual's mind in which all experience is organized, interpreted, forgotten, and remembered.[6] To gloss over this fact is to reify the world and to mistakenly assume that the objects which attract our attention broadcast and carry with them their own universal meanings. *Third,* the interpretations we build of our experiences and the purposes we give to our actions are social in origin. This is merely to say that it is only through continuous interaction with others that we can construct certain meanings for things in the world toward which we can then gear our behavior. Unless at least some meanings of the world's objects, facts, events, and relationships come to be mutually held by people, it would be impossible for people to engage in simple conversation with others, to behave toward one another in even a remotely civil fashion, or to simply make sense out of what goes on around them. In short, without developing some semblance of a shared system of meaning to guide our actions, the world would most certainly be a Hobbsian one, "a war of all against all."

The Interactional Origins of Meaning

How do shared meaning systems arise? From one perspective, we are said to "internalize" society's meaning system. Thus, for example, rules concerning what is good and what is bad are taught to us in childhood as "social values" which, after being properly learned and stored, provide something akin to a "blueprint for behavior" for us to follow throughout life. In this vein, basic biological urges such as eating and sleeping can be channeled into behavior modes which are approved by others as "proper forms." Such blueprints are learned through interaction with others and presumably grow more complex as we proceed from our mother's lap through other societal teaching machines such as the family, the school, the neighborhood, and the workplace. From this perspective, these learned social values serve as the primary determinants of what people do. These values constitute the bones of society upon which everything else is built. Meaning, then, is dependent upon the values that exist in a given society, and order among individuals is based upon the sharing of such values.

---

[6] I rely heavily here upon the social psychological work of Charles Horton Cooley, *Human Nature and the Social Order* (New York: Charles Scribner's Sons, 1922) and George Herbert Mead, *Mind, Self and Society,* ed. Charles W. Morris (Chicago: University of Chicago Press, 1934).

Behavior in such a world is merely the competent following of the rules that are given by society.[7]

But what of this most abstract version of society? We certainly can not see it nor feel it directly. And, like the concept of a social value, we cannot put society in a box and walk around it to carefully observe its behavior. Moreover, as the terrible and sometimes bloody arguments over what is to be considered good and bad, or right and wrong within a society make apparent, social values seem to be rather relative matters with each segment or group within a society improvising, as it were, their own interpretations for what should be considered appropriate behavior and what is not within their own sphere (and outside of it if they are powerful enough). Indeed, the only social values we can directly observe in use arise when we, as members of society, engage in face-to-face interaction in particular concrete situations. Consider, for example, the social value of "equality among members of the society." While such a value may set the tone for a stirring Fourth of July speech, it hardly conveys much practical meaning when considered apart or independent of a specific situation. Equality to, say, a black couple searching for a suburban home to purchase may well mean the right to select the home of their choice whereas, to the suburban home seller or real estate agent, equality means the right to select among potential buyers for the "good of the neighborhood." The social value that is then observed in this situation depends not only upon the outcome of the buyer-seller interaction, but also upon the observer's choice of perspectives from which to view the meaning of equality.

Society, from this perspective, originates in everyday life for it is here where our versions of the world are directly tested and the meanings we attach to our experiences can be compared, evaluated, and judged for their adequacy and accuracy. To the degree that our own meaning systems merge with others, we can then understand one another and perhaps engage in joint activities. Social values, in this sense, are not imposed from society on high but rather are constructed from the ground up as we observe and make practical use of them in a vast variety of both fleeting

---

[7] This brief passage hardly does justice to the subtleties of "social value" theory as formulated most completely by Talcott Parsons in *The Social System* (New York: Free Press, 1951). But the point I wish to make here is that this theory, for all practical purposes, reduces the role of the individual in society to that of a puppet on societal strings since the person is seen to have little or nothing to do with the construction of social values, which are viewed as existing somehow above and beyond the individual. My perspective is that "social values" (or, perhaps, more accurately, "shared meanings") are produced by people in everyday interaction and are therefore local, geared to the problems at hand, and are characterized by continual negotiation and change. Social value theory is therefore a somewhat misguided armchair effort to build a context-free science of human behavior. This is akin to an attempt to define social reality by fiat rather than to study it in its many forms.

and lasting interpersonal relationships. Society is what we make it, not what it makes us.[8]

Yet, understanding one another is always problematic. Certainly we know from everyday mundane experience that to discover "what is going on" is frequently a bothersome issue. We worry about whether we said or did the "right thing," and sometimes we have trouble knowing what another "really meant" by a particular remark. More dramatically, it is often difficult to know whether we love someone or merely lust after them, whether we are liked by another or simply tolerated by them, or even whether we are on equal or unequal footing with another. While we may possess firm beliefs about another person, direct experience with that other person may always reorganize our beliefs. When two people meet to conduct business, for instance, the behavior between them that follows cannot be attributed solely to the intentions and knowledge each brought with them to the encounter. Both must reevaluate their own stock of knowledge and intentions in light of the other's apparent stock of knowledge and seeming intentions.[9]

All this is to say that shared meanings must ultimately arise out of social interaction and each encounter tends to develop its own set of meanings that are tied directly to that encounter. People understand one another not only on the basis of the prior knowledge shared between them but also through the unfolding of the situation which brings them together. This is what is meant by the stiff but precise phrase, "the situated nature of meaning."

The Meaning of Meaning

Thus far we have been using the term *meaning* in a very loose and commonsensical way. This is hardly surprising since the term is a popular one that visits us many times during the day. In contemporary American life, we apparently encounter with varying degrees of frequency: "mean-

---

[8] I follow the lead here of Georg Simmel, who argued that individuals play out society within their own small worlds of interpersonal relations. From this standpoint, there is no such thing as society per se, only small circles of social interaction within which the meaning of society is carved out. See Kurt H. Wolff, ed. and trans., *The Sociology of Georg Simmel* (New York: The Free Press, 1950).

[9] This is merely to say that when another comes into our presence, we quickly try to gleen as much information as we can regarding the other person's identity and purpose so that we will know how to act within the situation. In many cases, physical appearances and what the person says about himself or herself are rather vital signs. Clothing, for example, serves as one of the best indicators of the wearer's identity and purpose, such as a person wearing a clerical collar or a police officer's uniform. For a good analysis of how we attempt to "read" intentions into the appearances of others, see Gustav Ichheiser, *Appearances and Reality* (San Francisco: Jossey-Bass, 1970). On matters of faulty readings, deceptions, and carefully faked appearances, see Erving Goffman, *The Presentation of Self in Everyday Life* (Garden City, N.Y.: Doubleday, 1959).

ingful jobs," "meaningful people," "meaningful films," and, of course, those much sought after "meaningful relationships." Several fundamental matters are tied into our use of the term, and it is worthwhile to examine these matters now, since they shed much light upon how meaning is constructed in everyday life.

Consider, for example, a person's involvement or membership in some social group, a neighborhood organization, a gun club, a baseball team, a work group, whatever, as a hypothetical segment of the world which may or may not be "meaningful" to a person. First, if people are to grant meaning to their membership, it must be seen as having at least one purpose; it accomplishes something—makes money, provides friendship, does good, and so on. Things that are meaningful to people stand for something; they are not neutral to them. Meanings, therefore, are essentially moral in character for they convey judgments as to a thing's goodness or badness and are sources of pleasant or unpleasant feelings. Second, for the social group to be meaningful to a member, it must be more or less predictable and fall into some kind of cognitive classification as a "type of group" that is different from "other kinds of groups." That is, the group must be recognizable to a person as something reasonably familiar and stable. There is a danger here, of course, since the familiar and stable may become too familiar and too stable so that it becomes altogether boring and routine, thus losing its value for the person.

These two vital properties of meaning, value and recognition, are the necessary and sufficient conditions required to build meaning into the world of objects and things. A waterfall, a sunset, a late model car, and current Paris fashions are either found meaningful to us on these grounds or they are found wanting. However, when we consider human relationships, such as our hypothetical social group, we must add a third dimension if we are to fully grasp the nature of meaning as it exists in the interpersonal domain. Specifically, for a social world to come alive, the people within it must see that their world is a responsive one; that, as participants in this world (be it a social group or even the society at large), they can exert an effect on it. In short, people must believe that their presence makes a difference to others in a particular social world such that their role can potentially be a creative and positive one. Consequently, if meaning is to be attached to an interpersonal relationship, an individual must believe that he or she can, in some fashion, control, manipulate, enrich, engineer, or otherwise influence the relationship. To the extent that this belief exists, a person can build a sense of purpose and a sense of belongingness to serve as bonds holding the relationship intact. If, however, these bonds are broken such that an individual comes to sense that he or she no longer can affect the nature and shape of the relationship, the meaning the relationship once held for the person will quickly vanish (as will perhaps the relationship itself).

From this quick description of meaning, it should be clear that different segments of the world provide people with greater meaning than others. *Recognition, value,* and *responsiveness* represent the sources of our attachments in the world. In a sense, they provide the markers by which we continually locate ourselves between the Janus-faced poles of individual freedom and social constraint. Meaningful segments of the world possess both security and adventure, permanence and change. Too much order is as destructive of meaning as too much disorder.

In each situation we find ourselves, therefore, the meanings we attach to it are patterned in terms of its value, recognition, and responsiveness. And, it is our capacity to build these meanings, to choose our own path that makes possible the social world. Take what one does for a living as a final illustration of these properties of meaning. For an occupational pursuit to be meaningful to a person, it must at least be one which has some value to the individual, that it represents a source of evaluation. It must also be uniquely distinguishable by the person as a particular activity in the world. Further, it must be viewed as one which is, to some degree, responsive to what an individual decides to do or not do on the job. For example, people must feel that they have some influence over the pace, shape, quantity, quality, and other characteristics of their work if it is to be meaningful to them. This is not to say, however, that the meaning of a particular job will be the same for different people. Clearly what the proverbial "boss's son" sees as pleasant, attractive work may be seen by the equally proverbial "coal miner's daughter" as uncomfortable, demeaning work. What this example shows is that in either case the occupation has been rendered meaningful to the individual, though the meaning itself is no doubt quite different. To one it is perhaps "great work," to another it is "rotten work."

We now turn to consider how such meanings can be both created and sustained. Since, as I have argued, reality rests not upon what meets the eye, but upon what symbols one chooses to see behind an appearance, how are such symbols selected? It is the premise below that the symbol selection process is a social one, but the process itself requires certain individual abilities or capacities before it can take place. These capacities are described below after first attending to some general definitional matters.

III.   INTERPERSONAL CAPACITIES

Everyday life is marked by the ordinary and common activities in which we routinely engage. It is that unquestionable part of life within which we dwell. Thus, we expect people to understand us when we speak to them just as we fully expect to, for example, understand them when they speak. Even when we move into a new scene, we assume that there will exist many familiar clues or clues upon which we can organize our behavior so that we will not heedlessly violate the propriety or sensibilities held by others in that scene. Beliefs of this type can be called *natural attitudes*, and they are of a variety that we rarely, if ever, make explicit.[10] By and large, these natural attitudes are taken for granted, and unless we are shocked into recognizing their inapplicability to a given situation, they will remain altogether tacit, hidden from view, yet, most influential upon the actions we take.

In brief, these natural attitudes allow us an everyday and practical life. They allow a real world to emerge for people through an almost infinite set of conjoint and not-so-conjoint interactions. In a sense, they are the building blocks of meaning that undergird all social interaction. Therefore, they represent the groundwork of all interpersonal relations and are fundamental to all human understanding. I will use the label *interpersonal capacities* to describe the natural attitudes we unhesitatingly take in the world. In essence, these capacities are the bedrock abilities which link all members of the human species together. And, as argued here, to be able to construct meanings in the world requires their use. They are then the foundations upon which culture and language are built.

Capacity and Behavior

To recognize and effectively use symbols of all varieties requires, of course, an enormous amount of learning. Furthermore, everyday life in our contemporary world is also increasingly complex and difficult. We must deal with persons whom we have never encountered before, adjust to circumstances that are changing constantly, enter situations the likes of which we have never seen, and make sense out of behavioral combinations we have not before witnessed. We purchase stamps, for example, from postal clerks we have not previously met; we live in neighborhoods among seldom-encountered neighbors; we adroitly steer our automobiles down streets we have never been on before. And, most crucially, we seem to do so rather routinely, often with dispatch, cunning, and skill.

It is true, of course, that we often misunderstand others, behave foolishly, become confused and uncertain, break the polite rules others expect us to observe, find that we are, on occasion, ashamed of ourselves for

---

[10] *Natural attitudes* refer also to such things as our belief that there is agreement in the world as to what is real and what is imaginary or our belief that when we speak, others will understand us as we ourselves do. In brief, natural attitudes are required for interaction to occur because without presupposing or assuming where others stand relative to ourselves, communication between people would be impossible. Such beliefs are not without their problems however, for they can be and often are ruptured in a particular interactive situation. See Alfred Schutz, *On Phenomenology and Social Relations* (Chicago: University of Chicago Press, 1970) for an extended but difficult treatment of the role natural attitudes take in everyday life.

making a certain remark, and so on. Clearly, the capacity for "correct" behavior that we all possess does not always protect us from error. *Capacity*, as the term implies, refers only to the necessary but not sufficient human *ability* to produce and understand behavior. It does not refer to the *actual* behavior produced or understood. To describe the observable or actual behavior, I reserve the term *performance*.

In language use, the distinction between capacity and performance is associated with what have been called the "deep" and "surface" structures or rules of speech.[11] At the deep level, persons who share the same language and wish to talk with one another usually know quite well what they wish to say on a particular occasion. Indeed, they typically know fully well how to say it and possess the necessary physical equipment to do so. But, for a vast variety of reasons, reasons that have nothing to do with their underlying knowledge of the meaning of words and the grammar of language, the actual speech performance that results is flawed. We cough, stammer, sputter, and lop off and slur words in everyday talk, all of which inhibit and restrict our conveyed impression and intended meaning. But these are merely surface difficulties and reflect only upon our ability to perform (to produce speech) in the moment. Such troubles do not reflect on our deeper ability or capacity to use the mother tongue. Furthermore, since any language can be used to generate an infinite variety of statements, an infinite variety of performances are possible even though each performance will make use of the same basic or deep capacities involved in using the language. From a few rules of grammar and a finite set of terms (the language itself), an infinite number of usages or performances can be produced.

Interpersonal capacity refers to an individual's ability to engage in social intercourse and, therefore, to potentially share meanings with others. Like language capacity, it is acquired only gradually as we come to experience and know the world around us. Interpersonal performances begin when we enter the world itself. Again, like language performances, interpersonal ones are those observable actions or behaviors of people in concrete situations. Interpersonal performances clearly are the basic material of which everyday life is constructed.[12] They come in an infinite

---

[11] The distinction between capacity and performance or, as it is also often put, competence and behavior is central to the study of linguistics—in particular, psycholinguistics. For a good introduction to the field, see Noam Chomsky, *Language and Mind* (New York: Harcourt, Brace and World, 1968). For a somewhat broader treatment of the capacity and performance issues as examined by sociolinguists (scholars concerned with the actual conversational or natural use of language as opposed to its underlying grammar or structure), see Del Hymes, ed., *Language in Culture and Society* (New York: Harper and Row, 1964).

[12] The view presented here is that language capacity is but a subset or special case of the more general interpersonal capacities we come to possess. That is to say that the ability to use language in our daily life depends first and foremost upon our most

variety but are based upon one's deeper capacities to generate purposeful or guided behavior. To do so requires that one has also become proficient at interpreting the behavior of others. The wink, for instance, does not announce its intention; only the observer (or winker) can decide that what lies behind the simple gesture is a sexual innuendo with future promise or merely an invitation to take the following activities unseriously. Interpersonal capacities stand behind our abilities to "read" the simple and complex signs, symbols, gestures, and appearances of the world. From a universe of potential meanings, we are able somehow to render the behavior of others understandable as well as make our own behavior understood. Mistakes are not unknown, of course, but even a mistaken and fully inappropriate performance is constructed upon the same raw materials or capacities as a skillfully executed one.

Three primary capacities are discussed below. Each can be thought of as similar to a structural property of the mind. These capacities allow us to generate and produce performances (even faulty ones) in any given interactional setting. They are acquired slowly throughout our lifetimes, and, depending on our experiences, they provide us with the interactional savvy to perform appropriately in everyday life. The three capacities are those mental operations which produce *temporal frameworks*, *categorization devices*, and *interpretive procedures*.

Temporal Frameworks

To produce a temporal framework suggests that the human mind has developed the ability to recall the past, remain aware of the present, and project a hypothetical future. Without this ability, social life would be impossible. We could not remember a face, predict a possible consequence of our actions, or attach meaning to our surroundings.

All behavior is, therefore, premised upon temporal frameworks which link past and possible future states into guides for present activity. Without such frameworks, causality would be both unknown and impossible, and meaning would vanish, since one event in the future would be as likely as any other. For example, consider a few of the temporal themes

---

basic abilities to communicate symbolically with one another. For example, to learn a language in the first place requires social interaction. Furthermore, to properly use a language requires that the user understand the situational embeddedness of concrete words and phrases. Indeed, it is the gestures, background features, rhythms, silences, tone dynamics, body idioms, and other expressive features that give color, melody, and, ultimately, meaning to conversational activities. Therefore, these nonverbal or social matters must be understood by persons if they are to fully participate in the social world. Coming to terms with language use, then, presupposes the existence of some very basic interpersonal capacities—such as those outlined in the text. See Pier Paolo Giglioti, ed., *Language and Social Context* (Baltimore: Penguin Books, 1972).

we attach to our lives: there is presumably a "time to weep, a time to laugh, a time to reap, and a time to sow." In a similar view, there are the seven Shakespearean phases of life wherein we are but players having our established entrances and exits on the world's stage. At a more mundane level, we know from experience that Sunday is different than Tuesday and that there are "blue Mondays" and "thank-God-it's-Fridays." We greet acquaintances with the well-worn cliche, "howya doin," fully expecting some variant of the trite but perhaps true response, "fine," in return. To be sure, our temporal frameworks occasionally break down (both in trivial and sometimes serious ways), but the point here is merely that we all possess the ability to construct them. This linking of the past, present, and future, then, is the first capacity that makes possible interpersonal relations.

Categorization Devices

Categorization devices represent the second basic human capacity. As the label suggests, these devices refer to the mind's ability to form categories for the recognition, classification, and, ultimately, understanding of experiences. Categorization devices underlie all thought. Indeed, we can only understand what an object is in terms of what it is not.

In everyday life, we know whether something is good or bad, proper or improper, attractive or ugly on the basis of where it fits in our mental classification schemes. For example, forms of address like "Mister," "Nurse," "Doctor," "Mrs.," "Sir," "Professor," "Miss," and even "Hey You," allocate people to certain social positions and order for us the kind of behavior we will expect in response to our selected form of address. At a group level, category schemes enable us to see "change," "stability," "harmony," or "conflict" among people. Even organizations and societies sort themselves out along numerous social and linguistic types—"capitalistic," "communistic," "socialistic," "peace-loving," "warmongering," and so forth.

The matter of categorization is closely tied to language use. Through classifying and naming, the experienced world of potentially infinite variety shrinks to a more-or-less manageable size and becomes both bearable and understandable. If we lived in a world where nothing was the same, this world would clearly be intolerable. While we perhaps may sit upon a one-of-a-kind chair which is chipped, broken-in, and uniquely recognizable, it, nonetheless, still belongs to a more inclusive category of chairs-in-general. Anthropologists refer to the outcomes of this universal human capacity as *semantic domains*. Such domains taxonomically order objects into certain classes with each class having at least one feature which can be readily identified by any cultural member to be in common with all other objects in that class.[13] Hot dogs and hamburgers, while distinct, are still sandwiches, whereas hot dogs and hamsters share little in common and most definitely are not both to be bitten into. Categorization devices enable us to typify things and, hence, order the world. For example, by using our categorization abilities, an unfamiliar sight can be classified in terms of what it is most similar to, thus it becomes possible to take action in relation to it, because it is now seen as a kind of "something." Therefore, through this capacity of interpersonal relations, the infinite can be tamed.

Interpretive Procedures

Interpretive procedures represent the third set of interpersonal capacities. These procedures refer to our mind's ability to construct, interpret, and understand on-going social interaction. Such procedures are rooted, however, upon our abilities to categorize experience and develop temporal frameworks. There are four major, but rather distinct, procedures central to this capacity.

First, as a species, we must be able to "fill in" the essential incompleteness that accompanies all social interaction. When a father asks his five-year-old son to "Put that down," the boy knows (usually) that what the father really means is, for instance, "Put that book of matches that you have in your hand down and do it right now." This interactional ability is called *glossing*, and we engage in it from childhood on, since we recognize that we always mean more than we say. That is, to carry on a conversation, we must be able to understand more than we can hear or see. If a college student were to say to another, "Take it easy," that student would no doubt be quite surprised if the other responded with a query as to what it was that he or she was supposed to take easy. Competent users of this slang phrase know perfectly well that what a speaker says is, under most circumstances, merely a convenient gloss for calling the conversation to an end. For practical purposes, however, glossing is made most clear when we come into contact with someone who cannot (or

---

[13] Semantic domains, as used in cognitive anthropology, refer to the way cultural members categorize or organize things of their world. A semantic domain represents a class of objects all of which share at least one feature in common which differentiates them from all other domains. If, for example, a child in school says something such as, "During class, most kids fool around," the child has indicated that there are at least three categories (semantic domains) within the school—classes, kids, and fooling around. Each of these categories begs further specification and, upon questioning, we would quickly discover that there are many different types of classes, kids, and fooling around. A semantic domain, then, is merely a category system which divides up and defines the world in which an identifiable set of people live. An excellent treatment of this topic geared for the beginning student can be found in James P. Spradley and David W. McCurdy, *The Cultural Experience* (Chicago: Science Research Associates, 1972).

chooses not to) gloss. Summarily, words and actions represent only the appearance or the exterior of the more meaningful interior detail we *expect* others who are "like us" to know and understand.[14]

Second, interpretive procedures include the competency to use what sociologist Harold Garfinkel calls the *etcetera assumption*. In essence, this procedure refers to the ability we have to "let-things-pass-for-the moment" in the hope that the future of the interaction will make clear what is presently unclear. Certainly, to understand the beginning of a written or spoken sentence requires one to read it or hear it in its entirety—"I was struck yesterday . . . (pause) . . . by the implications of Jane's remark." In games, the results are used by the players to inform them how well or how poorly they played during the game. Were we not to have the capacity of suspending meaning for the time being, interaction could never proceed past the opening moment, since doubt, uncertainty, and senselessness would quickly overcome us. We maintain a sense of understanding in an exchange, therefore, by letting the past clarify the present and also by allowing the present to clarify the past.

Third, interpretive procedures include the assumption that an *interchangeability of viewpoints* characterizes the understandings of all parties engaged in social interaction. In other words, unless we are explicitly shown otherwise, we take it for granted that were we to exchange places with the person with whom we are interacting, we would see the same world as we saw in our original location—that the world we both experience is one that is, for the moment at least, held in common. This implies that people assume that their action and conversation will be understood by others as they themselves would understand it were they in the other's position.

Fourth, and finally, the meaning of words and behavior are inherently tied into the setting in which they occur. Interpretive procedures include, then, the capacity to *index* actions to a shared feature of the situation. Meaning is situationally bound. When words and behavior are removed from one context and placed in another, they will acquire a different meaning. To "have another's ear" requires an entirely different interpretation were it to be mentioned over a Thanksgiving feast or in a Board of Directors meeting. The meaning of all interactional materials (be they grunts, acts, statements, gestures, and so on) are determined by people in light of the context in which they appear. The student who tells his roommate in the college common to "shut the fuck up" will be understood in a far different vein than the forgetful homecoming student, who, while dining in the family kitchen, tells his mother the same thing.

---

[14] See Harold Garfinkel, *Studies in Ethnomethodology* (Englewood Cliffs, N.J.: Prentice-Hall, Inc., 1967). And, for a somewhat more accessible explanation of interpretive procedures in general, see Hugh Mehan and Houston Wood, *The Reality of Ethnomethodology* (New York: John Wiley and Sons, 1975).

The Use of Interpersonal Capacities

These interpretive procedures, along with temporal frameworks and categorization devices, are the fundamental building blocks upon which social interaction is based.[15] This is not to say, however, that the use of these capacities makes for smooth, uninterrupted, and troublefree performances. Indeed not. Just as language capacity does not always generate adequate or correct language performance, interpersonal capacities may generate faulty assumptions about the world around us, as well as sound ones. Temporal frameworks may prove false, as is the case when our expected promotion, high grade in a college course, or invitation to a party fail to materialize. Categorization devices, too, may make for personal difficulties as might occur when we fetch a baseball out of some innocuous-looking bushes that turn out on first scratch to be of a poisonous strain. And, interpretive procedures may lead us astray when, despite our best efforts, we still misinterpret what another has said.

Yet all of these jogs and twists in the movement of our everyday life do not reflect upon our fundamental possession of the basic capacities for interpersonal relations; they only suggest that our particular use is inadequate in the situation. Children, for example, presumably begin life with these mental capacities, but they must first provide them with substance before they can be applied appropriately. From this perspective, at birth, these human capacities are present in all of us, but they are essentially devoid of specific content. They are akin to empty receptacles that will become increasingly full as experience accumulates and life proceeds. Indeed, each new situation faced by a person can bring about a subtle or a dramatic shift in the character and meaning of our temporal frameworks, categorization devices, or interpretive procedures.[16]

---

[15] I have relied extensively throughout this section upon a relatively new approach to doing social science called *ethnomethodology*. Fundamentally, ethnomethodology seeks to describe the way a culture, group, or individual (*ethno*) routinely obtains and uses information in the social world (*methodology*). As work in this growing area suggests, the procedures for making sense and orienting our actions in the world are invariably dependent upon our use of what I have labeled *temporal frameworks, categorization schemes,* and *interpretive procedures.* In addition to the works of Garfinkel, and Mehan and Wood, see H. P. Dreitzel, ed., *Recent Sociology* #2 (New York: Macmillan Publishing Co., Inc., 1970) and Roy Turner, ed., *Ethnomethodology* (Baltimore: Penguin Books, 1974). A useful though somewhat critical introduction to the many concerns of ethnomethodologists can be located in Jack D. Douglas, ed., *Introduction to Sociology* (New York: The Free Press, 1973), pp. 86–117.

[16] It seems safe to say that by our mid to late teens, most of us have acquired these basic interpersonal capacities. This is not to say that learning stops here for these capacities are, of course, filled in and elaborated upon throughout our late life as we become tracked into jobs, leisure pursuits, families, and other interactional settings. Indeed, we are forced by circumstances to learn new categorization schemes, to revise our temporal frameworks, and to apply in creative ways the various interpretive procedures we have developed earlier in life. The works of cognitive psychologists such

By focusing on interpersonal capacities in this section I have not had much to say about the actual materials that are managed by such capacities. It has been form, not content, that has been treated here. Clearly, an adult possessing simply a set of empty interpersonal capacities would be some sort of cultural monster who would not know when to act, to speak, to be silent, or even how to select a behavioral option from among the infinite repertoire of possibilities. Unlike ducks or ants, we do not have a life plan safely locked into our genes. All we do have is this set of interpersonal capacities which grow more concrete and complex as we experience more and more of the world about us.

The concreteness and complexity of the world lies, therefore, at the root of our performances in the world, and it is at this level that we first become familiar with the psychological and social rules that discipline the use of our interpersonal capacities. Performances represent the choices we make on how to present ourselves in particular situations, as well as how we choose to interpret the actions of others. It must be said, however, that the deeper cognitive structures explored here are always with us, allowing us to be informed more or less about the meaning of the world. Though we may perform atrociously in the world, we do so still on the basis of our interpersonal capacities. With this in mind, I turn now to consider reality as we construct it, recognizing that when our words or deeds go amiss in the world, it is not so much a matter of giving an incompetent performance per se that is at fault, as it is a matter of a competent performance given in the wrong world. It is our choice of reality that imprisons us, not our ability to create and act within one.

IV. THE CONSTRUCTION OF SOCIAL REALITIES

Reality is that part of the world that is experienced by people as existing over and above their everyday lives. It is apprehended through the use of our basic capacities, and we usually take an altogether unquestioning stance toward it since we assume, indeed must assume, that others live in it too. Yet, at least a part of this reality must be intensely personal since there are many things we cannot readily or easily communicate to others. Certain feelings, hunches, sounds, and even sights often fit into this category for sometimes they are quite difficult to articulate. Indeed, sometimes we just "know" something without being able to say why or how we "know" it. Nevertheless, much of our experienced reality can be poten-

as Jean Piaget, *The Construction of Reality in the Child* (New York: Basic Books, 1954), and Jerome S. Brumer, Jacqueline J. Goodnow, and George A. Austin, *A Study of Thinking* (New York: John Wiley and Sons, 1956) are good in this regard. A most thoughtful and elaborate application of this perspective (to playing jazz piano) is found in David Sudnow, *Ways of the Hand* (Cambridge, Mass.: Harvard University Press, 1978).

tially shared with others through the use of language which makes possible our involvement in interpersonal relations. Thus, much of our experience can be more or less regularized (institutionalized) wherein reasonably stable patterns of behavior can be framed temporally, categorized, and interpreted with some commonality across people. When such sharing occurs among people, we can speak properly of a social world within which shared meanings have come to exist among people. Hence, a reality has been produced such that members of this world can gear and direct their actions toward and away from one another with a reasonable degree of certainty that these actions will be interpreted by others as they themselves would interpret them.

However, as the title of this section suggests, this sharing of reality is highly problematic because, in part, the so-called modern world, at least the western part of it, is marked by not one, but many social worlds, each possessing its own version of reality which produces some rather highly variable patterns of conduct followed by participants in each of those social worlds. Moreover, people within these social worlds are not neutral towards them. Each world that is judged meaningful by a set of people provides its own moral standards for what is to be viewed as proper and just behavior within that world and what is not. Yet, these worlds sometimes collide within a society, and when they do, reality and the standards that go with it, become a matter of some concern to those who experience such collisions.

Reality Structures: Consensual, Emergent, Negotiable, Conflictual[17]

Since all knowledge of the world basically derives from social interaction, our knowledge or beliefs about reality are also social.[18] Reality, therefore, can be and most often is experienced as shared. The moon rises in the evening upon the sun's setting. Water always runs downhill just as

---

[17] This breakdown of "reality types" comes from Berger and Luckman, *The Social Construction of Reality*. My reliance on their work is substantial in this section.

[18] I should note that there is some debate as to how much our understanding of the world is a direct result of social mediation. Much of the debate centers upon what can be learned by a person prior to primitive language learning (preverbal) and what can only be learned after language development has begun. For instance, Roger Brown's studies—see *Language, Thought and Culture* (Ann Arbor, Mich.: University of Michigan Press, 1966)—show that certain concepts such as light, heat, and motion are learned by an infant in the preverbal stage. However, other concepts such as color, pain, kinship, love, and, most certainly, moral values require direct social intervention thus indicating the tremendous impact culture has upon our experienced and perceived reality. A brief but comprehensive introduction to how our knowledge of the social world emerges can be found in John Scott Fuller and Jerry Jacobs, "Socialization," in *Introduction to Sociology*, ed. Douglas, pp. 168–209. A more extensive review and introduction to the study of language and social learning can be found in Roger Brown's *Social Psychology* (New York: The Free Press, 1965).

smoke is always drawn upward. We die when we cannot take a breath. These represent features of the world that are more or less held in common and represent what we will call parts of a *consensual reality.* Such realities are bounded, however, and again the boundaries are social. For example, consider the practice of witchcraft. Indeed, to be a fully accepted member of some societies requires that one display a very healthy respect for magical rites. The presence of evil spirits and the tactics for warding them off are, furthermore, taken for granted by members of societies maintaining such belief systems. Witchcraft is seen to be in tune with the natural ways of the world, just as science is perhaps seen by the vast majority of Americans to be in tune with the natural ways of the world. However, it is also clear that reality is not always consensual even within a society. Certainly within mass societies, when people of very different backgrounds interact, they often discover that what one unquestionably takes for granted, the other does not.

If reality is not consensual at all times, then what is it? There seems to be at least three alternative states in which we can be said to exist at any given moment. First, we can be involved in an *emergent reality* wherein the meaning of what is going on is slowly unfolding as our own actions and the reactions of others take place. Consider, for example, a case in which we come upon an excited crowd clustered together on the public sidewalk all looking skyward. Initially, we may expect to see a plane or perhaps a bird. Children may even expect to see Superman. Or we may look to the ledges of surrounding buildings to see if anyone is perched there. We may even have to ask someone what is going on in order to determine where to look and what to look for. It may turn out, of course, that we have merely been taken in or put on by some practical jokester and there was nothing at all for us to see. Whatever the resolution, if any, the reality of the moment is an emergent one.

Second, the reality we experience may be a *negotiable* one. In fact, all reality is more or less negotiated by us at some time or other just as all reality must begin for us in an emergent state. By a negotiable reality, I mean merely that in coming to assess the meaning of our situation we find that there are several distinct versions available. We exchange views and then see whether or not we can reach an agreement about what is and what is not. For instance, in our crowd example, a person may, in fact, be upon a high and distant ledge of the building, but while some may claim that the person is suicidal and ready to jump, others may claim it is only a window washer taking a break. Both will, no doubt, marshall evidence to support their claims, and, depending on their arguments and interaction skills, one or the other may be able to make their definition of reality stick. Situations, therefore, are often defined as a reality *sui generis* only after some rather explicit period of negotiation has occurred.

Third, reality may be *conflictual*. This is to say that there are at least two versions of reality at stake and the supporters or followers of any one version are not about to give up their point of view. The negotiations in our man-on-the-ledge example may prove unsuccessful or break off. Indeed, in everyday life, realities are often in direct competition. Take drug use as an illustration. Some see it as a categorical evil, others view it as a necessary evil, still others see it as good and not evil at all, and another set of people may refuse to even think about it. Even if an agreement were to be reached on whether drug use was good or bad, there would no doubt still be much conflict over how such a view was to be applied in a concrete situation. Realities, indeed, can conflict, and, as the deep divisions that separate people from one another document, there are frequently no means available to settle the matter.

The reality within which we act can then be characterized broadly as consensual, emergent, negotiable, or conflictual. But humans are essentially practical theorists who are not as concerned with analyzing the properties of the everyday world per se as much as they are with overcoming the problems (routine and otherwise) they face in achieving their purposes in the world. Of course, the world can be problematic on many dimensions. The realities of the physical, moral, cognitive, and even mystical world can, on occasion, become matters of great concern to people. Natural disaster may, for example, shake loose our taken-for-granted physical reality. Indeed, people who have lived through terrible earthquakes often come to distrust the very ground upon which they walk, a feature of the physical world most of us very much take for granted. Moral realities, too, are often troublesome. Abortion presents an instructive illustration, for many of us are confused on the matter and find that our beliefs, emotions, and practical needs of the moment sometimes pull us in different directions. In contemporary argot, "we are not really sure where our heads are at." Indeed, there exist no clear-cut agreements in society at large about abortion as good or bad, natural or perverted. We may all agree that these are vital distinctions to be made, but many of us are not exactly sure what these distinctions should be or where they should be made.

However, as practical theorists, we do take positions in the world. In a sense, the individual plays out society within a small world of social interaction wherein the person's physical, moral, cognitive, and mystical theories of the world reflect the consensual beliefs carried by others within one's interpersonal sphere. One's view of the world, then, reflects the epistemic community to which one belongs. Workers, for example, view the organization by which they are employed more as a resource or a provider than will managers in that organization who will view it more in terms of a tool-to-get-things-done. Reality is never apprehended directly but is only seen through some sort of practical theory. Consider the cultural stranger who will experience a well of loneliness when moving from one culture to another for he or she is entering a different universe of meaning, one that is not shared or perhaps even known by him or her. Such loneliness results from the subjective isolation one feels at not having others around who are sufficiently similar to oneself to see the new world in the same fashion. As long as our theories remain unchallenged, however, reality is unquestioned. But, once challenged, reality suddenly presents a most practical problem, one that must be approached and if possible resolved. From this standpoint, the study of interpersonal relations does not lead to defining social reality; it leads, rather, to an investigation of its different versions and how they arise.

Culture and Reality

What I have argued thus far is that reality is frequently a problematic matter. Despite our universal and basic abilities to construct meanings, there is no guarantee that the meanings we construct will be shared ones. Significantly, the modern world is marked by and large by social realities that are not consensual (though we may take them to be), but ones that are of the emergent, negotiable, and conflictual variety. While we must build some version of reality to guide us in everyday life, the version we build will perhaps be confronted and tested continually against other versions. It is my belief that such tests are occurring with greater frequency in the world than ever before. In particular, western society is marked by many such reality tests.

We live in a time of vast change. A single walk around the block in any big city in America should be enough to convince virtually anyone of the presence of multiple, heterogeneous, competing, and thoroughly unique social worlds in which people live. Jesus freaks, business people, muggers, students, junkies, sidewalk musicians, hot-rod enthusiasts, panhandlers, rabbis, prostitutes, skateboarders, cops, winos, hipsters, Buddists, elderly loungers, transvestites, and priests, to name just a few, comprise the loose but picturesque mosaic of human strivings visible to any observer of the urban scene. This is hardly surprising since meanings, while socially bound, are potentially infinite. Since we all possess the capacity to order the world, many orders are possible. Thus, the view of the world which exists among people within any one order may vary from the view existing in other orders even though the material world in which all orders necessarily exist is more or less the same. Alfred Schutz captured this possibility well when he noted, "The same lifeworld lends itself to a magical interpretation by primitive peoples, a theological one by a missionary and a scientific one by a technologist."[19]

---

[19] Alfred Schutz, *Studies in Philosophical Phenomenology* (The Hague: Martinus Nijhoff, 1966), p. 29.

In mass societies (and especially in densely populated urban areas), many designs for living, each tuned to a somewhat different view of the world, are present. Each design is more or less distinguishable as a separate activity system with a set of special meanings, social rules of conduct, sacred symbols, and unique kinds of performances. In our society in particular, whatever hegemony of meaning that perhaps once was wrapped around our civil conduct by powerful institutions such as the family, the school, and the state seems to have disappeared or at least receded. Young people, for example, gather by the thousands in public parks across the country to joyfully smoke marijuana in bold defiance of the criminal law. Formerly taken-for-granted social norms regarding appropriate sexual conduct are challenged openly in many highly visible gay bars. Even polite standards of public conduct are disregarded on many occasions such as when we must fight with others to simply board a subway, cab, or bus. What lies behind these apparent rips in the social fabric? Fundamentally, this state of affairs reflects a growing social segmentation among people. Indeed, it reflects the growth and maintenance of almost separate cultures within the society.

Culture is information. It is that fact of human life learned as a result of belonging to a particular group. It is that facet, in particular, that is shared by all members of that group through interaction. To learn a culture implies that one learns how one is expected to behave in the group, what one can expect in terms of the behavior of others, and what the limits are for such behavior. In a sense, culture stylizes our behavior by providing us with a myriad of proper forms—a proper time to sleep, a proper way to eat, a proper way to think, and so on. From this perspective, culture places the moral limits on people in a way biology cannot accomplish. Culture includes, then, the inhibitions that govern us from the inside, the rules that apparently control us from the outside, the various customs and rituals that help define how we are to relate to one another, and, crucially, the languages and philosophies we use to edit and interpret our everyday experiences. In terms I introduced previously, culture fills up our "natural attitudes" toward the world.[20]

In places where geographic isolation, little change, and homogeneity mark the background experiences of the residents, culture is relatively unproblematic to people and provides a neat and encompassing life plan for all to follow. Certain activities which pertain largely to the group's

---

[20] Culture, in the sense I am using it, provides a person with an operational set of behavioral taboos ("you may not"), permissibles ("you may") and obligations ("you must"). Two different but rather good and recent statements on the role of culture in human affairs are Marvin Harris, *Culture, People, Nature* (New York: Cromwell, 1975), and Clifford Geertz, *The Interpretation of Cultures* (New York: Basic Books, 1973). For a similar, though distinctly sociological perspective on the influence of culture on behavior, see Peter Berger's very lively and readable *Invitation to Sociology* (New York: Anchor, 1963).

survival are parceled out according to tradition, and continuity is assured since the problems of one generation are the problems of the next. Kai Erikson, in a moving study of a community disaster, gives us a lovely description of one such culture that, before a flood wiped the community from the map, represented one of the few such cultural enclaves left in this country. The place is a remote hollow in the Appalachian mountains, and of it, Erikson writes:

> The environment required nothing in the way of planning and innovation, almost nothing in the way of personal and social change. And so a cultural style came into being on this frontier that remained largely intact for the better part of 130 years. There was no encouragement for change from within, since the old habits and old traditions seemed wholly adequate for the simple realities of everyday life, and there was no encouragement for change from without, since new ideas and new people rarely penetrated that vastness."[21]

Few frontiers of such stillness remain. Where they do, reality is reasonably complete, whole, and unproblematic. Meanings are, for the most part, consensual, though no society ever visited by mankind has been totally devoid of conflict. Yet, let us not wax too romantically over our loss, for such stability appears to come at only a high price. Poverty, in particular, is most often associated with such stable realities, and poverty is, indeed, a harsh taskmaster (perhaps second only to the insecurity triggered by anxiety over one's immediate physical safety). In brief, people who must work long and hard for most of their waking hours merely to survive, such as those described by Erikson, are sternly constrained by their practical situation. They can hardly take the time to examine and investigate other worlds. Yet, where time and opportunity allow, other worlds will be explored, since a basic curiosity and a desire for new experience characterizes humankind.[22] And, when these new worlds are explored, one's former world is likely to be disenchanted.

The Growth of Cultural Relativism within Society

One result of the kind of disenchantment discussed above is essentially the growth of cultural relativism. The spirit of this relativism is heard everyday in the "do your own thing" rhetoric of American public life.

---

[21] Kai T. Erickson, *Everything in its Path* (New York: Simon and Schuster, 1976), p. 113.

[22] While this may seem a sweeping generalization, I suspect that curiosity comes as close to a basic human "drive" (such as sleeping or eating) as anything else. From the Garden of Eden onward, people have always sought to expand their knowledge and experience of the world. Contemporary psychology has come close to recognizing this principle when it ponders such human propensities as the "need" for achievement, adventure, pleasure, change, self-actualization, and growth.

People who come together under such conditions must build situational standards to guide their activities, since a common cultural set of standards cannot be assumed to exist beforehand. Moreover, if the situations that require joint activity are regular ones in a society, common standards will begin to accumulate, but they will be standards applicable to only certain situations. Thus, in a world where many meaning systems exist, reality becomes tied to particular situations rather than across situations. Since the information germaine to these situations is shared only by the people who routinely interact within them, culture itself becomes highly specific and bounded.

The world then becomes segmented on the basis of what we are up to at any particular time. Hence, our specific purposes will at least partially determine the limits we will allow a situation to move. When we deal with George the shoe clerk, for example, it makes little difference to us whether George is sad or elated, cynical or sincere, as he goes about his tasks. What matters to us is merely that he is available, able, and willing to perform the function we need performed at the moment—to exchange our money for a pair of properly fitted shoes. In everyday life, impersonal encounters of this variety are made possible by focusing on only those meanings which appear to be "relevant" to our purposes at hand. Indeed, much of modern life takes place as we move in and out of situations where reality (and the culture it reflects) is highly circumstantial.

Equally important, the growth of cultural relativism results from some broader societal trends. Consider the great mobility that presently characterizes the contemporary American scene. Few of us now live in the communities of our origins, though it is true that throughout most of history, people were born, grew up, worked, and raised their children in rather self-contained and closed communities—communities wherein a rather uniform system of meaning existed. By moving about with such frequency, we have loosened our connections to local and shared standards of conduct and have come into contact with many new and different standards.[23]

Increasing education which also marks the contemporary scene has much the same effect as geographical mobility. In a sense, education represents a kind of intellectual mobility whereby our parochialism and common-sense morality is challenged by the knowledge that many other ways of life exist alongside our own. Thus, what may have been taught

---

[23] An interesting and similar analysis of the effect of recent social trends upon the individual is to be found in Orrin Klapp, *The Collective Search for Identity* (Chicago: Aldine Publishing Co., 1964). In particular, Klapp argues that rapid change weakens the sense of self we are able to develop. And it is not only discovering who we *are* that is problematic, but, moreover, it may be quite difficult to even discover who we *were* since many of us would have great trouble even recognizing the neighborhood of our origins so unrelenting have been the physical changes in the world. It may well be that Thomas Wolfe's figurative remark, "You can't go home again," has today become a literal one.

to us in childhood as the "one best way" or, in some cases, "the only way" (whether it was directed as viewing a painting, speaking to elders, or believing in God) is shown to be regarded quite differently by other people. And, furthermore, we can see that these other people seem to be getting on quite nicely in the world despite their nasty disregard for certain social and moral prescriptions that mark the world of our origins.

The media, too, are effective at promoting cultural relativism. Television, movies, books, newspapers, and other modern mass communication systems augment and spread news, ideas, and diverse information around the country with remarkable speed. The growth of these channels of communication seems to be particularly important in terms of broadening our horizons and increasing at least our simple awareness of the social variability around us. Take the ever popular TV situation comedies, the so-called sit-coms of today. However partial, stereotyped, and fundamentally inaccurate they may be, we nevertheless could on any given evening in 1977 at least vicariously share in the joys and the woes of: a black, widowed junk dealer in Los Angeles ("Sanford and Son"), a liberated middle-class housewife in suburban New York ("Maude"), a crusty and raw loading-dock worker from the Bronx ("All in the Family"), an aging though spry garage mechanic in Los Angeles ("Chico and the Man"), a divorced waitress with a teenage son who works in a diner in Phoenix, Arizona ("Alice"), and a psychologist who, with his wife, a schoolteacher, lives in a luxurious high-rise apartment in downtown Chicago ("The Bob Newhart Show"). These examples and the popularity they have enjoyed merely point to the rather pervasive introduction we all have had to the different and available ways of life that surround us.[24]

All this is to say that the simple and unquestioned life which perhaps once surrounded us is no more.[25] It is a time of great diversity and change, and our approach to the study of interpersonal relations must respect the

---

[24] It is worth noting that the effects of television on our lives is perhaps the most underresearched topic in all of social science. Despite the penetration of the "boob tube" into our everyday lives and the great outpouring of the vociferous resentment of intellectuals to the "debasing" character of popular TV programming, we know very little indeed about the behavioral implications of its presence in our midst. About all we do know is that children who watch a great deal of television tend to rely more on stereotypes than do children who watch less television. See Lotte Bailyn, "Mass Media and Children," *Psychological Monographs*, 73 (1959). Perhaps, because there is no chance for interaction with a television character, we can know them only as highly typified abstractions. But, to date, we have virtually no clue as to how this might or might not affect our interpersonal relations.

[25] Despite my remarks in the text and the many explicit challenges to the taken-for-granted social order during the last decade or so, cultural relativism has hardly destroyed the taken-for-granted world entirely. Indeed, there are still many beliefs and practices we put into use automatically. We assume when people cry they are normally sad or when another's brow is tightly knit together, that person is deep in thought. We still make use of the serviceable "excuse me" when we inadvertently jostle another in public—and expect it to be forthcoming when we are jostled. And, certainly we do not yet live in a world where all crimes against persons are defined as political acts.

basic facts regarding the place and time of our existence. Crucially, an assumption of "shared values" held by all members of society as the root metaphor upon which behavior is to be explained will no longer hold (if, indeed, it ever did hold).

Life as Theater

Given these considerations, a more appropriate root metaphor to examine the behavior of individuals and groups in the modern world is "drama." In brief, there is today a rather close analogy between individual acts in everyday interpersonal relations and the way actors self-consciously play out roles on the stage.[26] This is a particularly apt theoretical scheme for our times since a general self-consciousness pervades our everyday life such that we are often fully aware of playing a number of social parts ranging from mother to lover, from seller to buyer, from college student to grocery clerk, from serious churchgoer to jovial socialite, and so on. With fewer and fewer obligatory and transitional roles to play, people have developed something of a new psychological orientation to assume toward all the roles they play which reflect modern conditions, not traditional ones. While the overriding purpose of this psychological orientation is, no doubt, the same as it has always been—to be esteemed or at least accepted and not rejected by our fellows—its accomplishment has become more difficult since the social worlds in which we move into and out of today are so numerous and so distinct.

Let me backtrack for a moment. I have argued that when people enter a situation they must do so with an idea of what they expect to occur. They must also be able to type the behavior of others they observe in this situation as recognizable or, at least, categorically familiar and, therefore, meaningful. Finally, they must be able to understand the ongoing conversation and action that unfolds in the situation such that certain changing expectations, perceptions, and other circumstantial contingencies can be met and managed. These three interpersonal performances depend upon our interpersonal capacities to produce temporal frameworks, categorization devices, and interpretive procedures respectively. The content that char-

---

[26] For a very similar view on the practical usefulness of the metaphor of drama, see: Blumer, *Symbolic Interactionism*; Gregory Stone, "Appearance and the Self" in *Human Behavior and Social Processes*, ed. Arnold M. Rose (New York: Houghton Mifflin Co., 1962); Anselm L. Strauss, *Mirrors and Masks* (Glencoe, Ill.: The Free Press, 1959); Erving Goffman, *Presentation of Self*; *Encounters* (Indianapolis: Bobbs-Merrill, 1961); *Behavior in Public Places* (New York: The Free Press, 1963); *Interaction Ritual* (Chicago: Aldine Publishing Co., 1967); *Relations in Public* (New York: Basic Books, 1971); *Frame Analysis* (Cambridge, Mass.: Harvard University Press, 1974). For a brief but effective overview of the dramaturgic theory, see Sheldon L. Messinger, Harold Sampson, and Robert D. Towne, "Life as Theater: Some Notes on the Dramaturgic Approach to Social Reality," *Sociometry*, 25 (1962), pp. 98–110.

acterizes our use of these capacities will then define our reality for us. If, for example, we expect to attend a "boring party," encounter people who fit our a priori classification of "boring types" while at the party, and, in interaction, find that our basic orientation to the conversation in which we engage is of the "ho-hum" variety, we have constructed a rather encompassing reality to encase, frame, or in sociological terms, "define the situation."

It is possible, of course, that something might occur along the way to disturb this reality and nudge or perhaps jolt us into another one wherein the party may, in fact, be experienced as one that is truly exciting and fun. Certainly, our behavior in each of these two worlds is likely to be quite different. Thus, given a concrete situation, our interpretation of what is going on in that situation is the reality of the moment to which we must gear our thoughts and actions. Moreover, this reality may or may not be a consensual one shared by all persons also embedded within the situation. However, to characterize the reality of the situation itself as consensual, emergent, negotiated, or conflictual requires that we examine the perspectives of all those present, for ultimately there are no absolute grounds or criteria upon which the "correct" reality can be selected from among the alternatives.

Dramatic metaphors are of assistance here for they in no way rely on some assumed state of nature within which behavior must be bounded. Rather, they allow us to conceive of behavior as something that results from actors who consciously select certain lines of action. The selected actions, therefore, must always be seen within the context of the particular social stage upon which they are enacted. Thus, while we cannot always predict what an actor will do in certain situations, we can begin to understand what social actors may do, so that their behavior will be viewed as "proper" by others in that situation. Whether or not our social actors actually do the "proper" thing under specified and known conditions is quite another matter.

A Preview

The theory that lies behind this dramaturgic point of view on human behavior is outlined in the following essay. Briefly, I will argue there that three factors are of primary importance in coming to understand interpersonal relations. First, we must know something about social actors and the poses or stances they assume. Second, we must learn something about the social stages upon which these actors strike their poses. And, third, we must discover the available rules which guide the actors on stage in sustaining various stances without bringing discredit from the audience to whom they are playing. What we will find at the nexus of actors, situations, and rules is social reality, and what we will also discover is that if this reality is to be more than a fragmentary or fleeting one, it must inescapably be one that is collectively and cooperatively constructed. Reality, from this perspective, is an on-going social and moral venture, established, sustained, and sometimes drastically altered by everyday interpersonal relations as they occur in concrete situations.

3

The Self, the Situation, and the Rules of Interpersonal Relations[1]
by JOHN VAN MAANEN

In solitude we are least alone.

BYRON

I. INTRODUCTION

Drama and the Study of Human Behavior

For several thousands of years, dramatists such as playwrites, directors, actors, novelists, poets, and the like have demonstrated an exceptional understanding of interpersonal relations. The great dramatists knew well of human frailties and strengths, of human sorrows and joys. They knew well also of the key social events, issues, themes, and problems that characterized their times. So well were these known, in fact, that long before psychology, sociology, or anthropolgy burst forth as full-blown professions in the first third of the 20th century, the theatrical stage provided perhaps the best source of general knowledge about the human condition. Critically, the idea of comparing life to drama emerged probably at the same time drama itself began to be acted out in public settings. And this metaphor system, the borrowing of understanding from the theater and applying it to life, has been with us more or less explicitly ever since. Certainly, famous examples of just this are not hard to locate. Consider the work of Sophecles in ancient Periclean Greece, Cervantes in 16th-century Spain, Shakespeare in Elizebethan England, or Ionesco, Becket, and Genét in the modern European "Theater of the Absurd."

Drawing a close parallel between life and drama seems inevitable. Because the theater attempts to recreate and enact certain aspects of life, it

---

[1] This chapter was written specifically for this volume.

must fundamentally imitate life. A good imitation therefore must be grounded upon considerable insight into the experience and structure of social life, and, as I noted at the close of the previous essay, many social scientists have begun to make use of these insights. As a result, a number of "analytic tools" to understand human behavior have been developed (although it appears that such understanding has often come about in far more insensitive and heavy-handed ways than displayed by our predecessors). My use of the term *performance* in the last essay to denote individual behavior reflects, for instance, the use of this metaphor system to model interpersonal relations. To perform implies a degree of self-consciousness about the actions one takes in life. And, precisely, because of the consciousness-of-self, the dramaturgic approach provides a most appropriate means for describing the actions one takes before others who can be thought of as an "audience."

The Organization of This Essay

In the preceding essay, the central interest was upon how people, in general, render the world meaningful. As such, the objective was to describe certain primary aspects of the process by which cognitive understandings are gleened from raw experience. In this essay, I examine how actions are related to the information an individual holds in particular certain cognitive categories. Here, it is merely assumed that people can and do attach meaning to the situations they find themselves in. Thus, the emphasis of this essay is upon the different kinds of social information people must possess in order to behave appropriately (or inappropriately) in given situations.

In brief, there are three key elements to the analytic scheme presented below: the individual's sense of self, the social situations wherein the self resides, and the social rules which govern those situations in which the self is located. But, as in virtually all theoretical models which flow from observing the behavior of human beings, each element in this explanatory scheme is highly related to each other element. For example, one's conception of the kind of person one is can be expected to influence the sorts of social situations within which one allows oneself to become involved. Similarly, certain social rules are more likely to be discovered in some situations than in others. An adequate explanation for the behavior of an individual must therefore take into account all three of these cognitive elements simultaneously. Hence, while each of these elements is considered in relative isolation, the reader should keep in mind that in actuality they are tightly intertwined.

The material to follow is presented in four sections. The first section, Part II, considers that most important actor in everyday life, the self. In this section, the process by which an individual's sense of self develops is presented along with a discussion devoted to the ways in which our self-conceptions become fragmented thus allowing for the possibility that we possess both public and private selves. In Part III, several types of social situations are analyzed in terms of what individuals need to know about them in order to take action. Part IV describes various rules of social conduct with attention being directed toward the manner in which people make use of such rules as a way of regulating the behavior of themselves and others. Finally, Part V closes out this essay by suggesting a few implications (some good, some not so good) that flow from the foregoing description of the individual in modern society—a description that basically depicts the person as engaged in a continual struggle to exercise individual freedom yet still respond to certain omnipresent social constraints. This concluding section turns on the ironic observation that while we can be said to create our own reality, we must also live within it.

II.   THE EMERGING SELF[2]

The self, as it is thought of here, is a direct result of social interaction. We are not born with a self whose purpose it is to grow, mature, and die. But, rather, we are provided a self by others, many selves actually, throughout our lifetimes. We can be mothers, lawyers, socialites, sisters, secret sinners, devout believers, workhorses, aggressive lovers, shy speakers, politicians, gameplayers, and so forth. We can play several roles at the same time, change roles, fake roles, and still we tend to think of ourselves as somehow whole and unique. While the self may be thought of as our most personal and prized possession, it nevertheless resides ultimately in the hands of others who may choose to deny it, confirm it, ignore it, or change it. But before we can consider how these various selves are actually played out, we must consider how a consciousness of the self can be said to develop in the first place.

The Social Foundations of Self Awareness

The first and perhaps most critical piece to be used when putting together the puzzle that human behavior represents is the notion that indi-

---

[2] In this section we draw heavily upon those associated with the so-called Chicago school of sociology including Anselm Strauss, *Mirrors and Masks* (Glencoe, Ill.: The Free Press, 1963); Everett C. Hughes, *The Sociological Eye*, vols. I and II (Chicago: Aldine Publishing Co., 1971); Howard S. Becker, *Sociological Work* (Chicago: Aldine Publishing Co., 1971; and especially George Herbert Mead, *Mind, Self, and Society* (Chicago: University of Chicago Press, 1934). The bare requirements of the self, according to this perspective, include the ability to self-consciously manipulate symbols, take a position on one's own activities, and ponder the image that one presents to others. These writers are all closely aligned with the symbolic interactionist school of thought as mentioned in Chapter 1.

viduals become social beings only through interacting with others—in particular, interacting with others with whom they are involved on a daily, intimate, and face-to-face basis. Sociologist Charles Horton Cooley argued persuasively that the acquisition of personal characteristics such as a sense of fairness, justice, kindness, compassion, and cooperation all develop through situated social interaction in which a person learns to ascribe these labels to particular actions taken by others and to actions taken by one's self.[3] Just as we teach our children the meaning of terms like *uncle* and *aunt* not by reciting an anthropologist's definition of the kinship structure, but by pointing out to them the flesh and blood people who stand behind the labels of, say, "Uncle Jimmy" and "Aunt Kathy," we teach our children the meaning of fairness or kindness in the same matter.

Conceptions of the self are learned in an identical fashion. We learn as children, for example, we are "good" if we don't play with matches or bite the dog, and we learn we are "bad" if we do. Such learning is based upon our ability or capacity to subjectively understand our own behavior by placing ourselves in the position of others and viewing our actions as others apparently do.[4] This *looking-glass self*, as Cooley so aptly termed it, does not come about altogether smoothly as if by magic, but rather emerges quite slowly and problematically as anyone who has raised children knows empirically. The difficulty arises partly because the views people can hold toward our behavior are varied and partly because these views are most often only situationally specific. Thus, children may learn to use profanity at an early age, but it takes a considerably longer period of time for them to learn when, where, and with whom such profanity can be used without disrupting the situation.

The genesis of a consciousness-of-self then follows the same developmental pattern as other forms of consciousness. It is but a special case of meaning construction, no different in principle than the way we learn what anything means.[5] What sets it apart, of course, is the naked truth

---

[3] See Charles Horton Cooley, *Human Nature and the Social Order* (New York: Scribner's, 1922).

[4] This interchangeability of viewpoints can be put forth formally: An individual's gesture or act calls out symbolic responses from others which then provide the individual with both symbolic meanings for the self and for the gesture or act (and the situation within which the sequence is enacted). From the symbolic interactionist perspective, the gesture-response sequence is the most basic unit of analysis in social study. See Herbert Blumer, *Symbolic Interactionism* (Englewood Cliffs, N.J.: Prentice Hall, 1969).

[5] I should note that both the interactionist and dramaturgic analysis of everyday life has concentrated more upon the selves of actors than upon properties of social meaning and interaction per se. The theory of the self presented here is, therefore, a special case of the more general phenomenological theory of action. In other words, the self is a set of typifications no different in form (though, no doubt, considerably closer and more important to us) than the typifications we attribute to other objects, events, facts, and relationships we encounter in the world.

that the self rarely moves out of view; it is always with us even in our dreams. While we may take for granted some of the characteristics we ascribe to ourselves, such as being "good" or "shrewd" or "practical," the self, unlike other objects of our concern, is continuously present, thus theoretically always subject to the risk of possible disconfirmation.

According to many developmental studies which have been accomplished, we begin life apparently unable to distinguish the self from the environment surrounding us.[6] Slowly we learn that the self which acts on the world is biologically separate from the world that is acted upon. We learn that to bite our hand is altogether different than biting the hand of another, and that certain acts produce certain reactions from other objects (human or otherwise). These reactions are, however, purely symbolic in that we must learn to ascribe certain meanings to them by discovering what the reaction points toward. The smile, for example, may become a sign to an infant that food or affection or amusement are soon to follow. Feelings can then be tied to the emerging codes learned by the child, and, over time, the smile alone may become the generator of good feelings. In the preverbal world of an infant, such signs are taken as the representation of what the self means to others and constitutes the first step in coming to see the self as others do. The child visited frequently by smiling adults senses that it is the self which produced such pleasant and (not insignificantly) useful responses.

Such codes begin in a universal but rather restricted fashion but gradually become infinitely more specific and elaborate.[7] Thus, as we develop, the

---

[6] See, for example, some of the impressive empirical work of Jean Piaget: *The Construction of Reality in the Child* (New York: Basic Books, 1954); *The Origins of Intelligence in Children* (New York: International University Press, 1952); *The Language and Thought of Children* (New York: Humanities Press, 1959); and Jean Piaget and B. Inhelder, *The Psychology of the Child* (New York: Basic Books, 1969). A broader treatment of childhood learning can be found in Lawrence Kohlberg, "Stage and Sequence: The Cognitive-Developmental Approach to Socialization" in *Handbook of Socialization Theory and Research*, ed. David Goslin (Chicago: Rand McNally and Co., 1969), pp. 347–480, and in Norman K. Denzin, *Childhood Socialization* (San Francisco: Jossey-Bass, 1977).

[7] This increasing specificity may not be as universal as once thought. Anthropologist Basil Bernstein's notion of restricted and elaborated codes of interaction is helpful in this regard. Restricted codes are those interactional symbols that arise in close, intimate communication networks where the communication within the network is likely to be solidarity-supporting. Elaborated codes appear where the specification of meaning is all important as in the communication that takes place between strangers. Furthermore, class differences, according to Bernstein, exist in the use of these interaction codes. For example, the middle classes apparently switch back and forth between elaborated and restricted codes whereas the lower classes tend to rely on the restricted codes in all of their interactions. Seemingly, the middle-class child has greater opportunity to develop impersonal interpersonal relationships early on, and the learning that stems from these situationally specific interpersonal dealings is rather useful in such social settings as the school and the work place. This may well be one reason why lower-class children are so often labeled "less intelligent" than middle-class children by teachers and psychologists when they enter the public schools, for

signs taken as representative of the self are increasingly tied to our growing recognition of the acts we perform in the world. With language acquisition, for instance, we learn what it means to be "nasty" or "nice" and also discover, more or less simultaneously, that when our actions are seen by others as "nasty" or "nice," we are treated poorly or well. As a consequence, we learn to feel good or bad depending on the evaluations of the others who are close to us. As learning stretches out, our notions of the self become far more complex, concrete, and diverse as we learn from a vast number of others that we are viewed on certain occasions as dumb or smart, ugly or handsome, sad or happy, suspicious or trusting, and so on. A display of those qualities which are viewed by others around us as appropriate, correct, or desirable in the situation, bring both material and emotional rewards, and we learn, therefore, that it is in our own best interest to display them.

A person then develops a set of categories about the self. Such categories, like all categorization schemes, carry moral overtones for they increasingly provide the standards which allow persons to label their own actions as right or wrong. The more we move across different social circles and situations, the more differentiated these standards are likely to become. The more we move through similar social circles and situations, the more these standards are likely to remain the same.

Moreover, since self-classifications are interpersonal in origin, they can be altered by both the form and content of social interaction. It is, therefore, a matter of some concern to us that our actions are seen by others as morally acceptable under the circumstances—that they fit the standards of the social world we are operating in. Just as we construct impressions of another's behavior as morally justified or not, we construct self-impressions based on our own behavior. From these observations of our actions and the responses to them by others comes an always-emerging perspective on the self. It is necessarily an inductive and loose perspective based on an ever-enlarging chain of experience in which we attempt to manage our wordly performances such that others (particularly those others who matter to us) will judge our actions favorably.

The self, then, is both an integration and an abstraction of the views we think others hold toward us. As we progress through adulthood, these categories of the self must handle increasing amounts of information coming from others about "who we are." Significantly, the information is typically varied and sometimes conflicting since people will respond to us differently in different situations. The self, then, is always a fuzzy object, for while we may feel that there is a unique and complete self somewhere

---

these differences have been found in children as young as five years of age. See Basil M. Bernstein, "Elaborated and Restricted Codes: Their Social Origins and Some Consequences," *American Anthropologist*, 66 (1964), pp. 55–69.

behind the many roles we play, we will always have difficulty articulating that uniqueness and completeness since, like the words of a language, the self is only recognized fully in concrete situations.

From this standpoint, the self in adulthood resembles a large collection of behavioral repertoires ready to be plugged into different situations. While we may, for example, view ourselves as "happy persons," we must still try to generate under particular conditions the sort of behavior we think others will interpret as "happy." Thus, not only do we come to see ourselves as we believe others do, we must also manage our behavior in such a way that people will continue to see us in that light.

We also have, however, great generalization skills that allow us to pluck a value from here, an idea from there, a behavior, an attitude, or a fact from various sources and somehow put them together into a real or imagined perspective on our form of life. What we eat, what we say, the clothes we wear, where we live, the people we choose to be seen with, the manner in which we decorate our homes, where we spend our vacations, the cars we drive, and so on all suggest to others (and to ourselves) the kind of persons we have decided to be. The choices we make most often suggest that we struggle to maintain some congruency, uniqueness, and perhaps stability around certain "core classifications" we may hold about ourselves. Yet we still must move through many highly diverse social worlds in which our "core classifications" may be put to the test. If our response to the various testing episodes of our life is to be one that confirms our inner vision of the self, we must be able to manipulate our image of the self, complete with the performances and appearances that go with such an image, so that others' judgements of our actions will be reasonably congruent with our own. To say the least, we are not always successful on these grounds.

The self in any social situation, therefore, is inextricably tied to three components. First, there is the performance itself or the words, deeds, gestures, personal fronts, props, and so forth that describe our actions and appearances in a given situation. Second, there is our interpretation (reflective, immediate, prospective) of the response of others to our performance. And third, there is our own inner response or feelings attached to the performance itself and the feelings we attach to the response of others. In other words, all our behavior is both *instrumental* (in the service of some objective) and *expressive* (a symbolic representation of the kind of persons we are striving to be in the situation). As Goffman puts it, when hanging out the wash we are not merely drying it but hanging it out for others to see. Indeed, the most trivial of instrumental acts may turn out to be expressively the most significant of all.[8]

---

[8] See Erving Goffman, *Frame Analysis* (Cambridge, Mass.: Harvard University Press, 1974), p. 9.

From this perspective, all social interaction is potentially dangerous. Even in the most benign-appearing situations, a social trap may be present which may open to discredit, embarrass, or shame the unwary actor and lead to self-doubt as to the sterling quality of the actor's innermost character. To avoid such pitfalls demands the ability to create and maintain a performance that is taken by others as correct and to do so in such a way that one's own conception of the self is not damaged. This brings us back to where we began, for such performances depend upon our ability to know the other. Thus, while the claims we carry about ourselves may seem to be private property, these claims are fundamentally collective holdings since they must be sustained by others who may choose to honor them or profane them.

Self Conceptions

The learning involved in taking the position of another in order to know (subjectively) what others are thinking and doing is undoubtedly immense. It apparently can never be fully completed because throughout our lifetime we can be and often are surprised and taken aback by the behavior of others. To some extent, we are always in the process of "becoming." But, to "become" anything requires the ability to assume a reciprocity of viewpoints, particularly the ability to see our actions as others see them. The learning of reciprocity occurs perhaps most dramatically in childhood as we acquire our most basic notions about ourselves from those closest to us. As infants, we soon begin to understand to a degree what stance others take toward us, and, by so doing, we become aware of ourselves as something more than a gurgling bundle of baby fat and urges. To be seen as "good," therefore, becomes possible through our own actions based on our emerging knowledge of what others see as "good." And, if being "good" leads to certain creature comforts such as warmth, affection, food, and companionship, then "good" is what we will strive to be.

The work of W. I. Thomas is important here along with that of George Herbert Mead.[9] Both men argued convincingly that if we believe something to be real, it is real in its consequences. Thus, the beliefs people carry about a situation is the elemental reality of that situation. And the self is as subject to this law of interpersonal relations as anything else. Mead, in particular, noted that we are continually engaged in the process of building a set of beliefs about ourselves (self-conceptions) through our interpretations of the position others seem to take toward us by their gestures and use of language. Mead suggested furthermore that the self-conceptions

---

[9] See William I. Thomas, *The Child in America* (New York: Knopf, 1928) and Mead, *Mind, Self, and Society.*

we develop can be separated analytically into two fundamental parts— the *I* and the *Me*. The *I* is that part of the self that watches, as it were, the *Me* perform in the world. The *Me* is the object to which the *I* subjectively responds by seeing the actions of the *Me* as appropriate or inappropriate, as good or bad. In dramaturgic terms, the *I* is the performer or person who stands behind the role the *Me* is performing on any occasion. The *I* is, therefore, the unseen yet onmipresent other or audience to whom the *Me* must address all activities. When we carry on those familiar interior dialogues with ourselves about why we did such and such or said this or that, such dialogues represent the everyday substance of the *I* dealing with the *Me*.

Another piece remains to be fitted to our puzzle. Where does the *I*, the subjective sense of self, come from? Here again Mead's contribution to our dramaturgic model is crucial. Individuals, according to Mead, not only abstract themselves out of their given situated performance in order to evaluate it, they also form abstract conceptions of others' performances and responses across situations which can be used to measure, guide, and evaluate their own performances. This abstracted conception of others and the categories that go with it is called the *generalized other*, and it represents perhaps the most powerful but most elusive "they" of our lives. This "they" emerges from the crib onward as we learn that if we behave in a certain fashion, something we like will usually occur. Smiles, to continue my infant example, bring attention and visual variety. Kicking and hollering bring tightly drawn looks of scorn and perhaps a sting on our backsides. Whimpers and coos bring soothing pats and warm milk. Gradually the distinction between what we do and what occurs becomes recognizable, and, when it does, our sense of self begins to substantively expand and grow more sophisticated. The *I* which develops over a lifetime is then merely the generalized other or the forgotten and slippery "they" of an earlier period. The *I*, abstracted, refined, and infinitely nuanced, becomes analogous to our most critical audience of our everyday performances.

Several other aspects are important to understanding how the *I* develops. First, the notion of play is central. Mead argued that throughout childhood we play at and with certain roles drawn, however incompletely, from the adult worlds around us. We play at being fathers, mothers, cowboys, nurses, cops, and robbers, all of which help form the *I*. Through such play, our notions of justice, crime, sociability, human benevolence, and malice are slowly shaped. Second, these notions become part of our self-conceptions. Those that are most crucial come, no doubt, from the playing of roles associated with what are called the *significant others* of our lives. Such significant others represent those persons whom we know intimately and have come to care for, to both like and admire. Significant others are those whose evaluations of our performed self matter most to us. They may be teachers, relatives, parents, friends, or anyone with whom we have close contact. By looking at the world and ourselves as we imagine these significant others do, we come to develop our own conceptions of who we are and what we must do to be liked and admired by these significant others. Third, over time, the lessons emerging from significant others and through play become part of the generalized other, that silent evaluator of the mind that both prompts and assesses our performances in the world. The individual, from this standpoint, is not something the person invents. The individual is rather that someone whom other people have come to see, have come to believe in, and have come to treat the person as being. And, as a consequence, over time, the individual, too, comes to see, to believe, and to treat himself or herself as being.[10]

Some qualifications on the foregoing must be now suggested. Clearly, not everyone with whom we come into contact is important to us. Furthermore, because of the vast number of roles we play both in childhood and adult life, some roles will be treated more seriously than others. For many reasons, sociological, genetic, and psychological, we may be better at some roles than others. Thus, certain roles and the skills that go with them become emphasized over others. Reference-group theory is useful here for it suggests that embedded in everyday life are other persons whom we more or less consciously see ourselves as similar to and whom we positively evaluate. Thomatsu Shibutani suggested that people form conceptions of and attach themselves to certain reference groups which are not necessarily tied to any particular collectivity or location.[11] We do this, according to Shibutani, by selecting bits and pieces from the mass communication channels, our interpersonal networks, and our images of our self and fit them together into a perspective of some real or imagined group. Such groups represent audiences to whom we can gear particular performances. There are probably as many potential reference groups available to us as there are channels of communication available to us. Visibility is, therefore, a key aspect of the reference group concept.

The choice of a reference group to guide actions in a particular sphere of life is, unlike the choice of significant others, potentially wide. Images abound in American society. When courting a desirable young woman, a male in this culture may choose to be, for example, the virile sort of guy who reads *Playboy* or he may choose the more sedate image of the intellec-

---

[10] This point of view reflects the work of Erving Goffman more so than George Herbert Mead, who viewed the self-conceptions a person develops in life as relatively stable. Goffman, to the contrary, views self-conceptions as loose, fluid, and tied not only to particular situations but also to the ever-changing parade of significant others who come into and take leave of one's life. As the remainder of this essay indicates, I stand closer to Goffman than Mead. See, in particular, Goffman's *The Presentation of Self in Everyday Life* (Garden City, N.Y.: Doubleday, 1959).

[11] See Thomatsu Shibutani, "Reference Groups and Social Control" in *Human Behavior and Social Processes*, ed. Arnold M. Rose (New York: Houghton Mifflin Co., 1962), pp. 209–26.

tual who reads the "New York Review of Books." His preferred means of seduction may include hot dogs, beer, and tickets to a hockey game or it may include candlelight, pressed duck, white wine, and Bach. The "Johnny Carson Show" or *People Magazine* offer and endless parade of well-known celebrities who inform us as to their families, hobbies, diets, pets, and other mundane aspects of their presented selves and social worlds. Such images often provide the detail upon which we can partially manufacture a reference group from which our sense of "personhood" emerges.

Indeed, the power of the media to disseminate (and the willingness of segments of the public to adopt) various fads such as skateboards, pet rocks, yoga, and the Fonz suggests the importance of reference groups in various aspects of our everyday lives. While we are bombarded with a seemingly patternless set of alternatives to chose from when deciding what to purchase, how to spend our time, or even what kind of person we want to be, our selections from among this swirling set are anything but random. Tastes and preferences based on our idealized reference groups allow us to survey a universe of possibilities and then close-in on one. When selecting a dog, for example, we will prefer, say, an Old English Sheepdog to a Collie, Laborador, or Bassett Hound since we perhaps have come to see ourselves as a "country-squire" for whom the choice of an Old English Sheepdog is as natural as our casual smoking of a pipe and wearing of tweeds.

The reference groups we select for various aspects of our lives may be drawn from the neighborhood in which we live or wish to live, the colleagues we know or would like to know at work, school, or in leisure pursuits. They may be drawn from the media or from history or from myths and adventure tales. Indeed, the reference group need not even be present for our performances. We can and sometimes do perform for "mankind" or for "future generations." All that is required analytically of a reference group is that for certain performances, we have loosely in mind an intended audience whose assessment of our performance would matter to us were it to be given.

Summarily, the theory sketched out up to this point suggests that the self arises partly from experience and partly from imagining others' conceptions of us. Furthermore, the view we take toward the self tends to be that held by those whom we admire. Over time, these views become generalized such that a given performance in everyday life can be directed toward and evaluated by certain standards that we take to be our own. Relatedly, certain performances matter more to us than others. In those that matter, we can say that a part of the self is "lodged" in that performance.[12] Such performances, therefore, become self-defining. In these cases,

---

[12] On "self-lodging," see Norman K. Denzin, "Symbolic Interaction and Ethnomethodology: A Proposed Synthesis, *American Sociological Review*, 34 (1969), pp. 422–34; and Denzin's "Self and Society" in *Introduction to Sociology*, ed. Jack D. Douglas (New York: The Free Press, 1973), pp. 201–22).

it is a matter of some concern to us that we bring off a performance that is creditable—both to us and to others. The fundamental aim in interpersonal relations is then to present a performance that is accepted, perhaps admired, but at least not rejected by an audience that we care about and one that can actively or potentially evaluate our actions. If we are more or less successful in accomplishing this purpose, we can maintain an honorable sense of the self as one who is worthy of the respect of others (or at least the respect of others who matter to us).

Public and Private Selves

Respect, the view of the self as a ritual object fully deserving the deference and accord of others, is the key to my perspective on the emergent self. When respect is forthcoming in interpersonal relations, the foundations upon which the self is built are not threatened. But we do not invest ourselves in every performance we undertake in everyday life. For instance, a fender-bender traffic accident resulting from our not looking at a stop sign while we are on our way to work is unlikely to disconfirm any deeply held views about our self although to a bus driver with a flawless safety record, the same error committed while carrying a busload of passengers may have a slightly deeper effect.[13] Self respect is maintained not against absolute standards but against relative ones tied to particular situations and particular audiences.

This relative view of the self can be carried further by suggesting that we are able to generate many different public appearances for others which may or may not be tied to our crucial self conceptions. *Public selves* are confirmed by our abilities to perform competently in given circumstances—to appear organized, rational, fully in possession of our faculties when it is "correct" to do so. Public selves emerge around those recurrent performances of everyday life that are most often directed toward vocational, leisure, family, and intellectual pursuits. We act out a certain performance in the work place, for example, wherein we strive to appear razor sharp, hardnosed and knowledgeable. But upon walking through the door

---

[13] This may be somewhat of an overstatement. For example, a recent study of medical students and interns notes that via professional socialization, doctors tend to develop a notion of "self-validation." This notion apparently allows them to radically discount both overt criticism of their professional actions and actual mistakes made on the job. Such self-validation was found to be associated with having traversed the educational obstacle course leading to doctoring as an occupation. Once having passed the ordeal of training, a sense of mastery seemed to characterize the research subjects such that an obvious mistake in diagnosis, an error in treatment, or even a strong bawling out on the part of a senior physician would leave junior physicians relatively untouched and with their sense of competency still fully intact. If this finding holds up, one wonders what we are doing to people under the guise of professional education. See Rue Bucher and Joan G. Stelling, *Becoming Professional* (Beverly Hills, Calif.: Sage, 1977).

of our homes, we "let down our hair," relax, and take on the appearance of a casual, affable, and fun-loving sort.

We carry around with us perhaps what Erving Goffman elegantly calls "identity kits" which provide us with a great many public selves.[14] The use of the varied contents of these "identity kits" is tied to the particular recurrent situation or institutions in which our life unfolds. But many of the roles we play in life and the public selves pertinent to each of these roles become, over time, routinized, and we may well have our most valued self-conceptions lodged in them. In such cases, a *private self* can be said to be on the line. Such private selves refer to those self-conceptions which spell out to us the kind of person we believe we "really" are. Thus, when our more positive private selves are tested in public situations, the confirmation of our behavior as proper by others is indeed vital to us if we are to retain a view of ourselves as worthy. It is true, of course, that such private or "real" selves are visible only indirectly by way of our public performances, but, for the individual actor, there is typically little misunderstanding surrounding those situations wherein the private self emerges—though, to others, such an occasion may frequently be misread or missed entirely. Thus, interpersonal encounters in spheres which involve our private selves—which may or may not be cohesive and overlapping—are therefore quite significant to us because a performance taken as improper or repulsive by others in this sphere will discredit us not only in the eyes of the observers but in our own eyes as well.[15]

This raises the further possibility that we carry with us private selves that we do not wish to put on stage to be played out by our public self. No doubt all of us occasionally are subject to those nagging and troubling worries that we are not "really" the kind of person we make ourselves out to be. The "nice guy" may wonder about his "nasty streak" just as the "gentle sort" may sometimes ponder her "fighting side." A specific conception we carry of ourselves as a certain type is perhaps positioned somewhere on an axis of variation where we can at least imagine ourselves as polar opposites of the self we think we present to others. Maybe, for example, we carry private visions of our true nature as, say, cunning, cold, or afflicted with a hopeless "oral fixation." Yet, in interaction, we nonetheless manage to appear spontaneous, warm, and take care to keep our thumbs out of our mouths. Such dark and private selves may well exist within us all, but as long as they do not worm, ooze, or otherwise leak out during interaction itself, their status as "regulators" of human behavior must remain locked in the closet with other things that occasionally go "bump in the night." In other words, insofar as we are successful in keeping

[14] See Erving Goffman, *Asylums* (Chicago: Aldine Publishing Co., 1961).

[15] In most respects, the sense that I apply to the notion of the *private self* in this essay is very similar to the sense that Mead (*Mind, Self, and Society*) applied to the *I* of interpersonal relations as discussed earlier in this section.

certain private conceptions of our selves under lock and key, their influence upon interpersonal relations can only be remote.[16]

The Evolution of Self

The modern world requires that we take on in public many different appearances of which only some are perhaps central to our private (although often socially realized and communicated) selves. It is, in this sense, a Balkanized world we live in whereby we move from one role to another and act out quite separate public selves within each segment. Some roles are brief and transitory and others are enduring. A part of our private selves may be lodged in one sphere but not in another. To our colleagues on the bowling team, it may be important for us to be seen as energetic and genuine; to our fellow workers, we wish to be seen as slow, meticulous, and calculating. Our sense of uniqueness stems, perhaps, from whatever synthesis we can make of these enacted public and private selves. But even a most carefully constructed synthesis can change in its shape and content as the segments of life to which our public and private selves are tied also change. Indeed, to be married five years is to present a different public self than was presented after one year of marriage. To be married five years is also likely to create a quite different version of the private self as well.

From this standpoint, those recurrent social situations of our everyday lives are the foils against which both our public and private selves develop. There is a continual interplay between our subjective definitions of who we are and the perceived objective constraints under which our definition can be enacted. In our interpersonal dealings, we are most often more than we choose to present.[17] In general, we position both our public and private selves somewhere along a continuum of support for or against various perceived social constraints—institutions, rules, obligations, relationships, and so forth. The two may merge in some circumstances and widely depart from one another in others. But, since we are aware of others watching us, we can more or less manipulate the image we present

---

[16] This, of course, does not do justice to many of the insights coming from "depth psychology." My point here is merely that whatever effect one's unconscious or repressed needs, fears, or phobias may have upon ongoing interaction, it is not only difficult to pin down, it is largely irrelevant to explaining what occurs in the immediate situation at hand. A person may be transituationally "crazy" (in either a clinical or folk sense), but in interaction, the label will arise and stick on the basis of occurrences relevant to a particular occasion. In other words, if a "deep" diagnosis is to bear directly on interpersonal relations, it must be shown first to be related to immediate and concrete conditions.

[17] This follows Georg Simmel's notion that people always hold back a part of themselves and present only their social self in interpersonal relations. For the most part, what Simmel called *social selves*, I call *public selves*. See Kurt H. Wolff, ed. and trans., *The Sociology of Georg Simmel* (New York: The Free Press, 1950).

to conform to the image we believe others should take toward us. Whether or not we choose to actually publically present our private selves in the situation at hand depends upon the risk we feel would be involved were we to do so. Erving Goffman, as usual, makes this point best: "Our sense of being a person can come from being drawn in to a wider social unit, our sense of selfhood can arise from the little ways we resist the pull. Our status is backed by the solid buildings of the world, while our sense of personal identity often resides in the cracks."[18]

This dramaturgic view of modern people has been taken by some to be a somewhat disturbing one for it suggests that behind one mask lies another and that when all masks are stripped away there may well be nothing left except a thoroughly empty, discredited, and terrified being. We will reconsider this view again at the end of this essay, but, for now, our discussion will suffice without further elaboration, for it is all that is required to understand the next two essential elements in this model of interpersonal relations. After we have considered these elements—defining social situations and the rules of social conduct—we can then return to our social actor and see whether or not this image of the person as an artful juggler and synthesizer of calculated appearances which may reflect only a public but not private self is in fact as disturbing and empty as it may appear on first glance.

III.   DEFINING SOCIAL SITUATIONS

In the previous essay, I noted that the meaning of any action a person takes cannot be fully understood outside of the specific and concrete situation within which it takes place. In interpersonal relations, the construction of *situational definitions* represents the way we are able to render things "real" so that we are able to strategically accomplish the purposes behind our involvements in a given situation.[19] In this section, several properties of situational definitions are described that are crucial to recognizing how individuals are able to interact with one another. The content of situational definitions is considered first, then the various recurrent locales where situational definitions are built are presented, and, finally, the larger structure within which situational definitions are often contained is discussed.

On the Content of Situational Definitions

In everyday life, to have defined a situation means that the social actor has developed certain notions regarding the role he or she is to enact in

---

[18] Goffman, *Asylums*, p. 320.

[19] Thomas (*Child in America*) was the first to develop the notion of "defining the situation." It has since become a cornerstone in symbolic interactionism in par and social psychology in general.

that situation. Entering a subway car, for example, puts one directly in a social situation wherein the goal of unproblematically moving one's self from point A to point B requires adherence to particular codes of social conduct requiring the commuter to more or less play the role of a passive, preoccupied, and autonomous user of public transportation. The situation, if defined in this most instrumental fashion, requires one to sit quietly, appearing perhaps to be engrossed in one's thoughts, and taking care not to disturb the preoccupations of fellow travelers. Of course, other definitions for the subway situation are possible. Consider the pickpocket to whom the subway car is a work place or the so-called "bag ladies" of New York City who, after dark, define the subway car as home. Definitions differ, therefore, according to the purposes to which the situation can be put by a participant.[20]

In the first essay of this volume, I suggested that in interactional settings the meanings attached to particular objects, relationships, places, events, persons, and so on can be classified as consensual, emergent, negotiable, or conflictual. Situational definitions, since they provide meanings to people, can also be classified in such a fashion, and, like any meaning system, situational definitions contain moral overtones to them. All actions in interpersonal settings are organized around the critical judgments we make as to what we consider to be morally proper in the situation at hand. It is therefore a matter of some consequence to us that our behavior is consistent with our own notions of situational propriety as well as the notions held by others present.

Impression management is the term coined by Erving Goffman to describe the form and content associated with the way a person presents the self and its activities to others within a defined social situation.[21] It refers to the strategies we employ both to control the behavior of others and to control the opinions others form toward us. To successfully manage one's impression requires, of course, an understanding of the definition others maintain toward the particular situation one is in. Consider, for example, the policeman who tells his colleagues at work of his contempt, loathing, and disrespect for "niggers, spicks, and guineas," yet, in the privacy of his home he tells his family that he carries absolutely no anomosity toward others, believing in his heart that all people are equally deserving of respect. Which version are we to believe? Unfortunately,

---

[20] While it is true that not all of the situations in which we find ourselves are defined, and it is certainly true that not all situations in which we find ourselves are defined by us, it is also generally true that when we find ourselves in situations where a hasty exit is difficult and no obvious definition for what is going on is readily available, we typically go to great lengths to try to define the situation anyway. Consider Harold Garfinkel's *Studies in Ethnomethology* (Englewood Cliffs, N.J.: Prentice-Hall, Inc., 1967).

[21] See Goffman, *Presentation of Self.*

there are no guidelines to follow for it is entirely possible that the police-man may believe in one version on some occasions and the alternative version on others. It is possible that he may even believe in both versions at the same time. But, to the point of this discussion, the policeman in either case is responding to a particular social situation so as to enhance (or at least sustain) his status and position within it. From his statements we can infer, perhaps, something of the pressures upon him in each situa-tion and maybe something about the structure of those situations; how-ever, we are unlikely to learn much about his "true" feelings. Similarly, one can be meek at the office and a tyrant at home without necessarily rupturing the social fabric or making one feel undue strain in either set-ting. The point here is simply that the social situation in which interaction is located carries with it its own logic which, once developed, most often carries the person along by providing appropriate stances for individual participants to assume.

Understanding the logic of a social situation requires an appreciation for the total information each participant has of all other participants—their likes and dislikes, their goals in the situation, their knowledge of the situation, and so forth. The label *awareness context* refers to this aspect of interpersonal relations.[22] An awareness context can be "closed," wherein some participants know more than others about what has occurred, is occurring, or will occur in the situation. The con artists who pass off forged paintings as the real thing base their livelihoods on their ability to fabricate closed awareness contexts within which the "dupe's" situational definition is manipulated according to plan. Open awareness contexts, on the other hand, refer to those occasions wherein the situational definitions held by those on the scene are known to the participants. They may not always be the same, of course, but at least everyone knows where every-one else, in colloquial terms, "is coming from" (and "going to"). The doctor who shares the diagnosis (or lack of one) with the patient presents a convenient illustration of creating an open awareness context within which a situational definition can emerge. The patient may of course reject the diagnosis in which case the situational definition takes on a negotiable or conflictual character. Whereas closed awareness contexts always create emergent situational definitions in the sense that at least one party to the interaction knows more than the others and may or may not let them in on the secret, open awareness contexts may be typed in any of three ways—consensual, negotiable, or conflictual.

Situational definitions, therefore, can vary considerably from person to person dependent upon the awareness each party has of the context in which the actions are to take place. In general, to define a situation is to

---
[22] See Barney G. Glaser and Anselm L. Strauss, "Awareness Contexts and Social Interaction," *American Sociological Review*, 39 (1964), pp. 669–79.

be able to say one "knows" what is going on around one's self. In a sense, situational definitions represent commonsense theories about the occasions which allow a person to construct certain lines of action according to what he or she considers to be proper for such occasions. The actual content of these theories can be broken down in terms of their socio-temporal properties.[23] That is, in order for people to take purposive action, they must be able to say where they presently are located, where they wish to go, and how they plan to get there. And, in order to make such strategic choices, a situational definition is required to inform the individual as to the social space within which to act as well as the social time deemed appropriate for such actions. I consider social space first.

In any interactional setting, participants have respective parts to play—roles. We are listeners at times, speakers at other times. We sometimes act out the father role, the mother role, the boss role, or the humble servant role. When moving in and out of various interpersonal settings, the parts that people play represent that segment of the social structure that individuals must map if they are to fully participate with others in a given situation. Once mapped, these parts or roles provide guidelines for action and expectation.[24]

In particular social situations, individuals must have some idea of the behaviors that are representative of other persons in that locale and also some idea of the behaviors that others in the setting would be likely to interpret as going beyond the pale. For instance, when two previously unacquainted individuals come together to conduct business, pass the time, or, more generally, enter into some exchange that requires joint activity, both must infer whether or not the other's appearance, gestures, and utterances are typical of some other group or category of persons with which each has previously had some experience (real or vicarious). Once the other is typed, then a collection of more or less appropriate responses can be marshalled out by the participants to order the interaction. This allows a role for the other to emerge as well as providing the self with a proper role. And, to classify another as acting out a certain role is to inter-

---

[23] For a more extensive treatment of the sociotemporal properties of situational definitions, see John Van Maanen, "Experiencing Organization" in *Organizational Careers: Some New Perspectives*, ed. John Van Maanen (New York: John Wiley and Sons, 1977). This view owes much to the work of Mead, *Mind, Self and Society;* Garfinkel, *Ethnomethodology;* and Peter McHugh, *Defining the Situation: The Organization of Meaning in Social Interaction* (Indianapolis: Bobbs-Merrill, 1968).

[24] Cognitive anthropologists, social geographers, and developmental psychologists have all made imaginative use of the notion of mental maps. See, for example, E. C. Tolman, "Cognitive Maps in Rats and Men," *Psychological Review* 55 (1948), pp. 183–208; Kurt Lewin, *The Conceptual Representation of and Measurement of Psychological Force* (Durham, N.C.: Duke University Press, 1938); George Kelley, *The Psychology of Personal Constructs* (New York: W. W. Norton and Co., Inc., 1955); Kevin Lynch, *The Image of the City* (Cambridge, Mass.: MIT Press, 1960); and Peter Gould and Robert White, *Mental Maps* (Baltimore: Penguin Books, 1974).

pret the other's behavior—to make it meaningful in light of the situation.[25]

To construct a situational definition means, in part, that one can *normalize* the situation such that it becomes seen as a situation of a certain kind. For example, when we answer the knock on our door and discover a stranger on our porch, we are typically ill at ease, uncomfortable, and unsure of how to act until we can type the stranger as being of a certain kind—a salesperson, a pollster, a religious emissary, or perhaps a passing motorist in trouble. Normalizing the situation allows a culturally clear frame of reference to be built around it. And, within such a frame, we can predict how another should act and correspondingly how we should act. Thus, using our language skills and a few, quick observations, we are usually able to categorically define situations as of a particular type. To have normalized a situation means also that since the person can sense an order behind an appearance, the individual will be able to detect occurrences which fall outside normal patterns. Boundaries for appropriate behavior can then be said to exist.

David Sudnow, in a classic study of the situational definitions used by public defenders to order their work lives, reports extensively on what PDs considered "normal crimes."[26] In brief, Sudnow found that within the occupational culture of PDs, all crimes were classified into "typical" and "atypical" categories. Roughly 80 percent of their case load was comprised of the normal variety involving low-status defendants, crimes against property, no violence associated with the commission of the crime, and so on. The cases which fell under this interpretive frame of reference were then handled routinely with all PDs following a familiar and rather mundane plea-bargaining recipe. These "normal" crimes were not so much worked as they were processed according to preexisting, largely taken-for-granted plan. Actions taken by the PDs on cases falling outside the normality structure, however, were far less predictable. Each PD seemed to handle them in his or her own highly individualized fashion indicating that the situational definitions associated with the atypical cases were constructed idiosyncratically, based presumably upon whatever merits or demerits could be read into or gleaned from a particular case.

What this example highlights beyond the normalization characteristic associated with situational definitions is the fact that situational defini-

---

[25] As interaction episodes increase between the same people, the participants begin to develop what Harold Garfinkel (*Ethnomethodology*) calls "background expectancies." These expectancies rest on the interactional history the participants share and the common assumptions about one another that have been built up over the course of this history. For example, when we enter a neighborhood tavern where we are well known, the bartender may nod politely and then proceed to set our favorite drink before us without a word being spoken. Clearly, to understand what transpired in such a situation requires knowledge of the participant's "background expectancies."

[26] See David Sudnow, "Normal Crimes: Sociological Features of the Penal Code in a Public Defender Office," *Social Problems*, 12 (1965), pp. 225–72.

tions have also a probabilistic dimension built into them. To classify something as typical or normal is to suggest that the person has a particular expectation in mind. It suggests, too, that individuals assess the probability of an event as they do the event's normality and that this probabilistic assessment enters into the situational definition as well. Thus, a person observed to be crying may well be atypical yet still perfectly normal if it can be determined that the person is crying as a result of bereavement or drunkenness. The occurrence is relatively rare, but nonetheless, it is to be expected under the circumstances.

Finally, normalization implies that the individual has at least some idea of the "why" that lies behind an observed pattern of action, an idea grounded of course within the particular culture of which the person is a member. Situational definitions, therefore, carry with them everyday theoretical notions. In other words, to define a situation is to also be able to assign certain rudimentary cause-effect assumptions to the occasion's occurrence. Motivational schemes ascribed to persons are, for example, popular explanatory devices. Rightly or wrongly, they allow persons to make meaningful that which surrounds them. To most prisoners, for example, the treatment they receive inside their steel and concrete homes is a result of the dull and sadistic character of prison guards. In the work place, foremen contend with workers whom they see as "troublemakers" or "attitude problems." Such types are seen also to contaminate the otherwise "good workers," thus slowdowns, horseplay, absenteeism, and sometimes outright sabotage can then be "understood" by the foremen and assigned causal roots.[27]

Thus far we have noted that situational definitions provide a person with a sense of what is to be expected in the situation (normal forms), the probability of occurrences of all types within that situation, and some idea of the assumed causal structure that lies beneath the situation. Situational definitions also involve the person's conceptualization of time. Consider, for example, the newcomer in an organization who must begin to build a definition for the immediate work situation. To the novice, time is most problematic. One must discover: when to take a break, have lunch, quit work, when to read the paper (if ever), how long one must stay at a certain pay grade, when to ask the boss a question, and so on. The temporal framework the individual eventually develops provides both short-range timetables (which divide up the days and weeks into manageable compo-

---

[27] Of course, our commonsense theories of causation do not always rest upon the stereotypic categorization of others. Situational causes are not unknown. The underling in an office who sees the boss's smile turn into a frown when the workload increases has a ready-made explanation for the momentary cooling of the relationship. See Van Maanen, "Experiencing Organization." I should note, too, that much of what social psychologists have been up to of late under the tag "attribution theory" is very similar to the view put forth in the text. See, in particular, Harold H. Kelley, *Attribution in Social Interaction* (Morristown, N.J.: General Learning Press, 1971).

nents) and long-range ones (which provide notions of how one's career may unfold). As William James first suggested, the experienced present is rendered understandable only in terms of where one has been and where one wants to go.[28] Situational definitions that allow one to function effectively in the immediate moment must, therefore, provide for some continuity between the past and the future. The hard working, upwardly mobile medical student must believe, for example, that something is "out there" and is worth looking toward and preparing for if immediate experiences are to be meaningful.

The term *theme* is used here to denote that aspect of situational definitions that an individual uses to link the past, present, and future. A theme generates an evaluation of present activity not by interpreting the immediate moment itself but by interpreting the immediate moment's relation to the past and future. It joins the experienced past and anticipated future together whether or not that past and future are only seconds apart or years apart. A theme in the work place might be that one has an "interesting, challenging job with good prospects." Or, conversely, that one has a "dull, routine job with few prospects." Both themes postulate a pattern to one's activities in the work world and can be used to guide one's activities. Themes can, of course, be realistic (in the sense that they are continuously being experienced and documented) or fantastic (in the sense that they are never being experienced and documented). But the critical point here is simply that themes are necessary components of an actor's situational definition.

A theme serves largely to place the present within a normalized stream of life events. What occurs when one fails to document as expected a given theme is surprise. And surprise entails at least a momentary unhinging of the person from his or her constructed situational definition. The present becomes problematic because the future is hazy and the results of one's actions are undeterminable. Themes therefore are testable in the sense that a timetable for events can be partially constructed such that the person can more or less tell if the theme is an appropriate one or not. If, for example, a young woman wishes to define an association with a certain young man as "promising," this theme surely embodies notions of "getting closer over time" or "seeing more of one another." Conceivably, to the young woman, the test of this theme might have something to do with the number of times the young man visits her during the coming

28 William James, *The Principles of Psychology* (New York: Dover, 1950). On social time, see Julius A. Roth, *Timetables* (Indianapolis: Bobbs-Merrill, 1963); Steven Klineberg and Thomas S. Cottle, *The Present of Things Past* (Boston: Little Brown and Co., 1973); Mead, *Mind, Self, and Society;* Leonard Doob, *The Patterning of Time* (New Haven, Conn.: Yale University Press, 1971); and the classic work of Pitirim Sorokin and Robert K. Merton, "Social Time," *American Journal of Sociology,* 43 (1937), pp. 614–29.

month or so. If many visits are forthcoming, the definition of "promising" may hold. If, however, the visits are few, the "promising" theme will no doubt fade. Themes and their timetables are, like all reality generating equipment, subject to sudden twists of benevolent or malevolent fate.

The last temporal characteristic of situational definitions refers to the perceived ownership of a theme—the individual's real or imagined control over his or her fate. Situations vary as to the degree to which persons can by their own efforts create and sustain a theme. Civil service bureaucracies, for example, exert almost monopolistic control over the career themes of employees. Similarly, contracts and agreements provide narrow limits within which a union member can carve out an everyday work theme. In both cases, themes are most certainly present and are perhaps quite specific though the individual is unlikely to have had much to do with the authoring of the theme. While thematic revisions may occur, they are perhaps attributable less to individual efforts than to environmental conditions—the person being only a miniscule cog caught up in a situation he or she had nothing to do with defining. Ownership, then, is akin to the causal structure a person attributes to this temporal situation.

Summarily, situational definitions provide an individual with a practical theory for "what's going on" in concrete situations. Such a theory includes notions of what typically occurs in such situations (normality) and when it should occur (themes). Furthermore, the probability of an event's occurrence in the situation is tied to its normality structure in roughly the same manner as an event's timetable tests a particular theme. Situational definitions also include beliefs regarding why things occur as they do (causality) and the amount of control people believe they have over these things (ownership). Since this is somewhat of a complicated matter, an illustrative but very simplified case may help specify more clearly the essential ingredients of situational definitions.

Consider, for example, Harry, a hypothetical beat cop, a police officer who has been assigned to a particular skid row segment or district in his community for sometime. The situation, as Harry sees it on any given shift, might be partially defined in the following manner: The social space includes the corporate presence of "winos, pimps, whores, and other scrods" who, in Harry's view, are his normal clientele. He knows their troubles well and can rather accurately describe their interests, activities, relationships, and kinds of claims they make on him. He knows, too, that Charlie's Bar on the corner of 4th and Main is a "heavy hangout" and any call that directs him to go there is one to be handled with care. The Savoy Saloon, across the street from Charlie's, is, however, a "vaseline jar," but is a relatively calm and subdued establishment which presents few if any operational difficulties. Harry also has a lay theory in mind to explain the behavior of most of those he observes. His commonsense theory, perhaps quite like the commonsense theories of other policemen, tells him that the people he watches over are "losers, they are society's scumbags who are flat out failures through and through." By and large, Harry's theory works fine for him. Furthermore, it is one that is confirmed and reconfirmed continually, and, in fact, it is one that helps him make reasonable sense of the actions he observes day after day.

Harry has also developed some themes to attach to the temporal flow of activities he observes. One theme might be that more and more dope is being pushed in his sector. His timetable to test the theme might involve paying more attention than usual to the new faces on his beat which appear on those days when the welfare checks are released. Harry may even believe—though it is unlikely—that he has some control over this theme if he thinks that by cunning police work he is capable of reducing the flow of this dope through his district.

At any rate, to the degree that all of the spatial and temporal elements can be more or less accounted for by an individual acting in a given social situation, a definition for that situation can be said to have been constructed. It may exist in an open or closed awareness context; however, with increasing interaction among the parties within a particular situation, the definition under most conditions tends toward the open (though not necessarily consensual) variety. Thus recurrent social situations tend to carry with them certain definitions that guide the behavior of the participants within them. It is to these recurrent situations that we now turn.

Encounters, Scenes, and Relationships

Recurrent social situations fall into three generic types—Encounters, Scenes, and Relationships. All three types demand forms of joint action between people and therefore entail a certain amount of interpersonal risk. Indeed, when one commits the self to a particular line of action, the possibility arises that the other will not respond in the desired and expected manner. The other may not listen, may misinterpret what is occurring, may even ridicule one's presented self. All interaction is, therefore, potentially damaging to the conceptions of our public and private selves we carry with us. Feelings of embarrassment, frustration, shame, incompetence, confusion, and so on are always possible in any social situation.

As I have previously noted, all social actions must be viewed as both *instrumental* (designed to accomplish something) and *expressive* (providing others with a glimpse at our underlying character as displayed by the action).[29] A failure to maintain the integrity of our own or another's

---

[29] It is true, of course, that expressions are given off intentionally by people (as is the case with the clothing we wear or with whom we choose to be seen) as well as unintentionally (as is the case of our taken-for-granted table manners or with the way we speak). Ironically, we seem to regard the latter as more "real," since the former are seen to be more easily manipulated, hence, more "artificial." This makes for a

situational definition transforms both the instrumental and expressive properties of the interaction. For example, if a professor smiles or laughs at serious and earnest students seeking answers to what the students consider most important questions, the professor fails to maintain and honor the integrity of the students' definition of the situation as serious. The ridiculed students may well feel shamed at the disrespect accorded them (and their questions) thus causing them to redefine the situation, the professor, and perhaps even themselves.

Since social situations are potentially dangerous to our sense of well-being in the world, we have developed an almost infinite variety of ploys to minimize the minimizable risks. Foremost among these is the situationally selectivity we employ when deciding where we are to interact, with whom, and the sort of performance we shall present in such situations. We gear ourselves into some interactions and, when possible, out of others. We decide how much of our private selves to lodge in any given situation thus arranging to present certain performances only in front of certain audiences. Because of the vast number of interpersonal dealings we have in everyday life, we cannot become fully involved in all of them. To do so would be enfeebling and lead quickly to cognitive and emotional overloads. Impression management is hence both necessary and practical.

Situations can be classified in terms of their involvement patterns and impression management tactics typically displayed by persons within them. Three basic types are discussed below. Each situational type contains distinguishing characteristics which set it off from the others. It is, however, not always transparent to people what kind of situation they are in, and, of course, situations themselves change over time. The taxonomy presented here is, therefore, a loose and somewhat fluid one—one that is meant more to denote analytic types of situations than clear-cut empirical ones.

Encounters. The first and most tightly organized (constrained) situation is the *encounter*.[30] These situations are marked by their fleeting and transitory character and their general lack of personal involvement among the participants. Encounters represent primarily role-based behavior wherein the individualized quality of the interaction is minimized. Situations which fall under this label require only the copresence of people who perform rather predefined roles during the time the interaction is sustained. The encountering process itself is of little consequence to the persons who

---

difficult existence because slips in our presentations are, on occasion, magnified and intensified well beyond what we might consider their significance. Goffman puts this well with his remark: "The gestures which we sometimes call empty are perhaps, in fact, the fullest of them all." (*Interaction Ritual* [Chicago: Aldine Publishing Co., 1967], p. 91.)

[30] For a much more elaborate treatment of this form of joint action, see Erving Goffman, *Encounters* (Indianapolis: Bobbs-Merrill, 1961).

are engaged in it (unless it goes awry); only the results are of conscious concern. The alignment of the actions of persons in an elevator presents a good illustration of a basic encounter. Typically, what occurs is that the first person to enter takes over the controls, the second person entering after making his or her destination known, steps toward the corner farthest from the operator, the third person follows suit and fills another corner, and so on. Eye contact between travelers is avoided and conversations are usually minimal. The situation itself provides the instrumental roles to be enacted as well as the rules of behavior to be followed.

In a sense, encounters are interaction rituals for which a script is available to knowledgeable cultural members and a strict reenactment is called for by other cultural members in terms of the behavioral sequences required of the actors. Much of modern life goes on in this situational sphere. When we order dinner, make purchases in a department store, sit in on a class, shuffle out of the way of an oncoming pedestrian, excuse ourselves for an inadvertent affront to another, and so forth, we make use of the basic politeness and relational recipes of our culture and act out certain rather finely defined roles which provide us with routinized forms of proper conduct. The self that could be said to be on the line in an encounter is merely a situated, public, and rather anonymous one that has little or no life beyond the interaction itself. The roles assumed in such situations are only minimally embraced by the participants since they evaporate as soon as the encounter is closed. All that occurs is simply the coming together of persons who make indications to one another as to the official focus or purpose of their presence, conduct their "business," and then move on.

Despite its ephemeral character and the limited involvement of its participants, encounters, nonetheless, entail some interpersonal risk for people. In general, the risk that is run in an encounter is related to a major principle of all interpersonal relations: *to be observable is to be embarrassable.* A stutter, gaffe, stumble, blush, drool, mistake in identity, malaprop, or other blunder may crop up in any encounter situation subjecting the bumbler to potential complications. When the smooth flow of events is disrupted (a flow most of us rather matter-of-factly expect and count on), the disrupter has contradicted the polished and competent image one may wish to present. The disrupter may in fact bring the interaction to an awkward halt and wind up as a result feeling quite ill at ease and perhaps shamed. Remedial actions are usually called for to restore the situation to normal as well as bring some credit back to an already discredited self.

Certainly an isolated error is unlikely to cause much damage to an individual's sense of interpersonal competence, though repeated violations in encounter situations may well begin to eat away at one's conception of one's public and perhaps private self. Moreover, the principle of observability suggests that people achieve their purposes unmolested only by not standing out in appearance from other former or immediate participants in the encounter situation. Within the framework of an encounter, being noticeable and being regraded as deviant are intimately related and when people stand out, they are usually held suspect—"they are not like us." We can go about our mundane business comfortably and independently *only through the mutual regard of inattention displayed by others.* This almost Kafkaesque observation suggests that we all have more or less learned the terrible truth that achieving privacy and being left alone in everyday life is conditioned mainly upon our conformity to forms of behavior deemed socially appropriate by others.[31] Encounters, then, represent perhaps the most tightly arranged of social situations because proper conduct has been largely institutionalized.

Scenes. Situations that are less strictly defined are *scenes.* I define scenes here as those situations which people seek out and participate in primarily for the immediate gratification the situation provides.[32] Unlike transitory encounters where some concrete objective provides a focus for the interaction, the purpose of scenes is to be found in the interaction itself. Parties, commencements, lunches with friends, participant sports, certain kinds of business meetings, dating, parkbench sitting, weddings, bar mitzvahs, tavern episodes, corner lounging, funerals, all represent scenic occasions wherein the person is relatively free to become whatever the situation permits. Roles, serious or unserious, are typically embraced firmly, and involvement of individuals within the scene tends to be high.

Importantly, we usually are able to carry away from scenes a sense that something has happened as well as a sense of our fellow interactants. The roles assumed by people are not strictly instrumental but contain important expressive elements in which it matters to us that we be seen by

---

[31] I should note that it is not conformity per se that is at issue here, but rather the appearance of conformity. To be "natural" is to convince others that one is acting "naturally." Professional (and successful) burglars, for example, pay close attention to this rule as can be seen when they engage in afternoon work in a middle-class neighborhood dressed in business suits and driving late-model station wagons. Indeed, the burglars in this case take great care in being sure that there is little about their appearance that would distinguish them from those whom they are out to rob. The right to carry out their business as usual without undue interference is, therefore, more or less assured since they do not appear in any way incongruous in the situation. From this standpoint, it is perhaps easy to understand Goffman's only partially tongue-in-cheek quip: "Sometimes the best evidence could be the worst." (*Relations in Public* [New York: Basic Books, 1971], p. 327)

[32] John Irwin uses the term *scene* to distinguish those open and available social worlds people participate in voluntarily. Such settings are embellished with a set of special meanings, rules, symbols, and activities which have developed over time through the collective involvement of many people—the bridge scene, the bar scene, the disco scene, the surf scene, the hippie scene, the tennis scene, and so on. My use of the term here is quite similar though I place less emphasis on Irwin's insistence that scenes are exclusively expressive arenas. See John Irwin, *Scenes* (Beverly Hills, Calif.: Sage, 1977).

others in only a certain light—as gay or gloomy, deliberate or zealous, cynical or sincere, and so on. Indeed, scenes often are for immediate pleasure. Expression, more so than any instrumental pursuit, is the name of the game. Strictly speaking, appearances are the "be all" and "end all" of these occasions. In terms we introduced in Part II, *self-lodging* occurs in these situations, and aspects of our public and our private selves are on the line. Hence, we do not enter into scenes casually but rather exercise great care in selecting scenes to become a part of as well as choosing how to perform in the selected scenes. In selecting our scenes, we try to pick situations where we believe there will be people present who will behave well toward us. When we discover such scenes, we then selectively perceive as "good" the behavior of those present and try to evoke congruencies by presenting a self in these situations that others will see as "good." In short, we try to build a suitable image to present to others participating in the scenes we enter. To wit, the clothes we wear on scenic occasions are hardly accidental. They convey what we consider an appropriate personal front, one which will be regarded positively by others on the scene. In many respects, clothes are almost unspeakably significant when considering social scenes.[33]

The situational definitions that reign over scenes cover a broad canopy of meanings. Some scenes are for fun, some serious, some express the warm regard each participant holds for another, some exist for argumentative purposes, some are purely ceremonial, and so on. Our public presentations are built toward some scenes and away from others. Since many of the people present in such situations matter to us, discreditation of our projected self is likely to be disturbing, and pains will be taken to avoid such a condition. Yet scenes, because of the awareness each interactant has of the other, allow for more flexibility of action than is the case for an encounter. The normative system encompassing scenes is looser and, therefore, permits more expression of feeling than is possible in an encounter where feelings are largely considered to be irrelevant to the interaction. Furthermore, participants in a scenic occasion go to great lengths to avoid calling out another participant for public chastisement. To provoke the loss of face of another brings risk for the provoker. And, since interactants have carefully selected their scenes, the grounds for showing disrespect may be difficult to come by. Furthermore, even if such grounds are discovered, their use will surely rupture the congeniality of the situa-

---

[33] For example, on the ski slopes, clothes and equipment provide not only a clue to one's status in the scene (novice or expert), they also serve to provide people with something to talk about and, in the process, allow them to get to know one another on more than a fleeting basis if they so desire. "Where did you get those Olin IVs?" can serve, therefore, as a perfectly acceptable and safe opening gambit for a friendship one would like to develop on the spot. Other aspects of scenes also provide shared vocabularies and appropriate topics which function to bring people together—"Great snow today, eh?"

tion which, after all, is usually the reason for constructing the scene in the first place.[34]

Relationships. Some social situations represent relationships. This category of joint action is typical of marriages, work associations, friendships, and other long-term affiliations among persons. Here, common vocabularies develop, similar background expectancies emerge, and the events significant to one's sense of place in the world are interpreted. Obviously, much self-lodging occurs in these situations, and the parties to a relationship will typically view one another as sources of self-esteem. It is also true that within such situations, impression management is least self-conscious (given the awareness context is a relatively open one). Because of the closeness of relationships as well as the expectations the participants within them have of their likely continuation, individuals often present their "disgusting" side as well as their "virtuous" side without causing immediate damage to the definition of the situation which usually carries a potent mix of mutual caring, trust, and respect for the other. Indeed, before we commit ourselves, we typically take great care at being sure that what we define as a relationship is defined in the same manner by the other.[35]

To a great extent, relationships represent those situations wherein our selfhood is most developed. Here is where we may "let it all hang out" and present our "real" self. The posturing that accompanies encounters and scenes to a degree vanishes in the context of a relationship. All manners and moods of the other are important in a relationship. Whereas it makes little difference to us whether Fred, our mailman, is depressed on any given day just as long as our mail gets to us on time, such depression in Fred, our boyfriend, is unlikely to be overlooked.

It is true, however, that only certain kinds of selves tend to become lodged in a relationship. But those that do tend to become somewhat self-

---

[34] In general, it is probably the case that discreditation or embarrassment are more likely to come to a person from another who does not participate in the scene than from one who does participate. On most occasions, those partaking in the scene go to some pains to avoid close questioning which perhaps might embarrass a fellow participant. Such actions risk dissolving the entire scene itself. Take, for example, an "affair scene" where a couple is romantically dining in a quiet restaurant only to be disturbed by an acquaintance who happens by and inquires, "Hi, how's the wife?"

[35] I should note that encounters, scenes, and relationships are not mutually exclusive. Relationships, such as marriage, include both encounters ("Please pass the butter, dear,") and scenes (lovemaking, fighting, vacationing). Relationships, however, are built upon increasing interaction wherein the interactants gradually begin to define the interaction itself (and the purposes and activities surrounding the interaction) as pleasurable and its absence as negative or painful. In this fashion, relationships are built starting, perhaps, with only a quick encounter. Needless to say, however, most encounters never lead to anything more substantial. On "chains of involvement," see Howard S. Becker, "Becoming a Marijuana User," *American Journal of Sociology*, 1953, pp. 235–42. On the construction of relationships in general, see William J. Chambliss, "The Selection of Friends," *Social Forces*, 43 (1965), pp. 370–80.

defining and to some degree obligatory. Thus one becomes a good father, a forgetful sort, a passionate lover, an untidy housekeeper, and so forth. In essence, these roles grow from an ever-expanding set of interactional rules constructed by the parties to a relationship which define what is to be considered expected conduct within the mutual situation. Such everyday issues as how to display affection, accomplish work, dress accordingly, talk respectfully, and so on are addressed necessarily by participants and, over time, taken-for-granted styles of behavior emerge. From birth to death, these are the situations in which the more salient and important aspects of our selves are formed. Indeed, an almost iron law of human behavior suggests that the more we play out a role, the more we come to sincerely believe in it. And, when we think of where our most prized public and private selves are shaped, it is to our most significant interpersonal relationships that we must look.[36]

The Control of Situational Definitions

As indicated, definitions of the situation are associated with both passing and permanent occasions. These definitions tend to become both more flexible and refined as our knowledge of other participants in the situation and of the situation itself increases. Furthermore, the shape of everyday life forms around those situations where significant self-lodging occurs—scenes and relationships. We seek such situations out since, in them, we sense that we can successfully establish and communicate (perhaps discover) who we "really are."

This is not to say, however, that we all have an equal vote when it comes to defining situations. Certainly, definitions are also reflective of the institutional properties and context of the situation itself, the authority of the interactants in the situation, and the social resources and skills the interactants bring with them to the situation. The lives of children are, for example, far more determined than those of adults. Consider, too, that when some of the participants are organized and others are not, such as student-administrator or consumer-industry interactions, the situation as it is defined is likely to be be rigged so as to favor the organized participants disproportionately. Esteemed occupational roles also provide a sort of built-in power. Thus, doctors define situations for their patients, lawyers for their clients, professors for their students, and so on. And, in bureau-

---

[36] Because scenes and, more critically, relationships represent regularized moral orders with highly developed notions regarding proper forms of behavior, individuals can be said to have something akin to "moral careers" as they move through and across scenes and relationships. A person's self-conception is then changing continually in emphasis as one acts within these significant interactional situations. To have been working the same job for ten years is to be a different person than to have been working the same job for 20 years. See Goffman, *Asylums,* for an extensive treatment of the "moral career" idea.

cratic settings, the rules and duties which apply to the employee's situation are typically considered by most people in the setting to be more important than the individual's own interpretation of the rules and duties that "should" govern the situation. From this perspective, a definition of the situation is almost always to be found, but it is not always (or perhaps even ordinarily) one that has been invented by the people presently in the situation.

While it is also true that situational definitions are often negotiated, the culture itself may impose certain limits as to the acceptability of the argument we can use in such negotiation. In this society, for example, the increased level of interaction among people from tremendously varied backgrounds has played havoc with our previously secure and unquestioned ways. Shared meanings and recurrent situations are more difficult to locate in today's urbanized and segmented environment. This makes it relatively difficult to display, maintain, and retrieve a stable and viable sense of self in the world. Encounters and scenes seem to typify our social relationships more so than relationships. While we tend to avoid poorly defined situations, the situations we do find ourselves in are only loosely integrated. Individuals can, therefore, tie their many selves together in only a partial and fragmentary way.

The structure of modern life seems to be one in which social contacts are usually brief and somewhat superficial wherein each individual carries a range of identities (public and private) which are not cohesive but are easily altered to be in line with whatever the demands of a particular situation turns out to be. It is still true, of course, that if people define situations as real, they are real in their consequences, but it is not the case that the situation they so define as real will be altered by their definition. As Erving Goffman rightly notes, the world is too infinitely complex to be altered by a mere definition. While the meaning of an object, for example, may be found in its use, the users do not typically decide on how the object is to be used.[37]

Into our picture comes, therefore, the powerful institutions of the day such as the state and other large organizations which can and most often do provide very authoritative definitions regarding the uses to which individuals are put—the roles persons are to play in particular situations. Entering the picture, too, are politicians, experts, intellectuals, celebrities, social scientists, professionals, messianic leaders, administrators, and other guru-like public figures who all vie for legitimacy and control over the symbol-creating means by which situational definitions can be manipulated. Since the actors in everyday life must take pains to make their behavior appear rational and morally justified under the circumstances, these authoritative situational definitions handed down from high can

---

[37] Goffman, *Frame Analysis*, pp. 1–2.

potentially carry great weight. Still, the locus of meaning is to be found in immediate interactive setting, and, despite our appeals to what we might consider the most sacred of sources, if we fail to operate in terms appropriate to the situation, our immediate neighbors will no doubt be the first (though perhaps not the last) to let us know.

IV. THE RULES OF SOCIAL CONDUCT

The American social order is a complex one with multiple standards of social conduct in existence. Brief encounters of the impersonal sort typify our day-to-day lives, the scenes within which we involve ourselves rapidly change and do not necessarily overlap, and even our more stable relationships seem to break down with increasing frequency if we are to take divorce, geographic mobility, and occupational turnover statistics as indicators. The rules of conduct that perhaps once regulated our behavior across situations in such a way that life seemed simpler, more uniform, and, in many cases, safer appear to be gone forever.[38]

Traditionally, western societies have held that certain rules of conduct are absolute: Thou shalt not commit murder or adultery, bear false witness, or covet thy neighbor's wife. Rules, within this framework, are independent of social situations, persons, historical times, and so on. They represent unchanging moral standards which supposedly reflect the "natural order" of things. Even in matters of simple etiquette, this absolutist stance is typical: there being only one way to hold a fork, blow one's nose, or address a member of the opposite sex. In this section, I take issue with this absolutist and altogether simpleminded approach to understanding the rules of social conduct.[39]

In essence, rules are merely artifacts of a very human and social sort. They have been created by us to govern our interactions with one another, and, like any other social invention, they change over time, mean different things to different people, and always require a context before

---

[38] Perhaps the best depiction of the changes that have accompanied the passing of the traditional order can be found in Frederick Tönnies' classic study of *Gemeinschaft und Gessellschaft*, trans. and ed. Charles P. Loomis as *Fundamental Concepts of Sociology* (New York: American Books, 1940). See also Richard Sennett's more recent treatment of some of Tönnies' original ideas in *The Fall of Public Man* (New York: Alfred A. Knopf, 1974).

[39] Interestingly, most of the early studies of deviance were grounded upon just this absolutist perspective. Indeed, many of the original studies were undertaken for the purpose of eradicating evil. But, when a sort of journalist's fascination for the mean streets of city life began to emerge in sociology and researchers actually went into the field to see deviance for themselves first-hand, a rather sympathetic and contextual understanding of deviance took hold. A good historical trace of the study of deviance is provided by David Matza, *Becoming Deviant* (Englewood Cliffs, N.J.: Prentice-Hall, Inc., 1969) and Jack D. Douglas, "Deviance and Social Control," in *Introduction to Sociology*, ed. Douglas, pp. 537–60.

their meaning can be interpreted. Of course, some rules change more slowly than others, some are more uniformly adhered to than others, and some are more applicable across situations than others. Furthermore, some rules are written down, some are not. Some rules are enforced by the state and others are not. Some rules arise only in specific situations and then vanish forever, others seem ever present. And the violation of certain rules may result in merely a blow to one's ego struck by a friend, or the violation may result in a blow to one's head struck by a shrouded executioner. All of these matters are of our concern in this section and I will handle them, first, by examining some of the properties of rules of conduct in general. Second, I shall investigate four different kinds of rules: formal, cultural, contextual, and implementation rules. Finally, I will look at rule breakers and consider the role of deviance in interpersonal relations.

Rules in General

Rules of conduct are associated with all situations of our experience. They may be simple, complex, conflicting, vague, rigid, or difficult to precisely locate, but they are, nonetheless, manufactured and put to a variety of uses by persons in everyday life. Importantly, rules, selves, and situational definitions are constitutive of one another. That is, they go together. Once a situational definition ("What's going on?") has begun to be constructed by a person, rules appropriate to that definition can be brought into play to guide, justify, and evaluate one's actions. Yet, unlike the so-called subjective, intrapersonal definitions we develop regarding the situation and our role in that situation, the rules of conduct that are associated with these situations once defined represent the more objectively perceived conditions within which interpersonal conduct is constrained. In an important sense, rules serve as the foil against which the self in its moments takes shape. We can go with the tide or resist its pull, and the way we decide to move goes a long way toward defining who we are.

Six major characteristics associated with all rules are discussed below. These properties are neither exhaustive or analytically distinct. Certainly shorter (or longer) lists could be prepared, for several of the characteristics listed could fold into other categories (or, on the other hand, one could subtype some of the characteristics thus extending the list). The purpose here, however, is more mundane than presenting a precise theoretical description of social rules. My aim is merely to familiarize the reader quickly with some most important rule-related matters and then move on to consider the various kinds of rules that can be seen to govern social conduct.

First, rules cannot transcend the situation in which they are applied (though we often try). When deciding upon the use of a particular rule, the actor, of necessity, must take account of the context within which sanctionable actions take place. We may be both cognitively and emotionally bound, for example, to the Biblical dictum of an "eye for an eye and a tooth for a tooth," but, when the offender is our son or daughter, such moral absolutism is likely to understandably diminish. Rules are always situationally problematic. Indeed, many times we are forced to "play it by ear" even though there may be rules about. Consider a situation in which we are rushing a seriously injured friend to the hospital in the dead of the night and are stopped by a red light at an intersection where there is no moving traffic coming in either direction. The rules of the road clearly demand compliance to the red light though one suspects (and hopes) that there are few of us who would surrender to such rules.

Second, and relatedly, all rules have exceptions.[40] No matter what the rule, morally allowable justifications for its violation can always be constructed (though not always accepted). Even the most prized and endorsed rules of a society do not always lend themselves well to the on-going exigencies of day-to-day life. Incest, a most universal taboo, can occasionally be excused on the basis of ignorance or mistaken identity. "To kill or be killed" presents also a situation wherein the First Commandment prohibiting the taking of a life is often overlooked. Although claiming legitimacy for one's actions on the basis of appealing to universal rules is of obvious value when attempting to organize people or preach to them or guide them by constructing a code of ethics, such rhetoric conveniently overlooks how uncertain any rule can be for people when faced with a concrete situation. It is always difficult, too, to specify what precise meaning a rule will have for different people. A rule cannot specify its own applications; it takes a user to do so. And, crucially, while a rule may suggest what is considered "proper" conduct, such conduct is not always "smart" given an individual's or group's particular purpose. The archtype dope for instance is one who rather mindlessly adheres to a specific rule without attempting to see the rule in the light of the specific situation. The driver who remains at the red light while a friend suffers is a good illustration of this point. Indeed, strict adherence to a rule often reflects incompetence rather than competence, for the person displays by rigid adherence a rather remarkable ignorance of the specific context in which the rules as practiced must always be located.[41]

---

[40] The exception to this rule is the rule itself.

[41] This is to say that what is valued by society or a cultural system is not always practically available to people in their day-to-day existence. We should not, in fact, expect to find all the espoused values that perhaps lend coherence and rationality to a way of life expressed in the mundane activities of everyday life. The notion of "equality" is a good example here, for it clearly means very different things to different people in this society and can be taken in different ways on different occasions. Consider Edith Bunker's rather American perspective on this culturally esteemed value: "What's the point of working all your life if you only get to be equal in the end?"

Third, rules not only change over time, they are only selectively enforced at any given time. Historical periods bring with them different rules and enforcement policies. The 1960s, for example, saw a general loosening of the rules of sexual conduct followed by young people. This period, too, saw certain rules enforced against only certain groups as when antiwar demonstrators were arrested for activities the police ignored when they were engaged in by groups more supportive of American war efforts. Even the generally unspoken rules of common courtesy display remarkable flexibility. For a man to stay out of the kitchen is today more of an insult to women than a favor.

Fourth, rules, like all meaningful aspects of the social world, are negotiated. They come into being through the efforts of some to control the behavior of others. Rules, therefore, are only partial determinants of interpersonal relations, for people bring with them to interactive settings different resources, authority, skills, and so on. The situation cannot decide itself what rules are to apply, only the people involved in those situations can do so. And, to claim that a rule exists is a matter rather different from being able to invoke that rule. Like situational definitions, the rules that govern conduct often emerge only after some hard bargaining has occurred. Indeed, the presence of legal systems gives explicit testimony to the negotiated character of those rules set up presumably to regulate conduct among people. The production of a rule therefore exists in very close relation to the production of meaning. A transgression, like a meaning of a word, thing, or event, is always potentially negotiable.

Fifth, rules serve as resources to justify behavior after the fact as well as to guide behavior before the fact. They have a retrospective and prospective character to them. A man in fear for his life may follow the rules of survival though upon recollecting the situation later, he may find it more expedient to claim that he acted on the basis of the legal but sacred rules regarding the defense of property. The police officer who shoots a fleeing citizen in the midst of an emotionally charged public disturbance acts out such a drama, though in the officer's post facto report of the incident we are likely to learn that the shooting was based more upon concrete suspicions than the officer's "gut reaction" to personal terror—the citizen made certain "furtive" gestures, the citizen was a "suspected felon," the citizen was "endangering others," and so on. The point is simply that rules are used in a variety of ways, and their use as resources often enables people to insure that their actions come to be seen by others after the fact as morally justified—the rules were on their side.

Sixth, shame more so than any form of direct punishment is the great enforcer of the rules. Shame is that most powerful feeling that when fully aroused, paralyzes us, causes us to "flood out" emotionally, to wish that we were dead. Rules, in essence, are conditional upon their ability to engender a discovered violator's shame. If there is no shame, the rule in question hardly applies as intended. The remorseless is, in fact, society's deadliest enemy. Coercion is always possible, of course, though coercion is fraught with operational difficulty, and rule acquiescence must depend solely upon the watchfulness of the enforcers. For example, to many young people, to be caught smoking marijuana entails virtually no shame (though going to jail may), and, indeed, the rule prohibiting its use is seen as an anachronism. The popular John Prine song, "Illegal Smile," captures the essence of the prevalent feeling among the young toward the rule. Of course, a prominent older member of the community, a deacon of the church for example, may still be kept in line by such a rule as well as the ideology that surrounds the penetration of the prohibition in everyday life. At any rate, when discussing rules, shame is that matter that lies closest to whether or not a specific rule is to be accepted or rejected by those subjected to its use.

Given these sensitizing remarks about rules in general, I now discuss four basic kinds of rules. Since each rule-type displays the six properties laid out above, I will not often refer back to these characteristics but rather assume them in my discussion. It is, however, important to note that all situations (classified earlier as encounters, scenes, and relationships) contain a mix of the rule-types discussed below. Thus, while participants on certain occasions rely no doubt more upon, say, "cultural rules" than "formal rules," all four rule-types can conceivably be found at work in any concrete situation.

Formal Rules

Perhaps the least binding of all rules of conduct are those I classify as formal rules. This category refers to those explicit, usually codified and written rules that attempt to specify what people may or may not do in particular situations. Civil-legal rules, for example, prohibit certain actions individuals and groups may undertake. They presumably protect objects and their owners from harm. Consider organizational charts, too, which delineate responsibilities to people for particular functions by locating them in positions of more or less authority. Job descriptions also provide explicit behavioral guides for employees to follow while at work. Formal rules, in essense, represent a priori plans through which the actions of people can be directed. But, like all plans, their effect on human behavior is always problematic.

The situations to which formal rules apply are varied and are continually subject to differing interpretations. Any formal rule by its very nature must first be interpreted by its would-be users as to its situational applicability. Thus, there is always the possibility that a wide variation of interpretation exists among users. Moreover, when one examines those rules which have been "rationally" legislated to govern the behavior of members of society, we see great changes over time. Formal rules come and go, and, for that reason alone, tend, therefore, to be rather socially superficial. Consider, for example, the vast changes we have seen in criminal and property law in this country just in the last 25 years.

It is often argued, however, that formal rules make an orderly society possible by regulating the conduct of members in universal ways. This naive perspective implies that law and order somehow go together. Yet laws (or any other type of formal rules) have no relationship to order per se; they may even create disorder. Formal rules, for example, can create and maintain class privileges which foster strained interaction among people and perhaps even bloody conflicts between classes. Formal rules in the work place created by management to increase, say, efficiency by tighter supervision, a finer division of labor, and pressures for production through output quota systems often create vicious cycles wherein worker slowdowns are followed by the issuance of more managerially invented rules designed to break the slowdown, which are then followed by more worker activity to strike back at management.[42] Consider, also, the massive societal breakdown that would occur were we to actually enforce all the laws presently on the books. As the police know all too well, such a task would be impossible for the laws are so numerous and pertain to so many activities of our everyday life, few of us would remain out of jail after simply one day of enforcement. *Law* and *order* are terms that must be uncoupled for there is no necessary or automatic relationship between the two.

The formal rules are, however, quite useful as resources to justify one's behavior. In other words, they can be put into service for the purpose of convincing other people that one acted correctly. If a formal rule can be located that will excuse one's action, a moral justification has been created (though others may not be convinced this is so despite its formal character). In the same vein, formal rules are also useful as resources for insiders of a group or organization to present to outsiders. To point to an internal set of rules suggests to outsiders that the group or organization does not act capriciously but rather acts in rational and predictable ways.[43]

In general, formal rules overlook situational contingencies and the practical difficulties ordinary people have in determining just what a

---

[42] On this "vicious cycle," see Alvin W. Gouldner, *"Patterns of Industrial Bureaucracy* (Glencoe, Ill.: The Free Press, 1954).

[43] We should note, too, that the broader, more ambiguous the formal rule, the more serviceable it tends to be for those who wish to apply it. Diffuse rules provide great license to users. The police, for example, present a good illustration in this regard for they persistently and vocally resist the efforts of some citizens to specify more concretely the police right to stop and frisk "suspicious persons" or handle "disorderly ones" or, more generally, to do what they think is necessary to "keep the peace." See Peter K. Manning, *Police Work* (Cambridge, Mass.: MIT Press, 1977) for a good discussion on matters pertaining to the police.

formal rule means. Bureaucratic rules, for instance, lay out forms of proper conduct for people in terms of one's organizational position. But these positions are invariably personalized by an incumbant on the basis of that person's more or less unique past experiences, career goals, present circumstances, and a host of other contingencies. Even formal rules surrounding such matters as theft in an organization are sometimes interpreted in highly personalized ways thus allowing individuals to view their actions as morally justifiable under the circumstances. To pad an expense account or make off with the office's supply of paper clips may technically be labeled theft though one can be sure that the perpetrators of such doings will not see their actions in such a light.[44]

Some of the reasons behind the problematics of formal rules lie in the very fact that such rules can be made explicit in the first place. To be explicit suggests that the rule makers have in mind the precise behavior they wish to control. This is to say that formal rules do not necessarily express the "natural practices" of people to whom the rules are directed, that, in the past, breaches of the rule have been frequent enough to be noticed, and, once noticed, some person or group has become mobilized to put an end to such activity. In such cases, the rule stands in opposition to what certain people already consider proper or, at least, in opposition to what people have already done. The creation and enforcement of the rule, therefore, reflect power differentials more so than they reflect any "natural order" governing interpersonal relations, and, for this reason in particular, the examination of only formal rules typically reveals very little of the human condition.

Cultural Rules

Closer to the moral core of any group, organization, or society are cultural rules of conduct. Unlike formal rules, cultural ones are far less likely to be written down or made explicit. Cultural rules refer to the proper forms of interpersonal behavior an individual learns while becoming a member in good standing of a group, organization, or society. Enforcement of such rules, however, almost always resides in the immediate and face-to-face interaction network in which the person is involved. Cultural rules cover an extremely broad spectrum of behavior ranging from local customs such as how one orders food, takes leave of a group, or makes requests of others, to matters of wider significance (often also covered by formal rules as well) such as how to rightfully acquire property, how to

---

[44] On the moral justifications managers have invented for theft in organizations, see Melville Dalton, *Men who Manage* (New York: John Wiley and Sons, 1959). See also, Jack D. Douglas and John Johnson, eds., *Official Deviance* (New York: J. B. Lippencott Co., 1977).

exhibit the proper demeanor in passing public encounters, or how to redress perceived wrongs.

Generally, cultural rules fall under the rubric of what we call "commonsense." That is, we take most cultural rules for granted and usually find little about them to warrant attention. They are so much a part of our everyday lives, we have difficulty sometimes even finding the words which could express them. And insofar as explaining or accounting for them, the best response we usually can muster up resembles the dim and tautological expression: "because that's just the way things are."

Because of their implicit character, cultural rules are most often recognized only in their breach. When, for example, a woman is observed to be talking on a streetcorner to no one apparently other than herself, we become conscious of the cultural rule regarding keeping one's thoughts to oneself among strangers. The observed behavior reminds us of such a rule for it represents an obvious exception to it. Consider another example. We typically feel disturbed when an unknown clerk in a store seems to get too personal because we recognize a violation of another cultural rule which restricts the content of clerk-customer interaction to that of an impersonal kind.[45]

Cultural rules have, therefore, an "of course" characteristic to them. They deal with those actions we expect of others (and others of us) rather matter of factly. Indeed, we feel we have a moral right to expect cultural rules to be followed. Yet what is unproblematic to some may be problematic to others. It is useful then, to distinguish between the more problematic or varied cultural rules (surface rules) and the less problematic or shared ones (basic rules).

Surface cultural rules refer to the standards we follow regarding such things as politeness, dress, etiquette, ceremony, ritual, expression, neighborliness, and so on. Such rules find their expression most developed within relatively restricted social circles wherein members may well recognize the existence of other standards though they typically choose to follow their own. Within one's own circle, the following of such rules protects the person from local embarrassments and also furthers the solidarity of the group itself. Appearance, use of argot, demeanor, interaction styles, and even personal goals are often matters of some importance addressed by surface cultural rules. For example, in the bipolar status system of most public high schools in the United States, the

---

[45] In general, while cultural rules are known mainly in their breach, there does seem to be a somewhat more general framework which can be applied to these matters. The late Harvey Sacks (Unpublished lecture notes, University of California, Irvine, 1968–74) referred to the "rule of incongruity" as a way of distinguishing and recognizing cultural rule violations. A good discussion of this general principle can be found in Joan Emerson, "Nothing Unusual Is Happening," in *Human Nature and Collective Behavior*, ed. Thomatsu Shibutani (New Brunswick, N.J.: Transaction Books, 1970), pp. 208–22.

"soshes" can typically be distinguished from the "greasers." The "soshes" emphasize cooperation with authorities such as teachers, parents, and the police, participate in school activities, and try to approximate something akin to the just-scrubbed look of the proverbial boy or girl next door. The "greasers," on the other hand, emphasize toughness, stand in opposition to the authorities, and attempt to maintain a scruffy, rather rebellious look. Within any one sphere, to neglect any of these general rules is to commit something of a moral affront. For a male "greaser" to appear at school attired in Puma tennis shoes, neatly pressed cord pants, and a crew-neck sweater, for instance, would be certain to draw fire from fellow "greasers." Attempts to isolate, ridicule, embarrass, or otherwise shame the straying group member back into the approved boots, levis, and a leather jacket would be made. By and large, such social control is extremely effective, for the resources on hand for members of the social group to demand allegiance (or at least conformance) to their surface cultural rules are virtually limitless.

This is not to say that surface cultural rules do not run deep within any one individual. Indeed they do. The real test of understanding their use, however, is not found in one's knowledge or positive evaluation of the rules, but, rather, it is found when considering whether or not one can carry out the rules unhesitatingly and unquestioningly. Cultural rules that are consciously followed are, from this standpoint, similar to formal rules, and they represent, at best, a learner's crutch in interpersonal relations. The use of formulated rules is seen by members of a particular group to be as stilted perhaps as the local Mexican population views the American tourist who must turn to the guidebook for advice on how to order dinner, how to locate a hotel, or how to find a bathroom. The proper use of cultural rules requires one to throw away the formal rules and assume the casual role of a member where the knowledge about how to act, what to say, and when and where to do so comes naturally, without thinking. Like learning how to ride a bike, when the learner can say, "Look, Daddy, no hands," the formulated rules become passé and downright irrelevant to the performance. And, like learning to ride a bike, learners of cultural rules must eventually do without formulated rules if they are to bring off graceful, self-confident, and trustworthy performances in the group of which they are members.

Basic cultural rules, on the other hand, find their expression across many more situations than surface rules and are binding on far greater numbers of people. These rules are almost universally shared and hence are rarely violated by members of a particular society. So basic are these rules, such as those regarding public nudity, murder, and certain taboos surrounding death, religion, sex, and politics, that once learned they are never talked about except when socializing "young savages" (children) or "aliens" (foreigners) who do not yet understand or conform to such rules. By and large, since only anthropologists, diplomats, missionaries, immigrants, and other worldly sojourners have first-hand knowledge and intimate experience from living in other societies, our own rules tend to be unseen and therefore are largely taken for granted. But they do become quite visible when they are violated, for moral indignation of a most self-righteous sort results on the part of those who have knowledge of the violation. We are all the enforcers giving power to basic cultural rules.

Importantly, these rules refer to almost a residual category of rules. That is, even if we could write down all the rules we could vacuum out of society, other hidden rules of conduct would no doubt remain, since rules are potentially infinite (as are the situations in which they arise). Of course, even the deepest of rules can be discovered in the breach. In fact, the social stigma that comes from being labeled "mentally ill" is often a result of a person's violation of a basic cultural rule. The label is something of a catch-all for breaches in what is considered the most fundamental behavioral rules in society. A man who keeps his finger in his nose all day long, talks to the gods, wears invisible clothes, or makes up his own language has presented a most unusual and inappropriate performance in this society and is therefore in need of assistance, for it is obvious to all competent members that the person does not know the first thing about "reality." Such lost souls are thought to have "something wrong with them in the head" and are, therefore, perhaps dangerous and require isolation, for no one can know what they might do next. While an Azande tribesman may quite properly talk to the trees and hear the trees talk back in his society, it is quite a different matter for a card-carrying Rotarian in a three-piece suit to claim the same thing in our society.[46]

It is true, however, that the American society at large is becoming a more open and permissive one. Many formerly taboo matters have been confronted directly by various individuals and groups within this society, and, in some cases, sweeping changes have occurred in the wake of such confrontations. Indeed, over the past two decades we have been exposed repeatedly to the sometimes odd if not bizzare visions of the "good life" that in times past would have been seen as alien, crazy, and clearly beyond the pale. Esalen-molded psychologists have, for example, urged us to disrobe and plop ourselves into communal hot springs where, we are told, we can truely get in touch with our feelings (and perhaps other things as well). Silva mind controllers, transcendental meditators,

---

[46] The position I take here is that "mental illness" is rarely an organic or physiological defect associated with a person but, rather, that it is a label that has been successfully tied to a person. In other words, it is not one's behavior per se that determines whether or not one is to be called mentally ill, but it is the reaction of others in society to one's behavior that determines the distinction of the mentally ill from the rest of us. An impressive argument along these lines is located in Thomas J. Scheff, *Being Mentally Ill* (Chicago: Aldine Publishing Co., 1966).

"moonies," deprogramers, harikrisha devotees, flying saucer cultists, esters, ESPers all speak of a new and strange reality governed by rules few of us can comprehend.

More importantly, wider social movements have also questioned previously taken-for-granted rules of the society such as those concerning the "proper role" of women, blacks, students, homosexuals, and so on. Many of us, perhaps, have felt threatened by some of these movements for there is comfort in tradition. But it is true, too, that we have also felt liberated by other movements, for there is exhilaration that comes from change. But regardless of how we have reacted, our lives have been changed as a result of these movements. The basic-cultural rules of our society have also been changed as a result of these movements. It seems the case that some historical periods seem to produce more change than others and then are followed by periods which appear to produce a pulling back of sorts. Perhaps what sociologist John Irwin called the ancient theory of the pendulum works here where social change is perpetual, but the pendulum, without ever moving to precisely the same point, swings slowly back and forth from one dialectic pole to the other.[47]

Contextual Rules

Unlike formal or cultural rules, contextual ones are tied most closely to the immediate situations in which we find ourselves. These situations may be encounters, scenes, or relationships, but in them we often discover that formal or cultural rules provide only the sketchiest of outlines for appropriate behavior. Thus we must fill them in with situationally specific rules. Wherever recurrent interaction among people is found, contextual rules are usually also invented by the participants to protect themselves (and others) from embarrassment or shame which might, so to speak, stop the show and alter the situation. Contextual rules may refer to how work gets done, how emotions are to be managed, how one must act in front of others not usually present, what can legitimately be discussed, and so on.

There is a similarity between contextual and cultural rules in terms of content, but there is also an essential difference. In brief, cultural rules tend to hold relatively firm across situations where there are members of the same social circle present; contextual rules typically do not hold firm across situations—they vanish once the encounter, scene, or relationship has been terminated. For example, cultural rules must be modified to some degree when others who obviously do not share one's background or membership in a group enter into a situation. The modifications that come into being can be seen as contextual rules. Over time, of course, what begins as a contextual rule may well become a cultural one and may eventually

---

[47] Irwin, *Scenes*, p. 186.

even become a formal rule. But, like all rules, it has to be invented somewhere and this somewhere is always a specific situation. Consider Cain's
slaying of Abel. Such an event served, perhaps, as the primal occasion for
the prohibition against murder. What began as a contextual issue has
since become a most formal and basic cultural rule.

Erving Goffman is the master when it comes to describing the situational order held in check largely by contextual rules.[48] In his elaborate
and many-sided analysis of face-to-face behavior, contextual rules are
constructed such that if they are honored, they induce exchanges between
people of the sort that keep the situation on an even keel and allow
interactants to accomplish their purposes. For example, one's loss of poise,
slip of the tongue, slight of the other all threaten to disrupt a given situation. But, as Goffman points out, rarely do such potentially discrediting
lapses result in the distintegration of social situations, for fellow interactants have also learned to cover, as it were, for another's error. Eyes are
averted, contradictions in the presentation are ignored, jokes are made
to treat the potentially discrediting act unseriously, and, in general,
people help each other along in the situation so that everything continues
to move more or less smoothly (for example, "What you really mean
is . . ."). As Goffman suggests, when we interact with others, we presume
we have the others' attention, and, because of this, we are more or less
obligated to take the others into account when we decide on a particular
course of action. To break this contextual rule is to suggest to the others
that they are somehow unworthy of our respect. And, when mutual respect is not forthcoming in a particular situation, that situation typically
becomes untenable to all participants.

Contextual rules are slippery, though, because different situations permit people differing degrees of behavioral latitude. To wit, compare the
typically bland language we use in the presence of strangers to that sometimes earthy and raw language we employ when in the presence of friends.
Certainly the context of our actions can be overlooked only at our peril.
If, for example, we slight a colleague at work whom we hardly know by
not responding politely to his or her friendly "good morning," we run
the risk of being seen by this colleague as an "antisocial" or "stuck-up"
person, one who does not display the proper regard for others. On the
other hand, this same lack of response to a greeting given off by a colleague
with whom we are intimate is likely to be viewed quite differently. Our
colleague may believe we were busy, preoccupied, or troubled at the
moment. Our character is not in question in the latter case as something

---

[48] While all of Goffman's considerable work is pertinent to the contextual fabric of
social relations, his most recent book, *Frame Analysis,* is perhaps the most cumulative
and broadly theoretical. However, it is not by any means an easy work to digest, and
the beginning student is, perhaps, best advised to turn first to some of Goffman's
earlier and more accessible books, such as *The Presentation of Self in Everyday Life.*

to be diagnosed or deflated in light of cultural rules, rather only our specific behavior is of concern in light of contextual rules.

Contextual rules pertain also to the multiple roles we play across and within the various situations of our everyday life. We have all been both buyers and sellers, for example. As a buyer trying to negotiate a good price, we may sometimes try to project indifference about the object of our concern. Other times we may claim to have insufficient resources at the moment to make the seller's price or we may disagree with the seller upon the "fair value" of the object of our concern. On occasion, we may even suggest that we can get the particular object on better terms elsewhere. As a seller, however, we sometimes point out the scarcity of the bargained-for object; other times, we may attempt to project an air of unconcern for the potential sale or argue for a high value and try to show the buyer that because of certain altogether inflexible conditions, we are obligated to sell the object at only the asked-for price. This stylized interplay between a buyer and seller depends upon so many contextual issues (the object, the price, the setting, and so on) that no one set of rules could ever handle all the buyer or seller must know to competently perform in a specific exchange episode.

As a final example of contextual rules, consider certain research findings coming from studies concerned with the moral judgments and behavior of both adults and children. In brief, what researchers have begun to discover is that culturally disapproved actions such as cheating on tests, lying to others, or stealing small amounts of merchandise, money, and food are highly situationally specific. That is, the person who, for instance, lies in one situation, will not lie in another. The person who cheats will not necessarily steal. Even in very similar situations, moral behavior is rather remarkably unpredictable. The child who cheats on an arithmetic test will not do so on a spelling test. The reasons for such instability are as varied as the research subjects themselves, but one result stands out. Most subjects were easily able to construct some account or otherwise self-justifying explanation to excuse or rationalize their behavior. Whether such accounts were opportunistic or not makes little difference for our purposes since the point is that virtually every subject viewed each of the moral situations they encountered as quite different, and, therefore, they were able to follow quite different contextual rules on each occasion.[49]

---

[49] Lawrence Kohlberg, "Stage and Sequence," has attempted to isolate levels of moral development that correspond to Jean Piaget's stages in cognitive development. His work tends to show that the direction of moral awareness goes from the ego-centric ("What's in it for me?") to the social ("What will others say?") to the existential ("What's the principle involved?"). But, critically, research has also shown that the ability to conceptualize morality at these levels does not guarantee its production. Apparently, regardless of the so-called level of moral development achieved by an individual, the enactment of moral behavior turns on more situationally specific matters. See A. R. Havighurst and H. Taba, *Adolescent Character and Personality*

While contextual rules do not always contradict cultural or formal rules, on occasion they sometimes do. The difference between what people say and what they do is therefore problematic though it is hardly the great mystery some social scientists have made it out to be. People can not always say with any certainty what they will do until they discover the particular situation in which they are to act. Only then can certain rules be developed and applied which can guide their behavior.[50]

Implementation Rules

Implementation rules are, in essence, rules about rules. They refer to the manner in which we put to use, interpret, and sometimes justify our actions as appropriate to the situation. Implementation rules suggest whether one is to follow (or claim one followed) a formal, cultural, or contextual rule given in the situation at hand.

Rationality is a fundamental consideration when attempting to implement rules. Whether the rule is formal, cultural, or contextual, individuals making use of a particular rule are often called upon to defend their use, and, when they are, they will take pains to demonstrate that they have considered the relevant facts of the situation and are acting in ways that are consistent with whatever precedents can be dredged up from the past. In other words, the users of particular rules typically attempt to display their willingness to be "objective," to show their sincere belief that the rule they are following is appropriate to the situation, and, in general, to try to impress upon others that their actions were not undertaken randomly, capriciously, or with, as lawyers like to say, malice and forethought. At times, this means that individuals must first depersonalize their behavior so that others will not see their actions and the rules that are followed when attempting to justify their actions as oriented toward personal gain. Politicians who vote against precise accounting requirements for campaign expenditures must, for example, be quite careful when talking about their behavior lest constituents "misread" their actions as grounded upon only crass self-interest which, to the body politic, may well seem irrational.

The notion of *plausibility* is closely related to rationality, and it, too, is quite important when considering the rules about rules. Plausibility refers to a person's belief that a particular rule more or less fits the situation. It may not be the best rule to apply under the circumstances as they later unfold, but, given the information limits of the situation at hand,

---

(New York: John Wiley and Sons, 1949) and the now-classic experiments conducted by Harvey Hartstone and M. May, *Studies in the Nature of Character*, vols. I, II, and III (New York: Macmillan Publishing Co., Inc., 1928–30).

[50] For a brief but excellent discussion on the differences between talking and doing, see Irwin Deutscher, "Words and Deeds," *Social Problems*, 13 (1966), pp. 235–54.

the rule is justifiable. The police, for example, have been observed to follow rules of the chase that are acceptable at the time primarily because of their plausibility. Rules of the chase include looking for the suspect to always go downhill, not uphill, when fleeing the scene of the crime; to run, not walk away; to head directly out of town along the fastest route of egress; not to hang around the scene; and so forth. Police officers can therefore take action in such situations and can later justify their actions on the grounds of plausibility. Certainly other cultural rules could have been invented for these situations (for example, "Wait on the scene, for a criminal will always return.") though, to most American police, these particular rules of the chase are the most "natural" ones.[51]

Another primary rule concerning the use of rules is *practicality*. In fact, when we consider what members of this society deem rational or plausible, we find that practicality is of overriding importance. Regardless of how scientific, idealistic, legal, logical, or humane a postulated rule, it will be viewed as stupid, irrelevant, and maybe insane if it does not meet the practical requirements of the situation. Thus, the "thou shalt nots" of any society must be seen in light of the everyday life of members in that society. Any rule has its limits. Take, for example, table manners. It may be considered in bad taste to ever reach in front of another while eating. Yet, when another has both hands full and a request has been made for more gravy, one would be remiss not to assist in the situation even if it means reaching boarding-house style across the table for the gravy. All rules are conditioned upon certain operating and stop rules to be gleaned from what individuals consider practical in the situation.

When addressing the rationality, plausibility, and practicality requirements of rule use it is important to note that such considerations do not ordinarily arise in most situations of our day-to-day lives. We are not often called upon to justify our intended or observed behavior. These rules about rules stand largely in the unseen background and are matters of only peripheral concern to us since we typically assume that others will see the "obvious" rationality, plausibility, and practicality of our actions. But all rules must occasionally be defended. For instance, we sometimes go shopping with our personal fronts in disarray. Our hairdo is mused, our make-up out of kilter, and, in general, the surface decorations we have chosen for the mundane occasion are incongruous with the appearance we usually maintain. We, of course, count to some degree upon getting in and out of these situations unobserved by friends or acquaintances thus keeping our act together by saying out of view. However, if a neighbor gleefully approaches and greets us, we may well feel under some obliga-

---

[51] On a police officer's rules of the chase, see John Van Maanen, "Working the Street," in *The Potential for the Reform of Criminal Justice*, ed. Herbert Jacob (Beverly Hills, Calif.: Sage, 1974), pp. 83–130.

tion to account for our out-of-line appearance. Here is where the rules of rationality, plausibility, and practicality come dramatically to the fore. The account we manufacture, if it is to be believed, must have these characteristics. And to not provide an account for our "unusual" look is perhaps to suggest to others that we no longer care about how we appear (a moral affront in many social circles). Thus we come up with such disclaimers as "I must look a mess but I've been down with the flu for the past several days," and "I didn't have time to dress since the children have kept me busy all day." These hasty accounts usually get one quickly off the social hook providing, of course, one has not been observed playing tennis earlier in the day or that one, in fact, has no children.

It is true, too, however, that at times we are stumped and are unable to construct any account for our actions or to see any order behind the actions of others. Rationality, plausibility, and practicality notwithstanding, there are moments when the imponderability of life takes over and all we can express verbally is a "far out" or a "who knows" or a "no shit" or the remarkably serviceble "oh, wow." While we typically take care to normalize our actions and to make sense of the situations of our immediate experience, there are occasions, fleeting and presumably uncommon, where disorder is the best we can do. Like all rules, the rules of implementation have their times and their exceptions.

Rule Breakers

Deviance is the conventional social science term to denote any form of behavior (sometimes a thought or a feeling) that is believed by most members of a group, organization, or society to violate a rule they feel to be just and proper. The violated rule can be formal, cultural, or contextual, and, when a violation is charged, the rules of implementation come also into play. Certainly negotiation plays a huge role in defining deviance, for any act requires a charge before it can be claimed that the act violated any particular rule. And with charges come defenses. There are in this sense "moral entrepreneurs" who seek to implement certain rules to restrict the behavior of others as well as "moral provocateurs" who seek to challenge certain rules sometimes merely to flaunt them and sometimes in the hope of changing them. To implement any rule and call out violators invariably involves conflict over what is to be considered right and wrong both in general and in concrete situations.[52]

---

[52] For the best-known theoretical and empirical statement of the "labeling theory" perspective on deviance, see Howard S. Becker, *Outsiders* (New York: The Free Press, 1963). For some further refinements in this perspective, see Matza, *Becoming Deviant*; Edwin Lemert, *Human Deviance* (Englewood Cliffs, N.J.: Prentice-Hall, Inc., 1967); and Jack D. Douglas, *American Social Order: Social Rules in a Pluralistic Society* (New York: The Free Press, 1971).

From this standpoint, deviance is not an inherent quality of a particular act a person commits, but, rather, it is a negotiated consequence of the application by others (moral entrepreneurs) of a given rule to the offender (moral provacateur). The deviant, therefore, is best thought of as one to whom the label has successfully been tied. The power to enforce sanctions upon the behavior of others as well as the power to manipulate and change the rules that lead to the application of such sanctions are, of course, not evenly distributed across a society or even across the membership of a small interaction network. Social conduct, then, is at least partially determined upon the power resources a person has available to both avoid being seen as deviant and, at other times, to successfully charge others with being deviant.

We all have developed strategies for coping with deviance, however. When it comes to our own actions, our first and foremost tactic is to seek out locations that shield us from the view of those potential entrepreneurs who might take exception to our "provocative" behavior. For example, it is argued that saloons are typically only dimly lit and windowless for the purpose of hiding imbibers from the view of other patrons as well as passers-by (to provide a screen). The sanctity of the home is perhaps also premised upon such considerations, for within the home we are also unobserved and therefore have little need to be quite so chary about the rules of social conduct that hold in public locales.[53]

When it comes to stumbling upon the behavior of others that we consider deviant, our first and foremost tactic is, similarly, a discrete one. Typically, we make use of a convenient sort of tunnel vision that allows us not to see the "drunk," "streaker," "ragpicker," or the "obvious mental case" who drools over food in a restaurant or speaks to invisible companions on the public streets. Indeed, moral entrepreneurship is a role seemingly few of us relish and one in which we typically go well out of our way to avoid—though, no doubt, it is also a role all of us have played on occasions. Part of our reluctance to act out the moral entrepreneurial role is prompted by the trouble we believe we must endure when attempting to define a moral boundary because of the typically hazy and vague nature of the boundary itself. Part of it, too, comes from the potential embarrassment that would follow should we be shown to be wrong in our

---

[53] Another very popular strategy for coping with one's own actions that might be seen as deviant by another is to try to "normalize" them—to make them seem conventional and expected ("But, Mom, everybody else did it."). Consider Richard Nixon's well-known lament after the fall in which he claims in his autobiography that he should be let off the hook because his behavior in office merely followed the well-established precedents of those who came before him. See Nixon, R.N. (New York: Grossett and Dunlap, 1978). Such a strategy can be tried in reverse, too, as can be seen when moral entrepreneurs of the fire and brimstone ilk "abnormalize" behavior with atrocity tales. The Victorian caution against "self-abusement" because it would "grow hair on one's palms" comes to mind in this regard.

accusations. And part of our reluctance comes, no doubt, from having options available to us in the situation itself. Thus, most of the time, we can turn our heads, slip out a door, assume someone else will take charge, become preoccupied in other matters hoping that in the pause the offense and the offender will vanish. There are occasions, of course, when such strategies do not work and we are therefore plunged directly into a moral contest wherein our rules can be situationally affirmed or denied.[54]

It is important, however, to see deviance of all sorts in a functional as well as the more familiar dysfunctional light. By testing and retesting the degree of flexibility associated with certain rules, deviants can, for example, point to needed changes. Indeed, without rule breakers, we would hardly know what our rules of conduct were and would perhaps resemble computers who cannot blush, cry, laugh, or commit suicide more so than human beings. Deviance represents variety in our everyday lives and allows us to create niches in a world perhaps too often marked by its demands for conformity. It allows us to glimpse new worlds, and though we typically shy away from participating in them, their mere presence widens our conceptual horizons. Deviance allows also for emotional expression of all types, thus providing instrumental outlets for both rule breakers and rule enforcers.[55]

More importantly, many kinds of deviance must be seen as essentially creative acts. Whether it takes place in the realm of physics, art, science, or public morality, all important creative acts are, by their very nature, deviant. All such actions involve a person in a searching out and an inventing of new ways for doing things. This is, of course, not to say that consciously violating certain rules is necessarily good or useful. I am not making moral judgments here. Indeed, deviance typically doesn't work for people. To commit oneself to a deviant line of action is a difficult and painful decision; it puts one in all kinds of peril and requires more than a little situational courage to bring off such acts. More critically, it doesn't work for most people for they find that after a short experimental period they are ashamed of themselves and are hurt more than helped by their actions. Indeed, most forms of deviance never spread.

The so-called scientific explanations that stand behind deviance are

---

[54] "Interactional indirection" is the tag Goffman hangs on this strategy of avoiding moral collisions. He suggests that when we are involved in conversation and moral disagreements arise, we will avoid discussion of those disagreements and act as if the conflict were, for example, only about the facts. The strategy assists in avoiding the confrontation that might result from asserting, "What I say is moral and what you say is immoral." See Goffman, *Encounters*.

[55] Perhaps the finest statement about the positive social effects of deviance is Robert A. Dentler and Kai T. Erickson, "The Functions of Deviance Groups," *Social Problems*, 7 (1959), pp. 98–107. See, also, Kai T. Erickson, *Wayward Puritans* (New York: John Wiley and Sons, 1966) wherein it is argued that change is made possible only through the redefining of social boundaries accomplished by social deviants.

varied. The more common and apparently popular accounts associated with deviancy of the criminal sort propound such "reasons" as repressed childhoods, lack of opportunity, culture of poverty, social disorganization, and the presence of the infamous Y-chromosome. Perhaps some of these are occasionally true, but such universal accounts for deviant acts are quite limiting. No matter how one views the morality of a deviant act, it is, more or less, a creative one, nonetheless. And there can be many motives which lead people to violate rules of all kinds. The criminal, for example, may act out of a wish for gamelike excitement, to solve a pressing problem, in the momentary flash of anger, a desire for a better life, or simply out of a desire for a more intense experience than is to be found in the conventional work-a-day world. We cannot know directly of such things, but we can say that some sort of creativity and a willingness to stand in solitude outside of society (if only for a brief moment) is necessary when following any deviant path. Such creativity may be thoroughly brutish, nasty, and sadistic in character, but it is, by definition, an associative characteristic of most deviant acts.[56]

Finally, I should point out that deviance (or creativity) in all recognizably legitimate spheres of conduct is also accompanied by attempts to publically shame the deviant. Indeed, such attempts at public shaming in socially legitimate spheres may even be more intense than those that accompany criminal acts since criminals, when captured, are often willing to publically denounce their actions thus reaffirming the rules of proper conduct (the authenticity of such renouncements is, of course, never clear since a show of remorse may also save the criminal's skin). To the contrary, the artist, for example, who challenges the order of the day typically makes no such show of remorse; in fact, the artist often goads an audience by snubbing a public nose at contemporary standards. This is not an easy road to follow, however, and the history of art is littered with examples of incidents of an artist being publically shamed for breaking with the established rules of the show. Degas, Monet, and Cassatt had great difficulty exhibiting their impressionist works within an art world characterized

---

[56] It may be useful here to distinguish between the more proactive and singular forms of deviance and the more reactive and collective forms. The former involves considerably more creativity, courage, and willingness to stand alone than the latter which, in many cases, represents merely the more advanced stages of the former. The so-called "Hippie Trip" is interesting in this regard for the founding (proactive) members of the hippie scene discovered that once they began to recruit great masses of eager and willing (reactive) followers, they could not absorb them and still maintain the original and creative form of the scene. Indeed, after a few short years, the "Hippie Trip" was stretched into almost a grotesque shape and no longer was appealing to most of its original members. See Sherri Cavin, "The Class Structure of Hippie Society," *Urban Life*, 1 (1972), pp. 211–38. On the formation of the hippie scene, see Tom Wolfe's highly enjoyable *Electric Kool-Aid Acid Test* (New York: Farrar, Straus and Giroux, 1968). On the corruption of the scene, see Irwin, *Scenes*, and Joan Didion, *Slouching toward Bethlehem* (New York: Farrar, Straus and Giroux, 1968), pp. 1–18.

by classical-formalistic work. Duchamp and Picasso also found their cubist paintings ridiculed by critics who, by this point, did not wish to break with the impressionist standards. And the hissing and booing that were directed against Pollock, DeKooning, and Johns when they moved into the abstract impressionist style is almost legendary.

All this is merely to say that rule breaking is creative yet exceedingly difficult to accomplish. To view deviance as a categoric evil is to deny the contributions the creative act—even when it may seem almost criminally deviant at the time—has made to any society. Without deviance, change would not occur and the world would be a rather drab, timeless, and meaningless place since we would all be marching to the beat of the same drummer. And, if one believes that human beings are essentially creative, the great and pressing sociological question about deviance is not "How is it that people can do such things?" but rather "Why is it that people do such things so seldom?"

V. THE SELF REVISITED

I have argued throughout this essay that humankind is social to the core not just to the skin. Since our mass society is complex and multiple, filled with many noncohesive roles and rules of conduct, and social intercourse is typically fleeting with its meaning tied to specific situations, a new genre of citizen has seemingly emerged, the "actor" who self-consciously presents a stylized self to others. The structure of this actor's self can be seen as rather similar to a many-sided organic and ever-growing crystaline formation, one that reforms itself each time more substance of which it was created (social interaction) is introduced. On the surface of this structure are many reflective yet transparent panes of different sizes and shapes which mirror and sometimes distort the world around them. If one slices off a segment of the crystal, other segments may remain intact and unchanged. In an analogous fashion, the actor in contemporary society plays many parts and each part provides a different perspective on the world while presenting a different picture to the world at the same time. Some of these parts are enacted more successfully than others and, hence, become perhaps increasingly important to the actor. Other parts may fall flat in the world and are eventually abandoned. As people move from relationship to relationship, scene to scene, or encounter to encounter, changes in their conceptions of the parts they play (and themselves) take place. And, as we have suggested, these changes may well represent fundamental alterations in the nature of the individual's sense of the world and the individual's sense of the self.

This dramaturgic stance suggests that individuals self-consciously perform in the world so as to maintain or enhance their status in the eyes of others. Yet this perspective also suggests that people are aware that they are somehow more than what they present to others, aware that they are continually being watched, and are aware of, and concerned with, the evaluations of particular others. In short, actors strive to present only certain information about themselves so that most others will respond favorably to them. The question that now needs to be raised is simply what sort of psychology goes with this theoretical version of the individual?

Erik Erickson uses the term *Identity* to refer to our deeply held notions of self. In the sense that Erickson gives to the term, identity lies at the meeting between who a person wants to be and what the world will allow that person to be. Neither desire nor circumstance alone determine one's identity. Yet, this concept of identity as a single melting between freedom and constraint fits rather uncomfortably within the framework presented here. A person wishes to be many things and is held in check by at least an equally large number of social mechanisms—only some of which the person can even be expected to be aware. We move through many areas of endeavor and assume many different parts while doing so. Certainly a vague empirical sense of uniqueness may emerge from such travels since one person's patterns of involvement will never duplicate another's. Nor is one person's view of the world likely to match another's, for even if they belong to the same groups, they will not hold the same orientation to them. A neighbor may, for example, know our children almost as well as we do, yet this neighbor cannot feel the same sense of obligation to them as we do. However, Erickson's obscure sense of self rests primarily upon the integration a person can presumably achieve over the various selves presented and retrieved from the world at large, and it is precisely this notion of integration that is so problematic as a theory of the individual in the modern world.[57]

From the frame of reference introduced in this essay, a stable sense of identity would seem to require a relatively stable set of institutions and situations within which the self can take shape. However, for most of us, the bedrock institutions of the society (such as the family, the school, the

---

[57] To be fair to Erickson's most influential work, he does postulate a developmental or moving view in which the self is allowed to change shape across one's lifetime. Yet, in contradiction to my perspective, Erickson fails to appreciate properly how the sense of self is, in large part, organizationally generated—a result of the recurrent situations in which we find ourselves. Moreover, those following Erickson's normative (though scholarly and cautious) lead have rather unabashedly capitalized on our human desire to know ourselves and have built what today can be called the "self-awareness" industry within which the key concept of "personal growth" is a much abused one. This is not to say that Erickson's work carries no value—indeed, it does, for much of it hints at ways we may be able to resist the all-too-seductive pull of outright conformity. But I do wish to make clear that I consider Erickson's "integration of self" idea to be a hopeful, not empirical one. See, for example, Eric H. Erickson, "Identity and the Life Cycle," *Psychological Issues*, 1 (1959), pp. 1–171 and *Identity: Youth and Crisis* (New York: W. W. Norton and Co., Inc., 1968).

state, the local community, and the church) which perhaps used to supply a reasonably coherent design for living have lost their once-sacred and authoritative character. They have become demystified as cultural relativism continues to advance. Take work for example. In the past, occupations provided the major badge of identity for many people. Indeed, we used to take our names from the occupations we followed—Miller, Baker, Smith, Farmer, Carpenter, and so on. But today there is growing evidence to suggest that work has lost its appeal to people as a provider of a special place in the world.[58] Bureaucratization, geographic dislocation, standardization of tasks, and so forth have all contributed to the loosening of one's attachment to and involvement in work. Through increasing specialization, few occupations are even remotely describable in a few words in terms of what the people who follow these occupations might actually do let alone contribute to our collective well-being—an electroencephalographic technician, a word processor, a sanitation engineer, a community relations administrator, or an incentive clerk. Suburbanization moves us further from our places of work thus creating a larger geographic and perhaps psychological gap between work and other of our life's pursuits. And change itself is the order of the day in the economic sector. Business cycles fluctuate widely, occupations radically reorganize themselves on the basis of rapid technological change, and automation creates machine feeders and fixers out of once skilled craftsmen. To be sure, affluence is one result of such vast change, though one of the prices that we have paid for our relatively recent affluence has been a turning away from traditional sources of psychological commitment and pride.

If identity seems to be loosened from the major institutions of the day, where then do we look for our sense of the self? Our analysis suggests that we must look anywhere and everywhere human beings are to be found comingling with one another. In this vein, Goffman's suggestion that we maintain at best only "situational identities" appears to be a good one.[59] Unlike Erickson's integration-of-selves idea, Goffman's notion implies that as our circles of interaction enlarge and become more varied, the more

[58] The demystification-of-work idea can be found in The Department of Health, Education and Welfare recent report, Work in America (Cambridge, Mass.: MIT Press, 1973). Some enlightening first-hand accounts about work in contemporary society can be found in Studs Terkel's Working (New York: Pantheon, 1974), and a scholarly treatment of this same idea has been provided by Peter Berger, "Some General Observations on the Problem of Work," in The Human Shape of Work, ed. Peter Berger (Chicago: Henry Regnery, 1964), pp. 211–91. All of these authors suggest that work and occupations have, in general, lost their once-sacred character. I should note, however, that while "hard times" may, in fact, restore the once-glorified sacrifice of the self in work, it is also quite tempting to suggest that the sacred view of work represents drudgery carried to an excess. That instead of lamenting the passing of a traditional source of attachment in the world, we should rejoice at the new avenues of endeavor that have been opened up as a result.

[59] Goffman, Presentation of Self.

differentiated we are likely to become and the more futile it is to seek core typifications of the self. Thus, when the occasion demands it, we can act as salesperson, moralist, customer, teacher, father, loner, or lover. When the situation calls, we can be calm, irate, intense, intimate, hostile, forgiving, and indignant. We can appear in business suits or leisure suits; we can decorate our homes in traditional Early American furniture or in a demimonde style resembling early Sparta; we can even change our hairstyles as often as we can the oil in our station wagons or sports cars. The modern world is, in short, an actor's world. Of course, associated with this world is the unsettling fact that there is no necessity for us to believe in the essential authenticity of any one of our performances. It is the appearance that counts, for the appearance is all that we can be judged upon.

Such a version of the self without question lightens the moral yoke we must carry in the world. Unlike the Puritan who is born into sin and must struggle for redemption, as actors, we merely must avoid taking the evil parts on the world's many stages. From this standpoint, there are no bad people, just bad parts. If we wish to change our so-called innermost character, all we need do is modify slightly our behavior. Our essential character is, therefore, little more than skin deep.

This view that appearances are masks and the person behind the mask has only the illusion of a separate and stable self may touch a raw nerve or two. It suggests that we are both creators and prisoners of our momentary appearances. Certainly the people that populate Goffman's writings are a somewhat sorry and disquieting lot since they are forever struggling fearfully to save face, avoid hassles, make good impressions, engage in deceitful games, and so forth. But, crucially, such dishonorable, ignoble, and petty actions do not necessarily flow from self-conscious acting.

Goffman has perhaps been a bit too cynical and overimpressed with the many forms of gross self-interest. Certainly the actor model allows for a wider range of possibilities. Behavior in the dramatic posture is not necessarily demeaning, shallow, silly, or frivolous. Self-conscious actions can be aimed at a vast variety of legitimate and socially desirable ends. There is no reason to believe that people can't act as self-consciously to promote ideals such as equality, harmony, and trust as they can act self-consciously in the service of their own personal and perhaps narcissistic ends. Nor is there reason to believe that equality, harmony, and trust cannot be personal ends as well. Just because one is responsive to the judgments of others does not require one to behave pitifully or selfishly. The young man in love tries to be honest and sincere in his actions toward the object of his affections not because he is a hypocrite, but because he wants to be honest and sincere. There is nothing inherently debasing about wishing to be seen in a favorable light.

The actor model, despite some claims to the contrary, also allows for individual variability and creativity. Since we move in a world where shifts from one social category to another are somewhat frequent, we carry relatively "open" situational identities. That is, we are free within the limits of the situation to become whatever we can convince others we have become. Our society has broken with certain past traditions such as the omnipresence in everyday life of the symbols of rank, background, and class which virtually predetermined one's role (and the response of others to that role) in interpersonal settings. Since, in traditional societies, people carried their station in life on their sleeves or on their tongues, they could hardly be expected to suddenly present themselves to others (strangers or friends) in a new and daring light. The actors moving on the modern stage, however, have great latitude to experiment with new social selves. The film *Saturday Night Fever* is a good example in this regard, for the movie depicts the adventures of a working-class hero who is able to periodically transcend a drab, day-to-day world by becoming an elegant master of the evening whose twists and turns on a disco dance floor draw applause and admiration from all those who witness his weekly performances.

The social order of our time appears to open up more avenues of life for people. The traditional scheme where one was locked into (ascribed) only a few possible roles provided perhaps great stability and predictability for an individual, but it also made sure that the world would be comprised of only a few winners and very many losers. Failed merchants or farmers, for examples, brought down on themselves (and their families) dishonor, and there were few areas of life available to them to recoup their social status and social respect. Nowadays, there seem to be far more winners and fewer losers in the scheme of things, for there are more areas of life to enter and fewer barriers of entry to be crossed in most of them. The so-called plateaued bureaucrats can win the respect of their neighbors by taking first place in the local tennis tournament; the unpublished professor can enter and perhaps come close to winning the Boston Marathon; the awkward athlete can excel in biochemistry. The housewife can take charge and successfully direct a state-wide political campaign. Indeed, there should be no tears or despair over the passing of a stable social order, for far more opportunity exists for people to follow varied and potentially creative paths today than ever before.[60]

This is not to say that today our segmented lives are idyllic. All group life is marked by the recurrent tensions between order and change, be-

---

[60] In general, it seems rather "natural" for human beings to strive for both achievement and dominance in life. Indeed, wherever we look, people create symbolic status systems. For example, clothing, recreational interests, club memberships, and even the magazines we leave "casually" on the coffee table when guests come over all potentially elicit attention from others and perhaps communicate one's noble position in the scheme of things social. Even in subcultures that strive for equality, such striving itself can be the mark of a person's respectability and superiority. The point here, however, is simply that the social circles in which such strivings are typically expressed have become more numerous in modern times.

tween individual desires and group constraints. To choose to enter and act within a group gives one order, companionship, and perhaps some degree of stability and obligation in the world, but it also excludes other pleasures such as entering new situations, making new friends, and trying out new social activities. Increasingly, however, we have been able to create times in our lives where we can "break out" of our various realities and engage in somewhat unserious behavior such as vacation times, bar times, party times, and even jogging times. In these brief episodes, the self is free to try out new attire, experiment with new acquaintances, and, in general, engage in new activities. Like the function of play in childhood, such occasions furnish the experiential base wherein new selves can be tried out and old selves reevaluated. We can then return to our former situations refreshed, renewed, and maybe even somewhat changed.

Regardless of the occasion, however, there are always rules of social conduct to follow. All recurrent social situations maintain a certain order whether such situations represent those rather *tightly organized activities* such as work on the assembly line, reading in the public library, or attending the Sunday morning service at the local Baptist church, or whether such situations represent those rather *loosely organized activities* such as searching for ecstacy through mystical practices, doing science, or taking psychotropic drugs. But, as we cross back and forth among our many pursuits, we also discover that all situations leave some room for individual variability (some, no doubt, more so than others).[61] And, as our lives unfold, we begin to gear ourselves more to those social spheres where we are made to feel most comfortable. To do so entails sacrifice and loss, of course, and the coming to terms with the social guidelines present in those spheres. Yet such coming to terms rarely strips away our sense of uniqueness in the situation since we are always able to contrast ourselves with others on the immediate scene (though to outsiders, we all may look the same). It is through such small, localized, and individually significant contrasts between ourselves and others that we are able, therefore, to locate our own special voices.

Perhaps affiliation in the modern world is a little like playing a musical instrument in a jazz quartet. We are free to improvise as long as we do so

---

[61] There are, no doubt, some partial exceptions to this rule. In particular, the so-called rehabilitation or "people-changing" organizations of the sort Goffman calls "total institutions" (for example, prisons, mental hospitals, military boot camps, and so on) leave a person little room to display a unique self and still allow the person safe passage through the setting. Total institutions exist largely to tear down and strip away a person's entering sense of self, such that a new, organizationally approved sense of self can be substituted for the old and entering one. The personal space available to one to carve out an individualized place in the setting is quite restricted, since those who control the setting are ever present and matriculation is dependent solely upon the person's ability to act in ways deemed appropriate by the controllers. See Goffman, *Asylums.*

in keeping with the beat. The beats of our lives may be social obligations such as dinner at six and regular family outings or the work tempos of the day, week, or year. The beat changes, no doubt, throughout our lifetimes, but it continues as long as we have interests and obligations in the world. The beat, of course, curtails our solos, but it does so in peculiar ways. If we are too still and hear only the beat, our lives will probably follow an uninspiring and conventional path—akin, perhaps, to playing "The Surrey with the Fringe on Top" over and over. If we are too raucous and forget the beat, we can be sure someone will let us know—witness the fate of free jazz, word jazz, and all-that-jazz. The trick, of course, is to soar like an Ornnett Coleman or a Charlie Parker while still maintaining a sense of the underlying order within which our solo takes place.

The dramaturgic view of the individual, however, still has its problems even when we open up pathways for improvisational activities. Primarily it remains at best a descriptive view that is perhaps too close to a modern person's own conception of everyday life for comfort.[62] If we examine a few of the broader psychological implications of this perspective, we can quickly see some of the difficulties raised by the dramaturgic view of the world. Most critically, there is a withdrawal danger that is carried with dramaturgic beliefs. Since the actor must be careful on most occasions to conceal certain information about himself or herself, authenticity and spontaneity become crucial issues in everyday life. In a society where the appearance of civility in public may be just that, the actor must look to other, more private, locales for relaxed, easeful, and playful interaction. One must be wary in public situations, for embarrassment and perhaps loss of face are at stake. One may easily be deceived by the appearances of others, thus the establishment of intimacy, disclosure, and trust becomes a precondition for letting down our social guard. The trouble comes, of course, from the plain fact that in modern times we do not seem to let this guard down much in public. And the gap between what we say and what we feel grows, while public spontaneity and genuineness shrink.

Relatedly, because we withdraw as a way of guarding ourselves in the world, much of our public experience is that of detached observation and silence. Indeed, one of the basic rights we seem to fight most aggressively for in today's world is the right to be left alone, the right to privacy. Tocqueville, commenting upon Americans more than a century ago, captured this point quite nicely: "Each person withdrawn into himself behaves

---

62 For example, in our everyday dealings, we talk frequently about others as "good actors." Usually, however, these "good actors" are seen in rather negative ways—they are thought to be people who perform smoothly in public interaction but are presumed to feel nothing in the process. Indeed, we often beseech each other to "get down," "be ourselves," "quit playing a role," "get off of it," "stop putting on airs," and so on. All of these common events offer explicit testimony to the extent to which the social scientist's dramaturgic view of social life mirrors the lay actor's commonsensical view.

as though he is a stranger to the destiny of others."[63] And, indeed, this form of self-absorbtion seems to typify much of our modern experience. Since strangers have no right to talk to one another, we come to know the world only as it appears to us, and appearances can easily include illusions.

Self-absorbtion can lead toward many other troubling issues as well. Consider increasing consumption as an example. Because it is our appearance to others that matters, we must take great pains to see that it is an enhancing and correct one. Increasing consumption becomes, therefore, a way of bettering one's expressive position in the world. Ironically, Marx, of all people, was prophetic in this regard, for he was the first to point out that goods were more often consumed in industrial societies on the basis of their status value rather than on the basis of their direct use. And the cardinal principle on Madison Avenue today is that to have a "successful" product, the good must express the "personality" of the buyer. We buy dresses, for example, because of the way they make us "feel." Thus one chooses to be chaste or sexy depending on the dress the "real you" slides into. Expressive behavior is perhaps coming to be seen as more vital, perhaps more "real" than behavior in the instrumental modes. Candidates for political office emphasize, for instance, their "credibility," their "integrity," and their remarkable "self-control" more so than they do their particular ideas about government, and they seem to win votes by doing so. We seem more convinced as voters with discovering what kind of man or woman the candidate "actually" is than with the past actions or espoused programs of the candidate. To know one's self and to know others is perhaps becoming an end in itself rather than a means to know the world.[64]

In a sense, if we believe that one is merely what one appears to be, we must hold that people who present different appearances are, in fact, quite different people. This certainly reflects the American legacy of individualism which in its present "do your own thing" reincarnation has become something of a modern creed. Odd mannerisms, queer dress, and even

---

[63] Alexis de Tocqueville, *Democracy in America* (New York: Random House, 1945), p. 138.

[64] It seems true, too, that at a time when the power structures of government, business, and labor seem to be growing larger at the national and international horizons, our own personal political creeds paradoxically seem to reflect increasing concern for localism. The image that appears to best attract voters in this country is one of independence and autonomy. The politician tries, therefore, to create a "personality" or "public persona" as a kind of rugged individualist who stands in sharp contrast to the vast and remote institutions of the society (whose main vice, it would appear, is, to a voter, their very "impersonality"). Our great compulsion today is to know our leaders "as persons" and not as "instruments" who just might aggressively pursue certain interests (which might also include our own interests). On the "cult of personality" in politics, or, as some observers have put it, the "triumph of form over substance," see Murry Edelman, *The Symbolic Uses of Politics* (Urbana, Ill.: University of Illinois Press, 1964) and *Politics as Symbolic Action* (Chicago: Markham, 1971).

loose talk become tied to one's "personality" since they are seen as direct expressions of the "inner self." To concentrate on appearances is then to suggest we can know others merely by observing them in concrete detail. Spontaneity becomes set against conformity and makes the proverbial "free spirit" a deviant in the scheme of today's dramaturgic belief system. Since spontaneity entails the risk of disclosure and oozes feelings that are sparked by the moment, one must be careful because such "leakages of personality" may potentially damage the image we wish to sustain in the situation and thereby interrupt the smooth flow of interaction. Since we typically do not desire such a condition, the tendency is to stay in line, keeping our act together, as they say, by closely managing our manageable impressions.

But what of our intimate relationships? Does the critique of the actor's model of the world penetrate into these spheres? Perhaps. Consider the following argument of social historian Richard Sennett, who suggests that our capacity to display sociability and build relationships based on respect for one another has been badly damaged by our concern for an understanding of the actor's image-making abilities in the modern world. In brief, Sennett suggests that because appearances are so often deceiving, when given the opportunity, we quickly set at work to discover another's most close-to-the-soul thoughts and feelings.[65] Cocktail parties, for instance, are full of comments of the sort: "I know that is your official position, but what do you *really* think?" It is as if we will not allow a public position to pass as true feelings and thus must probe like amateur psychologists into the recesses of another's being. As a result, we put great pressure on those close to us to "break the barriers" of manners and customs in order to establish a relationship based on candor, frankness, and mutual criticism. The expectation here is that when relations are visibly open and free from social convention, they are also warm, understanding, and honest. And, perhaps as many of us have wondered, the accuracy of such a social calculus seems questionable.

Today there is something of a growing cult of intimacy about. The so-called self-awareness or human potential movement is a popular and apparently a rather seductive social movement that is gaining converts and true believers rapidly. One identifying characteristic which typifies most self-awareness groups is the almost instantaneous results they claim for their programs. If one seeks intimacy (as most of us do), it is claimed that we must, in the process, come to know others inside out and that this is a relatively easy matter to accomplish. From this standpoint, beliefs about one's self and others must pass into the immediate situation wherein sensation and concrete behavior in the "here and now" become the crucial elements of interaction to be concentrated upon. And, to a certain extent, this "be here now" perspective has made itself felt in our culture.

[65] Sennett, *Fall of Public Man*, pp. 257–340.

One must be cautious here because the evidence is far from clear that by localizing human experience to the point where it is only that which is close to the immediate and intimate circumstances of people that is to count as "real" is necessarily the optimum or most satisfying way to exist. No doubt such experiences have brought great pleasure to some who have followed the well-trod path to "self-discovery." But it remains to be seen whether or not this compulsion to know where another's "head is at" brings more joy and sociability in the long run or more pain and fratricide. Historically, intimate relationships take time to construct, are based upon common grounds, and slowly build situationally relevant rules to express warmth and affection. Instant intimacy of the sort fostered in many social settings today may force people to discard a particular mask, but there is little guarantee that the mask that replaces it is any more the authentic one than the one removed. To believe that the only source of truth about another is to be located in the immediate situation seems a trifle naive.[66]

At any rate, the dramaturgic view of interpersonal relations has great power still in explaining what we do and why we do it. Like any theory, it has its problems. It is most definitely not a normative theory that prescribes how people *should* behave toward one another. And, as I have tried to point out in this concluding section, some of the social implications that flow from the theory are rather troubling. But it does seem safe to say that within the foreseeable future, people will continue to make decisions, select courses of action, choose careers, create works of art, consume goods and services, play with one another, execute heroic as well as not-so-heroic deeds, fulfill their social obligations, associate with one another in groups, try out new modes of conduct, and generally act within a sense of performing in front of others with a concern for the evaluations of those others. To say much more about humankind is difficult, for it is certain that we will continue to be the sometimes chained, sometimes free beings that we are.

---

[66] A most interesting illustration of this phenomenon can be found in some of the so-called innovations in office and business architecture. For example, designers sometimes argue that the destruction of office walls increases efficiency among clerical workers because when people are exposed to one another for long periods of time, they are not as likely to gather together to chat and gossip about nonwork matters as they would were they afforded some private areas. But there are hidden costs carried along with such schemes, for it also seems to be the case that when everyone is under everyone else's surveillance, sociability in general decreases as does morale and people seem to keep to themselves more. In this regard, Edward T. Hall, in *The Hidden Dimension* (New York: Doubleday, 1959), suggests that for Americans to be sociable with one another, some distance from others is required. Thus, it may be the case that what appears to get in the way of knowing another may, in fact, enhance it. From this standpoint, the "barriers" of manners, polite distance, and respect for another's private spheres of life may not be barriers at all, but rather serve as important aids in truly getting to know others. There may be much peril involved, therefore, in attempting to strip away the "barriers" to interpersonal relations. On these matters (and more) see Sennett, *The Fall of Public Man.*

Emotional Expressions in Interpersonal Relationships[1]

by WARREN BENNIS

> ... *I wish to show here an inward picture which does not become perceptible until I see it through the external. This external is perhaps quite unobtrusive but not until I look through it, do I discover that inner picture which I desire to show you, an inner picture too delicately drawn to be outwardly visible, woven as it is of the tenderest moods of the soul.*
>
> SOREN KIERKEGAARD, *Either/Or*

This essay represents an attempt to search out the basic emotional transactions between people: the emotions that exist for no visible instrumental end. I wish to reckon with, following Kierkegaard, the "tenderest moods of the soul"; so I will be speaking of feelings that bind and estrange, feelings that contort into angry knots of discord and those that grow into natural affection, feelings that flow directly into action and those that are transformed and disguised into devious paths, feelings that overwhelm and inspire and those that depress and disgust. This section, then, holds up an imperfect mirror to phenomena that can be only indirectly observed and crudely measured—the raw, almost incomprehensible experiences, at the edge of verbal awareness, we call *interpersonal feelings*.

There are four parts to this essay. Part I, which follows immediately, discusses the perspective brought to the problems I see in the study of the emotional expressions in interpersonal dynamics. Part II samples a few schemes and frameworks for ascertaining the existence and strength of interpersonal feelings. Parts III and IV represent the core material of

---

[1] This chapter is a revised version of the essay which appeared as the Introduction to Part I of *Interpersonal Dynamics*, editions 1, 2, and 3.

this essay. In Part III, I present a typology of the emotional modalities expressed in interpersonal relationships; Part IV examines three basic interpersonal expressions of feelings: "going toward" (love), "going against" (hate), and "going away" (alienation and withdrawal).

I. SOME PRELIMINARY CONSIDERATIONS

Scope and Definition of Interpersonal Feelings

An interpersonal relationship is an irreducible element of reality. Just as we cannot have a line without the presence of two dots, we cannot have an expression of an interpersonal feeling without the existence of two people. I hope to avoid the "myth of isolation" and to stress the "connectedness" of human encounters.

Second, I will focus only on those interactional dimensions which have an emotional base, that is, the interdependencies and transactions that involve the expression of feelings by the participants. Thus *this essay will be concerned with that class of human interactions where feelings are basic and pivotal in the interpersonal exchange.*

Third, I regard interpersonal feelings—the emotional or affective transactions—as the basic, raw data of interpersonal relationships. We do not need to argue about whether these feelings can be reduced to more genotypic categories, such as instincts or impulses; or do we need or desire to assert that certain feelings are "better" or "deeper," or are derivatives or causes of each other. Questions about the causal pairings of interpersonal feelings, or whether one is the obverse or precipitate of another or whether they are instinctive, acquired, or learned need not concern us here. Love is as *basic* as hate and as *real* as loneliness. What I do assert, however, is that the expression of interpersonal feelings is basic to the existence of the relationship, that interpersonal feelings can be ascertained and measured, that they are causal elements in how people will behave, that they have real effects, and that they can be studied without recourse to a physiological or instinctual theory.[2]

These emphases—the irreducibility of the relationship, the primacy of feelings and their "reality"—characterize this essay. One further thought should be added before going on. Arthur Lovejoy, the historian of ideas, coined the term *metaphysical pathos* to describe the subtle and imperceptible, even unconscious, attitudes that guide one's theoretical predilections. Nowhere is this temperamental disposition so visible as it is in the study of personality and interpersonal relations. There is only a thin line between what one is and what one wants, between descriptive realities

---

[2] This is a far more complicated problem than it's made out to be. These oversimplified assumptions will be useful later on as more complex issues are discussed.

and normative desires. It is not only true, for example, that Hobbes and Freud developed theories different from Gordon Allport or Carl Rogers; they also brought to their theories a completely different world view. My own metaphysical pathos, too, tinctures this essay. Wherever I can, I try to make it explicit. My hope here is to penetrate "reality" wherever it leads.

The Present State of Theory

There is as yet no single, comprehensive theory of interpersonal relations. Sociology, social psychology, and psychiatry have offered important insights to the understanding of interpersonal phenomena, but the area still escapes superarrogation by one discipline.[3]

As I point out later on in this essay, when the main theoretical influences feeding into the study of interpersonal feelings are reviewed, I have had to draw on a wide range of disciplines and concepts. The plethora of terms used to describe interpersonal feelings testifies to the range of theories and disciplines. For example, here I use such terms as: *assumptions, needs, interpersonal response, traits, orientation, impulses,* and *feelings.* They are all used to circumscribe the class of behavioral events I am calling *interpersonal feeling.*

The Languages of Interpersonal Theory, Scientific and Humanistic

It might be useful at this point to say a few words about the problem of discussing interpersonal feelings in a quasiscientific way. This presents something of a dilemma, for interpersonal feelings have to do with one's private experiences. One's visceral reactions, experiences of pain and pleasure, delight or disgust, love, fear, and boredom are all intensely private and only partially communicable. These matters have long been considered to be the domain of the humanities. Science, on the other hand, may be thought of as a device for investigating, ordering, and communicating the more public of human experiences such as sense experiences and the intellectual experiences of logical thought.[4] Loosely speaking, then, the cultural elite, the humanists, have constructed a language which roughly expresses the existential situations of individuals in their worlds while the scientist creates a precise language which deals with objects which are independent of human beings.

Any language, though, is a process of symbolization. This is as true for

---

[3] See the first two essays in this volume for a more detailed statement on the "state of theory."

[4] Aldous Huxley, "The Only Way to Write a Modern Poem about a Nightingale," *Harper's Magazine,* 227, no. 1359 (1963), pp. 62–66.

poetry as it is for mathematics. What makes matters more difficult for the language of feelings is the fact that feelings are reflexive by nature; that is, the object of analysis, people, do their *own* abstraction and symbolization. (The physical sciences can avoid this difficulty as they avoid the study of people.) Because of this "reflexive dilemma," the language of interpersonal feelings has stubbornly defied logical analysis or even adequate description.

Today in the social sciences, two languages compete for primacy: the language of the "game" and the language of the "myth."[5] Game languages follow the model of the physical sciences by defining all terms operationally and in formal terms. ". . . Analysis of social interaction is made in terms of moves and countermoves. . . . In all these fields the trend toward miniature systems is indicative of the model of a tight situation, rigidly defined, where individuals can be assumed to conform to a set of rules which can be completely specified."[6]

The language of the game seems most appropriate for the class of interactional problems that are devoid of affect, where the rules are explicit, where formal models can simulate a "tight situation, rigidly defined."

But what of the problems which hold the most interest for us, interactional situations *with* affect? How would the language of the game treat the following passage from a book of fiction?

> Her back seemed mysteriously taut and hard; the body of a strange woman retains more of its mineral content, not being transmuted, through familiarity, into pure emotion. In a sheltered corner of the room we stopped dancing altogether and talked, and what I distinctly remember is how her hands, beneath steady and opaque appraisal of her eyes, in nervous slurred agitation blindly sought mine and seized and softly gripped with infantile instinct, my thumbs. Just my thumbs she held, and as we talked she moved them this way and that as if she were steering me. When I closed my eyes, the red darkness inside my lids was trembling, and when I rejoined my wife, and held her to dance, she asked, "Why are you panting?"[7]

The language of the game could not easily untangle or encompass the range of interpersonal feelings and interactions described. Yet the excerpt is altogether unextraordinary in good fiction. This type of human experience requires a more complicated and subtle expression than the language of the game.

Back suggests as an alternate language—the "language of the myth." It is a language adapted to the human capacity to grasp the complexity and nuance of vital human problems, which game languages might sacrifice to increasing precision.

---

[5] K. W. Back, "The Game and the Myth," *Behavioral Science,* 8 (1963), 66–71.
[6] Ibid., p. 68.
[7] John Updike, *Pigeon Feathers* (New York: Crest Books, 1953), p. 176.

The language of the myth becomes the means of expressing those theories of social science which try to encompass an unlimited field of applicability, which appear to contain some truth but seem fated to be subject to unending controversies over interpretation. They frequently revert to the use of accepted mythology to make a point clear. Freud's theories, for example, fit closely the definition of a theory couched in the language of the myth. The concepts which he uses, such as ego, id, superego, have no precise denotable referent. The meaning derives from the experiences of the listener, and it is clear to him that something beyond the simple concepts, which are practically personifications, is meant.[8]

I cannot endorse completely Back's analysis of the two languages of social science. It is somewhat oversimplified, and he tends to exaggerate the differences through polarization. At the same time, there is no denying that the language we presently use to denote the expression of interpersonal feelings falls short both of the precision of the game and the beauty of the myth.

With these three preliminary considerations spelled out, we are now in a better position to come closer to the core material of this essay. In the following section, I will sample a wide array of approaches which encompass different aspects of interpersonal feelings.

II. A BRIEF SURVEY OF APPROACHES TO ASCERTAINING INTERPERSONAL FEELINGS

As mentioned earlier, there is no single, comprehensive theory of interpersonal feelings. There are, though, a number of researchers and theoreticians who have attempted to ascertain and conceptualize the properties of interpersonal feelings through a variety of techniques. It is useful at this point to sample a variety of these approaches in order to grasp the main dimensions of the field.

This section is organized in terms of the two principle ways of ascertaining interpersonal feelings. In this way, two things can be accomplished at once: to acquaint the reader with these methods, but also, more basically, to examine the way theorists have conceptualized the domain of interpersonal feelings.

The two principle ways of ascertaining interpersonal feelings are some form of *self-description* and some *observation* system, whereby an observer scores interpersonal interactions, usually act-by-act.

Self-Rating Methods

My main example of the use of a self-description inventory to identify and measure interpersonal feelings is FIRO, deriving its name from the

---

8 Back, "Game and Myth," p. 69.

"Fundamental *Interpersonal Relations Orientation.*" The FIRO is a questionnaire developed by W. C. Schutz[9] which consists of a check list of 54 statements designed to measure an individual's propensities along three interpersonal dimensions. These three dimensions were derived partly from a factor analysis done by Schutz[10] and partly from a theoretical disposition favoring the group theories of Bion.[11]

Schutz's work starts from the assumption that each individual has different intensities of needs and different mechanisms for handling them but that all people have three basic interpersonal needs in common:

> The need for *inclusion.* This is the need to maintain a satisfactory relation between the self and other people with respect to interaction or belongingness.
>
> The need for *control.* This is the need to maintain a satisfactory relation between oneself and other people with respect to power and influence.
>
> The need for *affection.* This is the need to maintain a satisfactory relation between the self and other people with regard to love and affection.

Thus, *inclusion* has to do with the degree of commitment, belongingness, and participation an individual requires in human interaction; *control* has to do with the degree of influence and power an individual requires; and *affection* has to do with the degree of closeness and intimacy an individual desires.

One additional factor has to be mentioned in order to present Schutz's theory in more or less complete form. For each dimension we can imagine that an individual *expresses* a need toward other people and that he or she *wants* a need fulfilled for him or her by another person. For example, on the inclusion dimension, we can see how one person may have a strong need to include others, to bring them into his or her groups easily and quickly. This same person, though, may have a low need to *want* inclusion; that is, he or she may not care if others include him or her. Thus, one aspect is what we *do* with relation to other people; this is called *expressed behavior.* The second is what we *want* from other people; this is called *wanted behavior.* Figure 1 shows the extreme types along the three dimensions.

A second example of the kinds of dimensions of interpersonal feelings which can be ascertained from self-descriptions is shown in Figure 2. This

[9] W. C. Schutz, *FIRO: A Three-Dimensional Theory of Interpersonal Behavior* (New York: Holt, Rinehart & Winston, 1958); and "Interpersonal Underworld," *The Planning of Change,* ed. W. G. Bennis, K. D. Benne, and R. Chin (New York: Holt, Rinehart & Winston, 1961).

[10] Ibid., 1968.

[11] W. R. Bion, *Experiences in Groups and Other Papers* (New York: Basic Books, 1959). The work of D. Stock and H. Thelen, *Emotional Dynamics and Group Culture* (New York: New York University, 1958) is also associated with the FIRO dimensions.

108

FIGURE 1
Extreme Types on the Three Interpersonal Dimensions

Expressed Behavior		Dimension	Wanted Behavior	
Extreme High	Extreme Low	Dimension	Extreme High	Extreme Low
Oversocial	Undersocial	Inclusion	Social-compliant	Countersocial
Autocrat	Abdicrat	Control	Submissive	Rebellious
Overpersonal	Underpersonal	Affection	Personal-compliant	Counterpersonal

From W. C. Schutz, "Interpersonal Underworld," in *The Planning of Change*, ed. W. G. Bennis, K. D. Benne, and R. Chin (New York: Holt, Rinehart & Winston, 1961), p. 298.

list, summarized by Krech, Crutchfield, and Ballachey,[12] presents 12 primary response traits (equivalent to Schutz's needs and what I am calling *feelings*) derived from self-descriptions. These were classified into three arbitrary categories and purportedly are representative of the salient interpersonal dimensions.

Observation: Act-by-Act Analysis

One deficiency of self-rating forms is the absence of validating data. Individuals frequently do not see themselves as others do and it is obvious that our interpersonal relations contain important areas of misperception due to inadequate information, systematic distortions, and selective inattentions. For example, Bennis and Peabody[13] showed that self-ratings on FIRO were not significantly correlated with observers' ratings. It will be profitable to examine this discrepancy between self and observers' ratings in some detail.

Sullivan[14] explores this idea in his analysis of interpersonal communication. It is his contention that we systematically *experience* feelings which we do not admit to ourselves and which would therefore not appear as salient on any self-rating inventory. Feelings such as hostility or aggressiveness, for example, are part of the total person and are occasionally experienced. But to all intents and purposes, as the individual construes it,

---

[12] D. Krech, R. S. Crutchfield, and E. L. Ballachey, *Individual in Society* (New York: McGraw-Hill Book Co., Inc., 1962).

[13] W. G. Bennis and D. Peabody, "The Conceptualization of Two Personality Orientations and Sociometric Choice," *The Journal of Social Psychology*, 57 (1962), pp. 203–15.

[14] H. S. Sullivan, "Psychiatry: Introduction to the Study of Interpersonal Relations," in *A Study of Interpersonal Relations, New Contributions to Psychiatry*, ed. P. Mullahy (New York: Hermitage Press, 1949), pp. 98–121.

FIGURE 2
Some Primary Interpersonal Response Traits

Role Dispositions
  Ascendance (opposite: social timidity). Defends rights, does not mind being conspicuous; not self-reticent; self-assured; forcefully puts self forward.
  Dominance (opposite: submissiveness). Assertive; self-confident; power-oriented; tough, strong-willed; order-giving; directive leader.
  Social initiative (opposite: social passivity). Organizes groups; does not stay in background; makes suggestions at meetings; takes over leadership.
  Independence (opposite: dependence). Prefers to do own planning, to work things out in own way; does not seek support or advice; emotionally self-sufficient.

Sociometric Dispositions
  Accepting of others (opposite: rejecting). Nonjudgmental in attitude toward others, permissive; believing and trustful; overlooks weaknesses and sees best in others.
  Sociability (opposite: unsociability). Participates in social affairs; likes to be with people; outgoing.
  Friendliness (opposite unfriendliness). Genial, warm, open and approachable; approaches other persons easily; forms many social relationships.
  Sympathetic (opposite: unsympathetic). Concerned with the feelings of others; displays kindly generous behavior; defends underdog.

Expressive Dispositions
  Competitiveness (opposite: noncompetitiveness). Sees every relationship as a contest—others are rivals to be defeated; self-aggrandizing; noncooperative.
  Aggressiveness (opposite: nonaggressiveness). Attacks others directly or indirectly; shows defiant resentment of authority; quarrelsome; negativistic.
  Self-consciousness (opposite: social poise). Embarrassed when entering a room after others are seated; suffers excessively from stage fright; hesitates to volunteer in group discussions; bothered by people watching him or her at work; feels uncomfortable if different from others.
  Exhibitionistic (opposite: self-effacing). Is given to excess and ostentation in behavior and dress; seeks recognition and applause; shows off and behaves queerly to attract attention.

Source: D. Krech, R. S. Crutchfield, and E. L. Ballachey, *Individual in Society* (New York: McGraw-Hill Book Co., Inc., 1962), p. 106.

they are not part of the experienced self; hence, they make up the "not-self" or "denied-self."[15]

Sullivan[16] tells of a hypothetical couple, Mr. and Mrs. A. Mrs. A, according to an observer, makes a derogatory remark to her husband, Mr. A, after which Mr. A becomes quite tired. Mr. A is not aware of being offended; he is only aware of being weary. He becomes more withdrawn and preoccupied with his weariness. Under cover, according to Sullivan, Mr. A retaliates in a dominantly hostile, noncollaborative way: "A and Mrs. A are not collaborating in an exchange of hostility. She has acted against him, perhaps with full awareness of her motivation; but he "suffers weariness" while unwittingly acting against her, in his weariness ceasing to be aware of her relevance in his motivation. . . ."[17]

Mr. A, in fact, experienced, lived through, and underwent the hostile action of his wife; he reacted to it and then suffered what at first glance seemed like an irrelevant state: weariness. But if we studied Mr. A more closely we would see that this is not the whole story. Sullivan points out that if we had a slow-motion camera and some rather special equipment we could observe that Mr. A experienced something connected with Mrs. A's remarks. For example, we would be able to detect postural tensions in some parts of his face and increased tensions in various parts of the skeletal structure.

> Now if also in our apparatus for augmenting our observational abilities, we had included a device for phonographically recording the speech and adventitious vocal phenomena produced by Mr. A, we would have found interesting data in the field of his peculiarly expressive behavior. There would appear a series of phenomena, beginning, perhaps, with an abrupt subvocal change in the flow of breath. There might appear a rudimentary sort of gasp. A rapid inhalation may be coincident with the shift in postural tension that we observed in the skeletal muscles. There may then have been a respiratory pause. When Mr. A speaks, we find that his voice has changed its characteristics considerably, and we may secure, in the record of his first sentence, phonographic evidence of a continuing shift of vocal apparatus, first towards an "angry voice" and then to one somewhat expressive of a state of weary resignation. In brief, *with refinements of observational technique* applied to the performances of Mr. A as an organism, we find that we can no longer doubt that he experienced, even if he did not perceive, the personal significance of Mrs. A's hostile remark.[18]

This discussion points to a dilemma frequently encountered by students of interpersonal behavior: the discrepancy between self-reports and ex-

---

[15] W. G. Bennis, "Interpersonal Communication," in *The Planning of Change*, ed. Bennis, Benne, and Chin.

[16] Sullivan, "Psychiatry."

[17] Ibid., p. 106.

[18] Ibid., p. 108. Italics added.

pressed behavior observed by others. Both methods are obviously "valid"; self-ratings ascertain self-image and observer reports detect how others perceive the self. The concern here, however, is not the idea of "congruence"; rather I am concerned with the range and complexity in the expression of interpersonal feelings and the need for behavioral measurements to augment the self-rating method.

A number of reliable systems for observing microscopically the act-by-act interactions between people have been developed. Perhaps the best known of these is the Interaction Process Analysis devised by Bales.[19] Figure 3 shows the system of categories used as well as a key to their meaning. Of the 12 categories, notice that only six of them deal with the social-emotional sphere of human interaction; categories 1–3 and 10–12 deal with positive and negative emotional acts, respectively. The remaining six categories, 4–9, deal with instrumental problem-solving processes; numbers 4–6 signify initiating acts and 7–9 signify receiving acts. According to Bales, both instrumental and social-emotional acts are necessary for effective problem solving. The main interests in this section are the socioemotional categories.

There are other systems more specifically geared for observing and recording interpersonal *feelings*. For example, Leary[20] developed a measurement system of 16 interpersonal variables based on the theories of Harry Stack Sullivan. All expressed emotional behavior can be categorized in terms of two orthogonal dimensions: hostility-affiliation and dominance-submission. Also, Mills[21] developed a Sign Process Analysis based on sign theory and sociological theory which categorizes *objects* discussed (such as group member, "boss," and so forth) and what *valuation* is expressed toward the object, positive or negative. And Mann[22] developed an observation scheme which was designed to assess and record the implications of each act initiated by a group member for the state of that person's feelings toward the leader of the group. Mann's scheme consists of three main areas: (1) *Impulse Area,* which includes hostility, resisting, withdrawing, guilt-inducing, making reparation, identifying, accepting, moving toward; (2) *Authority Relations Area,* which includes showing dependence, independence, counterdependence; and (3) *Ego State Area,* which includes expressing anxiety, denying anxiety, showing self-esteem, expressing depression, and denying depression.

---

[19] R. F. Bales, *Interaction Process Analysis* (Cambridge, Mass.: Addison-Wesley, 1950).

[20] T. Leary, "The Theory and Measurement Methodology of Interpersonal Communication," *Psychiatry,* 18 (1955), pp. 147–61.

[21] T. M. Mills, *Group Transformation: An Analysis of a Training Group* (Englewood Cliffs, N.J.: Prentice-Hall, Inc., 1964).

[22] R. D. Mann, *Interpersonal Styles and Group Development* (New York: John Wiley and Sons, Co., 1967).

FIGURE 3
Interaction Process Analysis

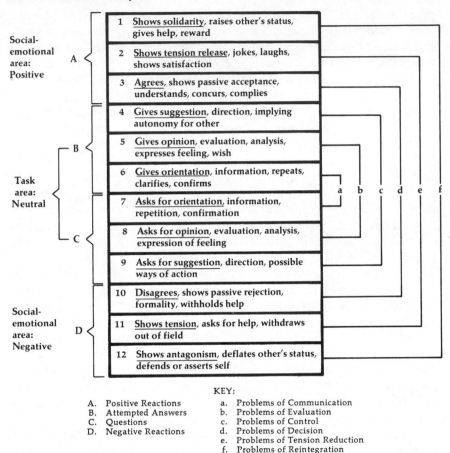

KEY:

A. Positive Reactions	a. Problems of Communication
B. Attempted Answers	b. Problems of Evaluation
C. Questions	c. Problems of Control
D. Negative Reactions	d. Problems of Decision
	e. Problems of Tension Reduction
	f. Problems of Reintegration

Source: R. F. Bales, *Interaction Process Analysis* (Cambridge, Mass.: Addison-Wesley, 1950).

It is possible that Mann's interaction scheme, while focusing exclusively on expressed feelings in member-leader relations, may be applicable to member-member relations. If so, this may be a reasonably comprehensive system which enables one to describe in molecular detail emotional responses heretofore inferred. Ego states and impulse areas, most particularly, govern an important segment of interpersonal behavior. It is possible now to record these phenomena as they are expressed.

Of course, act-by-act observational schemes have their drawbacks, too. As indicated in the first essay of this book, the problem of *inference* is perplexing. How do the observers gauge the intent of the remark? Do they even try or do they look only at the effect of the remark? Do they reckon with the unconscious as well as conscious purpose? How do they score multiple meanings? What about such puzzling phenomena as silences? How unambiguous can a statement be? How do observers determine what a unit is? Could it be that adding atomistic and molecular units of behavior will miss the possibly greater impact of *one* remark? All these are questions which the act-by-act observation schemes have to cope with in one manner or another.

It was not my intention to delve deeply into the methodological problems or to describe in microscopic detail the self-description and observation scoring systems for ascertaining interpersonal feelings.[23] Rather the major goal was to present an array of approaches or orientations to the area. The reader has undoubtedly noticed, and may have been bothered by, the proliferation of terms coined to describe what I am calling *interpersonal feelings: needs, assumptions, orientations, "who-to-whom" interactions, emotional states, impulses, interpersonal response traits,* and so on. Although the operational referents may vary, the terms are concerned with the same class of phenomena: emotional expression in interpersonal relationships.

Before going on to Part III of this essay, one final point should be made concerning the kinds of measurement employed to ascertain interpersonal feelings. Both the self-rating inventories and the observational systems have their advantages and limitations. This can be demonstrated more clearly through the use of Sullivan's interpersonal theory.[24]

We can assume, first of all, that people vary with respect to levels of awareness. We saw in the example by Harry Stack Sullivan that Mr. A was simply not aware of the feeling he experienced. But we saw how an observer could have identified the feeling Mr. A was experiencing, leading to the discrepancies between self-rating and observer ratings commented on earlier. To complicate matters even more, it is possible that Mr. A was *concealing* something from the observer or his wife which neither could detect. After all, patients can "fool" their analysts and we have all learned to dissemble—or simply to conceal aspects of our self to others. So we not only have unconscious distortions, but also conscious *concealing.*

In order to portray this problem more graphically, the reader should refer to Figure 4.[25] Quadrant I is the area of greatest congruence, the sector of behavior where there should be no significant difference between self-rating and observer ratings. Quadrant II is the "blind area," a result of not being able to see things in ourselves which others can detect. This case is

---

[23] The interested reader should consult the original sources to gain more detailed information with respect to these scoring schemes. I merely wanted to display, not demonstrate, these schemes.

[24] Sullivan, "Psychiatry."

[25] This analysis and Figure 4 are adapted from the work of J. Luft, "The Johari Window," *Human Relations Training News,* 5 (1961), pp. 6–7.

FIGURE 4

	Known to Self	Not Known to Self
Known to Others	I. *High congruence* "Announced self"	II. *Blind area* "Denied self"
Not Known to Others	III. *Concealed area* "Concealed self"	IV. *Unknown* "Unknown self"

similar to the one Sullivan describes, and it is this phenomenon which accounts for the discrepancy between self and other ratings. In Quadrant III is the "concealed" area, that domain of behavior that represents things *we* know but do not reveal to others. Finally, Quadrant IV is the "unknown" area, a deeply buried unconscious area that can be revealed only through depth analysis.

What derivations can we make now about the ascertaining of interpersonal feelings? First, an important variable is the *"congruence" or integrity of the individual.* If one is "out of communication" with oneself—that is, Quadrant II—the self-rating inventory will not be a good indicator of one's interpersonal behavior. In fact, there should be a discrepancy between what an observer detects and what persons observe in themselves. A second variable is the degree of *trust* or *psychological* safety in the situation. Lack of trust leads to the case of Quadrant III, where the individual knows something but does not want to reveal it. In this case, a self-rating inventory would be better than the observer scoring—or, certainly, the scores should be discrepant. Finally, the strength of the instrument *depends on the interpersonal area to be ascertained.* A deep, unconscious motive may not be visible to the ordinary instruments used. In other words, a feeling can be ascertained only if there is some social expression of it.

In conclusion, one can say that a self-rating inventory and observer scores may be equally valid in Quadrant I; observer scores would be superior in Quadrant II; self-ratings would be more valid in Quadrant III;[26] for Quadrant IV only depth interviews or projective tests could detect these feelings.

---

[26] This, of course, depends on who is going to "see" the self-rating forms. If the person trusts the tester or if the tester is an unknown, but safe, person, then the self-rating inventory may be accurate. More complicated—but more interesting—are the games we play with ourselves, quite apart from Quadrant II where we deny seeing certain things in ourselves or Quadrant III where we conceal things from others. I am referring to that class of "self-dissembling" where we choose certain responses on a personality test, for example, knowing full well it isn't "us" we're describing, but a pleasant version of ourself. It's a bit like cheating at solitaire. This case can't be explained by any of the four Quadrants in Figure 4. It is not concealing or denying *or* public. We are playing a game—not vis-à-vis others—but with ourselves, our conscious ego-ideals.

III. THREE THEORETICAL APPROACHES
TO INTERPERSONAL EMOTIONS

Early in this essay I noted that there was no single, comprehensive theory of interpersonal relations. At this point, I would like to go beyond this preliminary statement and consider several different but influential theories—psychoanalytic theory, interpersonal theory, and existential theory. My hope is to identify their basic elements so that the substructure of interpersonal feelings can be more fully understood.

I have found it convenient to divide the theoretical structure of inter-personal feelings into three branches: *instinct theory* or psychoanalytic theories associated with Freud; *interpersonal theory* or the theories associated with Harry Stack Sullivan and some neo-Freudians; and *existentialist theory* associated with May et al.[27] As shown in Figure 5 we can organize these theories around three features: source of conflict, source of anxiety, and goal.

Source of Conflict

All the above approaches imply that emotional states are aroused in order to cope with a *conflict* situation. In the case of *instinct theory*, the conflict is between humans and their basic biological nature, the physical aspects of the organism. As tempting as it is to "psychologize" these biological conditions—and even orthodox Freudians are guilty of this—there should be no question about the basic biological nature of instinct theory.

Interpersonal theory focuses on the person-person tensions; essentially, interpersonal theory is a theory of human relations. In contrast to the instinct theory, impulses, drives, striving toward goals are considered by the interpersonal theorists as useless abstractions necessitated by the narrow bioneurological vision of psychoanalytical theory. As Sullivan

FIGURE 5
Three Approaches to Interpersonal Feelings

Theory	Source of Conflict	Source of Anxiety	Goal
Instinct theory	Person/Nature	Lack of impulse control	Adaptation, pleasure
Interpersonal theory	Person/Person	Lack of consensual validation	Valid communication
Existential theory	Person/Self	Lack of meaning and/or integrity	Identity

---

[27] R. May, *Existential Psychology* (New York: Random House, 1961).

said: "So if a person really thinks that his thoughts about nerves and synapses and the rest have a higher order of merit than his thoughts about signs and symbols, all I can say is, Heaven help him."[28] Interpersonal theory, then, is the study of the processes that result from person-person tensions.

Finally, *existential theory* concerns itself primarily with a person in tension with one's "self." Ludwig Binswanger, leader of the European existential psychiatry movement, held that the main weakness in psychoanalytic theory—a weakness he considered profound enough to prevent him from becoming a "Freudian"—was its omission of a person in relation to itself.[29] But the self, as the existentialists know it, is a very complicated mechanism:

> My "being"—which by definition must have unity if it is to survive as a being—has three aspects, which we may term "self," "person," and "ego." The "self" I use as the subjective center, the experiencing of the fact that I am the one who behaves in thus and thus ways; the "person" we may take as the aspect in which I am accepted by others, the "person" of Jung, the social roles of William James; and the "ego" we may take as Freud originally enunciated it, the specific organ of perception by which the self sees and relates to the outside world . . . the point I do wish to make strongly is that *being* must be presupposed in discussions of ego and identity, and that the *centered self* must be basic to such discussions.[30]

The self is the center of existential theory, and the major conflict is the self in tension with the ego and the person.

When the Conflict Situation Is Not Satisfactorily Resolved, Anxiety Ensues

The key concept here is *anxiety*, and each approach to interpersonal feelings employs it in a crucial way. For *instinct theory*, anxiety occurs when biological impulses, the instincts, overwhelm the ego. In its most primitive form, we can observe this in Freud's writings when he asserts that: ". . . the aim of the death instinct is to undo connections and so to destroy things.[31]

In *interpersonal theory*, the presence of anxiety indicates the lack of "empathy" or, at a more primitive level, a "not-understood state." For Sullivan, effective human relations can occur only when individuals develop "consensual validation," a state where the primary, referential tools

---

28 As quoted in H. Guntrip, *Personality Structure and Human Interaction* (New York: International Universities Press, 1961), p. 176.

29 May, *Existential Psychology*, p. 32.

30 Ibid., p. 48.

31 Sigmund Freud, *An Outline of Psychoanalysis* (New York: W. W. Norton & Co., Inc., 1949), p. 20.

of communication are shared. Not to be understood is not to exist, to be destroyed. Anxiety for the *existentialist* is the threat to *being* caused by a lack of *meaning* for the self. It is that state where the self is not coterminous with the ego or the person and where the lack of integrity leads to despair and state of meaninglessness.

How Is Anxiety Reduced?

The organism, in *instinct theory*, avoids anxiety by reaching some desired state or goal, by seeking some adaptation or pleasure which, in turn, lessens the conflict. In other words, the ego must be able to maintain some balance between its biological impulses and the outside reality.

For the *interpersonal theorist*, anxiety is reduced when the interpersonal unit has reached a state of "valid communication." That is, when participants in an interpersonal encounter have reached the stage where they have developed methods for achieving and testing consensus, they have successfully reached the goal.

For *existentialism*, "identity" is the desired anxiety-free state. In the famous quote from Sartre, "We are our choices," he is implying that existentialism means centering on the existing—that is, deciding—person. There is no such thing as truth or reality in existential thought aside from the human beings participating and experiencing their identities.

What derivations can one make with this typology? First of all, interpersonal theory is the only one of the three approaches that makes interpersonal feelings per se pivotal to the theory. Instinct theory and existential theory encompass interpersonal feelings, to be sure, but only as derivatives of "deeper" motives. *Others* are important in existential theory, but only as agents in *self-actualization; others* are important in instinct theory, but only as they lead to more effective impulse control.[32]

This classification scheme also allows a number of different approaches to interpersonal feelings and allows them to be sorted out. It should be apparent, for example, that the FIRO theory of Schutz[33] and the Sullivanian scheme of Leary[34] belong in the interpersonal theory sphere. The group theory of W. R. Bion,[35] the interaction scheme of Bales,[36] and the

---

[32] This statement, as it now stands, is too blunt and unqualified. But the *emphasis* should be clear. The important work of the ego-psychologists (Hartmann, Kris, Erikson) and the English psychoanalysts M. Klein and W. R. D. Fairbairn stands out as an exception to this emphasis.

[33] Schutz, *FIRO.*

[34] Leary, "Theory and Measurement."

[35] Bion, *Experience in Groups.*

[36] Bales, *Interaction Process Analysis.*

philosophical speculations of Martin Buber[37] must also be located there. While there are differences among these various theories, some trivial and some important, they all place primary emphasis on the relationship of person to person.

Existential theory, as mentioned, stresses concepts focusing on the "self." Existential psychologists such as Rogers, Maslow, and May tend to use concepts such as a "self-actualization," "existential loneliness," and "identity." It is interesting to note that when existentialists discuss loneliness, they often regard it as an affectively positive state;[38] interpersonal theorists, on the other hand, tend to treat it as a morbid, even psychotic, state.[39]

Finally, it should be stated that approaches like Mann's[40] fall into the instinct theory sector because of their reliance on the expression of impulses.

There are some difficulties with the typology which should be mentioned. Most significant is the fact that some interpersonal and personality theorists cannot be so easily categorized. Erik Erikson, for example, falls into the "ego-psychology" school of instinct theory; on the other hand, his governing theoretical concern has been "identity." To make matters even more complicated, he is considered by some as an interpersonal theorist, his entire theory of development resting on interpersonal dimensions. We find the same problem in the work of the English branch of the neo-Freudians, M. Klein[41] and Fairbairn,[42] who have developed an "object relations" psychology. Where do they belong? They cannot be omitted from the interpersonal sphere. This is particularly true of Fairbairn, who places primary emphasis on object relations and contends that libido is not primarily pleasure seeking but *object* seeking.[43]

Despite these qualifications, this classification system will help guide and organize the next and final section of this essay.[44]

---

37 M. Buber, *I and Thou* (Edinburgh: T. & T. Clark, 1957).

38 C. E. Moustakas, *Loneliness* (Englewood Cliffs, N.J.: Prentice-Hall, Inc., 1961).

39 F. Fromm-Reichmann, "Loneliness," *Psychiatry*, 22 (1959), pp. 1–15.

40 Mann, *Interpersonal Styles.*

41 M. Klein, *Contributions of Psychoanalysis, 1921–1945* (London: Hogarth Press, 1950).

42 W. R. D. Fairbairn, *Psychoanalytic Studies of the Personality* (New York: Basic Books, 1952).

43 As discussed in Guntrip, *Personality Structure*, p. 253.

44 I cannot resist a speculation on a possible future direction of a creative synthesis in the theory of interpersonal feelings. It can be foreshadowed, I believe, in the work of Erikson, Klein, Fairbairn, Sullivan, and the ego-psychologists. All these theorists emphasize, to a greater or lesser degree, the autonomy and integration of the ego, the reality and significance of relationships and environment in personal development, and the significance of adaptation. An integration of these theories holds genuine promise for the theoretician.

IV. STYLES OF INTERPERSONAL FEELINGS

The discussion which follows is organized in terms of a classification system of interpersonal styles developed by Karen Horney.[45] It consists of three styles of modalities of how people relate to each other: (a) characteristically relating to others by moving *toward* them; (b) characteristically relating to others by moving *against* them; and (c) characteristically relating to others by moving *away* from them. These styles have to do with love, hate, and aloneness or alienation. Let us begin by examining the interpersonal aspects of moving toward: love.

Going Toward: Love and Interpersonal Intimacy

The advertising blurb on Erich Fromm's classic work reads: "Love—a short word that means so many different things. Everybody wants it; far from everybody can give it. Yet we all think we know what it means. Is it something natural that we don't need to think about or is it art? . . . To practice the art of loving is more difficult than ever under today's pressure . . ."[46] This statement on "love" represents a more-or-less average attitude toward the topic: puzzlement and confusion, chagrin and awe, yet fascination with its "curative" and harmful effects. And yet with all the cosmic and religious overtones, the concept of love, complicated and elusive as it is, must serve as one of the basic dimensions of interpersonal feelings. It *is* a complicated topic, primarily because of its rich heritage in spiritual, physical, and psychological thought. To a zoologist, like Kinsey, love can be defined in terms of orgiastic potency; to a theologian, it can be explained or understood only in terms of mankind's relation to God; and to a psychologist it is often either an embarrassment or a source of an argument about operational referents.

In any case, its primacy and importance in the sphere of interpersonal feelings are assured because of its instinctual, human, and philosophical nature. Terms which are derivative of or synonymous with love pervade psychological literature: *libido, eros,* and object-relations from psychoanalytic theory; "intimacy" from the first phase of adulthood in Erikson's theory[47] and the second step in "group maturity" according to Bennis and Shepard.[48] Bion speaks of "pairing,"[49] Schutz of "affection,"[50] Sorokin of

---

[45] Karen Horney, *Our Inner Conflicts* (New York: Norton, 1945).

[46] Erich Fromm, *The Art of Loving* (London: Unwin, 1962), frontispiece.

[47] E. H. Erikson, *Childhood and Society* (New York: W. W. Norton & Co., Inc., 1960).

[48] W. G. Bennis and H. A. Shepard, "A Theory of Group Development," *Human Relations,* 9 (1956), pp. 415–37.

[49] Bion, *Experiences in Groups.*

[50] Schutz, FIRO.

"altruistic love,"[51] Murray of "synthesism,"[52] Wolff of "surrender,"[53] Harlow of "heterosexual affectional systems,"[54] Fromm of "overcoming of human separateness."[55] These examples could be multiplied but the point hardly requires more evidence.

It is tempting, though perhaps foolhardly, to make some tentative statement about "what love is." The work of Allport,[56] Frankl,[57] and Fromm[58] can be examined in this respect.

Those authors, alas, as thoughtful and penetrating as they are, leave us wistful, imbued still further with a Faustian restlessness. The fact is that modern psychology has failed to come to terms with love.[59] It tends to be treated in a number of ways: like a "hot potato," or starched into crisp abstractions, or elevated beyond human comprehension or capacity. But one shouldn't blame modern psychology for this "flight from tenderness" any more than the mortals who participate in the exodus.

Here, I attempt to "come to terms" with love in a particularly *normative* way: Love is a relationship between two people which allows a full and spontaneous impact. "Full and spontaneous" means: *All. Here. Now.* Love is a kind of fusion with the essence of the other person, but where the two people concerned clearly see their boundary conditions, they know where one begins and the other stops; there is no confusion about "who's who." Love is where two people can care for, show responsibility and respect for, and understand each other.[60] Love is where there is an active concern for the growth and development of the other. In addition, love is adapted to an external reality: to work, to developing a family, to relating to some external social institution.[61]

Love is satisfying what the psychoanalyst calls an "object relationship," what Sullivan and others would refer to as "valid communication," and what the existential theorist would term "existential union." But none of these phrases gets close to the basic, deep, potent experience which can

---

[51] P. Sorokin, *Explorations in Altruistic Love and Behavior* (Boston: Beacon Press, 1950).

[52] H. A. Murray, "Synthesism," *Daedalus*, 90 (1961), pp. 552–63.

[53] K. Wolff, "Surrender and Religion," *Journal for the Scientific Study of Religion*, 2 (1962), pp. 36–50.

[54] H. Harlow, "The Heterosexual Affectional System in Monkeys," *American Psychologist*, 17, no. 1 (1962).

[55] Fromm, *Art of Loving*.

[56] G. W. Allport, *Personality and Social Encounter* (Boston: Beacon Press, 1960).

[57] V. E. Frankl, *The Doctor and the Soul* (New York: Alfred A. Knopf, 1962), chap. 4.

[58] Fromm, *Art of Loving*.

[59] Allport, *Personality and Social Encounter*, p. 199.

[60] Fromm, *Art of Loving*, p. 25.

[61] See P. Slater, "On Social Regression," *American Sociological Review*, June 1963, pp. 339–64.

make us competent and helpless, savage and tender, jealous and posses-
sive, rational or insane, productive or slothful, lewd or prim, hopeful or
cynical. In fact, what other human experience can account for the presence
of such complex and polar emotions?[62]

Going Against: Hate and Fantasy

Moving against people has to do with anger, irritation, hostility, competitiveness, exploitativeness, hate. Its biological counterpart to sex is
death and its ubiquitousness is profound. In fact, hate has much in common with love: it is active; it is direct contact; it is an encounter. In fact, it is
as difficult to untwine them in life as it is in science: where love is, hate is.

Its centrality to the study of interpersonal feelings is no less than love.
Thanatos and aggression play an important part in Freud's theories; coun-
terpersonalness is featured in Schutz's work and fight and counterpairing
in the group theory of Bion. But we do not need to turn to theory or
concepts to corroborate the existence of the aggressive emotion; we have
only to observe our everyday experience. A section from Saul Bellow's
novel, *The Victim*, brings this point out well:

> People met you once or twice and they hated you. What was the reason;
> what inspired it? . . . You had only to be yourself to provoke them. Why?
> A sigh of helplessness escaped Leventhal. If they still believed it would
> work, they would make little dolls of wax and stick pins in them. And
> why do they pick out this, that, or the other person to hate—Tom, Dick or
> Harry? No one can say. They hate your smile or the way you blow your
> nose or use a napkin. Anything will do for an excuse. And meanwhile this
> Harry, the object of it, doesn't even suspect. How should he know some-
> one is carrying around an image of him (just as a woman may paste a
> lover's picture on the mirror of her vanity case or a man his wife's snapshot
> in his wallet), carrying it around to look at and hate? It doesn't even have
> to be a reproduction of poor Harry. It might as well be the king of dia-
> monds. . . . It doesn't make a bit of difference. Leventhal had to confess
> that he himself had occasionally sinned in this respect, and he was not
> obviously a malicious person. But certain people did call out this feeling.
> He saw Cohen, let us say, once or twice, and then, when his name was
> mentioned in company, let fall an uncomplimentary remark about him.
> Not that this Cohen had ever offended him. But what were all the codes
> and rules, Leventhal reflected, except an answer to our own nature? Would
> we have to be told "Love!" if we loved as we breathed? No, obviously.

---

[62] The "metaphysical pathos" I spoke of earlier with respect to normative wishes
tinctures accurate description. The very idea of "love" is a normative concept, almost
by definition. Hostility or hatred seems less so; perhaps we are more confident of its
presence. Or perhaps because most social science has to date been accomplished by
men, the study of hatred is more popular since it is viewed as more "manly" than discovering the riddle of love.

> Which was not to say that we didn't love but we have to be assisted whenever the motor started missing. . . .[63]

The fictional character quoted, "the victim," communicates a desperate, fruitless complexity about the nature of hostility. He knows hostility is real, that it appears inevitable and impulsive, and that the targets of hostility, the victims, are selected without reason. We can say all this about love, too. We seem to be left with some of the same ambiguities and complexities when we try to become analytical about hate as we do about love, and perhaps for the same reasons.

There are things we do know about hostility; we know that hostility is related to "frustration," or to some tension the individual is undergoing. However, this explains both too much and too little; individuals vary tremendously in their tolerance of frustration as well as what they perceive to be frustrating. In addition, frustration is only one kind of stimulus which may lead to aggression. So the "frustration-leads-to-aggression" hypothesis is useful, though a bit too restrictive for our analytic purposes.

It is preferable to take a broader perspective and identify the *threatening conditions* that lead to aggression. Some of these threatening conditions are known to be related to hostility: competition, jealousy, envy, deprivation, status-anxiety, forms of social degradation, thwarted aspirations, to name only a few. One can see more clearly now that "frustration" in the usual sense it is employed is only one form of threat, "that motivational and emotional state which results from persistent blockage of goal-directed behavior."[64] One can also see that threats can emanate from without or from within. An example of the former is a feared boss or a hated rival who spitefully jeopardizes the career of a highly motivated subordinate. An example of the latter is the flood of emotion experienced by an individual during an anxiety attack. In either case the threat imperils —or is perceived to be imperilling—the ego. Thus, the formulation regarding the expression of hostility would be:

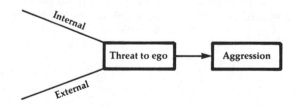

This formulation advances us a little, but we still have to know more about the elements of a threatening situation and how different types of

---

[63] Saul Bellow, *The Victim* (New York: Viking Press, Compass Books, 1958), pp. 80–81.

[64] Krech, Crutchfield, and Ballachey, *Individual in Society*, p. 134.

individuals react to these stimuli. We also need to know far more than we now do regarding the people "chosen" as victims. If we can gain more understanding of the interpersonal exchanges between aggressor and victim, we will be on our way toward a theory of interpersonal relationships. This means adumbrating the complexity of the unconscious collusion between the oppressed and the aggressor and the peculiar meaning of the exchange for both.

Some light can be thrown on this issue by examining the special case of "prejudice."[65] James Baldwin[66] points out that one reason white people hate the Negro is because the Negro reminds them of those conflictual areas in their personalities which white people struggle to repress: sexuality, rampant impulses, id forces they do not "own up to." The same argument was made about anti-Semitism in Hitler's Germany. In both cases we can see that hostility was expressed to certain targets in order to alleviate inner conflict. By identifying these impulses in others and then projecting them outward, the individual is able to reduce his or her own anxiety. Note two factors in this process: (1) that hostility is a defensive maneuver entered into in order to avoid anxiety; (2) that the targets selected are not random, that they relate to conflicts the aggressor has and cannot consciously face.

This formulation permits us to understand more fully the role of hostility in *interpersonal* relationships. What we can detect is an interesting parallel between the origin of hostility in individuals when they select a particular target to discharge their anger, and the origin of hostility in a pair or group when it selects a certain target. In both cases we can identify the basis of conflict *via* understanding the victim and the peculiar meaning of the victim for the aggressors. Vogel and Bell, in their research on the role of scapegoating in family settings, show that the targets of hostility are not accidental, that the person selected is intimately related to the source of tension: "If the parents' most serious unresolved problems were with male figures, the child chosen to represent the family conflict was usually a male child. Similarly, sibling order could be a strong factor. If one or both parents had difficulties with older brothers, an older boy in the family might become the scapegoat."[67] Some victims of hostility are

---

[65] I am talking here and throughout this section on "going against" of excessive or defensive hostility. I do not have in mind *appropriate* hatred or rage as that, for example, which might be directed toward a destructive person. Prejudice, by definition, implies a type of hostility which is excessive, off-target, and caused by reasons quite often unconscious to the aggressor; there is *always* some distortion of reality in prejudice. Realistic or appropriate hostility, as I define it, is based on some legal constraints and ethical codes; it is willful, directed to the appropriate source of threat, and conscious.

[66] James Baldwin, *The Fire Next Time* (New York: Dial Press, 1963).

[67] E. Vogal and N. Bell, "The Emotionally Disturbed Child as the Family Scapegoat," *The Family*, eds. N. W. Bell and E. F. Vogal (Glencoe, Ill.: The Free Press, 1960), pp. 382–97.

"satisfactory" and others are not. Victims are satisfactory only if they enable the attackers to alleviate some important conflict within the aggressive pair.

Another example of this unconscious maneuvering can be seen in an analysis of a case of severe aggression toward a group member who emerged as an informal leader of the group while the formal leader was absent.[68] When the formal leader returned, the substitute leader was excessively attacked for no apparent reason. I should point out that this particular person was selected as the informal leader because of a perceived resemblance to the formal leader. It was inferred that the critical rage vented toward the substitute was due to the feelings of revenge which could not be expressed openly toward the "deserting" leader. Thus the substitute leader was the victim of hostility which was felt, but unexpressed, toward the formal leader. This enabled the group to avoid, for the time being, their negative impulses toward the formal authority, a more anxiety-producing and threatening object for them than their peer.

From these examples, the complicated vicissitudes of hostility can be detected. It serves a number of purposes simultaneously. First, it avoids anxiety in the organism whether a pair, a group, or a person. Second, it identifies the source of the anxiety and projects it outward, thereby doing two things at once: discharging hostility and destroying what one can't face internally. Third, the victims frequently unconsciously collude with the aggressor in becoming the target of the aggressors' rage.[69] Fourth, and most centrally, *hostility preserves distance and precludes a full and spontaneous relationship between the oppressed and the attacker.* This is equally true for the "cooperating oppressors" (the husband and wife who scapegoat a child) as it is between couple and child. Continued scapegoating causes a lack of communication, which in turn prevents discovery of the sources of their conflicts. But as long as the conflict is not discovered and "worked through," the scapegoating continues.

And now we can return to Saul Bellow's victim and his profound questions: "People met you once or twice and they hated you. What was the reason; what inspired it?" We are still unable to formulate a satisfactory answer for him. What may be put into clearer focus, though, is the idea that in a relationship of hate, neither the victims nor the aggressors can influence or change the nature of their emotional exchange until their own relationship is more fully understood. There is an essential helplessness

---

[68] Bennis, "Defenses against 'Depressive-Anxiety' in Groups: The Case of the Absent Leader," *Merrill-Palmer Quarterly*, 7 (1961), p. 3–30.

[69] This is highly speculative as well as complicated. In the above study (Bennis, "Absent Leader"), it was found that the two individuals who drew the most hostility during the formal leader's absence were attacked because they persisted in reminding the group of his absence. In both cases the fathers of these two men died during their childhood. Thus, it seemed possible that they were evoking hostility as a way of draining off guilt associated with an earlier loss, a loss for which they feel in some degree responsible.

for the victims; they cannot "do anything" when they are used and exploited as targets for "projective identification";[70] the aggressors are equally helpless for they dimly perceive that the anxiety they are attempting to ward off may have only peripheral relevance to the victims.

So far I have discussed hostility as an altogether undesirable state, as a defense against anxiety and as a "distancing" factor in interpersonal relationships. There are, of course, positive and productive aspects of hostility. Freud[71] believed that civilization springs from instinctual renunciation; repressed aggression leads to work under many conditions, and sublimation and substitution are often channeled into the service of "good works." Also, Semrad and Arsenian[72] have contended that hostility may lead to increased productivity in group settings. Mills[73] shows, in an ingenious experiment, that certain forms of hostility—toward the person in authority—may be extremely functional for work in interpersonal settings.

Both love and hate, as we said earlier, share some common properties. They both mobilize affect and involvements; they represent the basic currency in interpersonal changes. Let us go on to the third modality now, "moving away."

Going Away: Isolation and Withdrawal

In his essay "On Narcissism," Freud[74] pointed to the "introversion of the libido": the fact, often observed in the clinic, that people seemed to have withdrawn their attention and feelings from the external world to themselves. Horney describes this type of interpersonal style in the following manner:

> The underlying principle . . . is never to become so attached to anybody or anything that he or it becomes indispensable. Another pronounced need is for privacy. The person is like the person in a hotel room who rarely removes the "Do Not Disturb" sign from his door. His independence, like the whole phenomenon of detachment of which it is a part, has a negative orientation; it is aimed at not being influenced, coerced, tied, obligated.[75]

Loneliness, withdrawal, isolation, estrangement, alienation are all words that seem descriptive of this interpersonal style; catatonic stupor,

---

[70] The concept of "projective identification" developed by Melanie Klein appears to fit all the cases under the heading of "prejudice." M. Klein, "On Identification," in *New Directions in Psychoanalysis* (New York: Basic Books, 1956), chap. 13.

[71] Sigmund Freud, *Civilization and Its Discontents* (London: Hogarth, 1930).

[72] E. Semrad and J. Arsenian, "On the Concept of Billets" (Boston: Massachusetts Mental Health Center, 1958), unpublished manuscript.

[73] Mills, *Group Transformation.*

[74] Sigmund Freud, "On Narcissism: An Introduction," *Collected Papers*, IV (London: Hogarth, 1953).

[75] Horney, *Our Inner Conflicts*, p. 64.

depression, and psychosis are all clinical correlates of what we have in mind by "going away."

Let me be clear about what I do *not* mean by "isolation and withdrawal." I do not mean that condition of life where persons broaden and deepen their humanity through an experience of "loneliness." Moustakas,[76] for example, tells us movingly about his "gripping, painful, exhilarating, and beautiful experience of being utterly alone and separated from others." I do not mean isolation or withdrawal caused by "reality factors," such as moving into a strange city or the self-imposed withdrawal due to "role imprisonment." Woodrow Wilson wrote to friends about his own loneliness caused by holding public office which brought him only "irreparable loss and desperate suffering."[77] I do not mean by withdrawal those temporary aberations sometimes noticed as a pathological reaction to stress and referred to by Greenson[78] and Strassman, Thaler, and Schein,[79] as "apathy." Nor do I have in mind, when talking about isolation and withdrawal, those individuals who think of themselves as "mavericks" or "independent thinkers" who refuse to conform or those individuals who view themselves as vigilantes of dissent.

"Going away" is a characteristic orientation toward the outside world and interpersonal relationships which can be summarized by Sartre's: "Hell is other people." It is a *chronic* withdrawal from involvement with the environment, a loss of contact with external reality. This kind of loneliness and isolation is similar to Fromm-Reichmann's notion of loneliness: it is nonconstructive and disintegrative. It is not, "independence" or "autonomy" or "self-actualization" or any of those "peak experiences" individuals report when they are "at one" with themselves. It is that state of human affairs, possibly as unbiquitous as love and hate, which realizes its aims through reduced contact with external reality.

It is something of a contradiction to talk of isolation and withdrawal as an *interpersonal* style. The "moving against and moving toward" styles are in contact with their environments, while the "moving away" style is detached and dead insofar as other people are concerned. There are, however, at least three types of "going away" which evolve in an interpersonal context with resulting unique interactions.

1. First there is *narcissistic withdrawal*, or what Slater refers to as "the withdrawal in strength." The narcissist doesn't "need" people in the conventional sense; he or she appears autonomous and ingenious, a person with power, fascination, and charisma.[80] The paradox is that the narcissists —the most inward of people—seem to have a certain seductive fascination

---

[76] Moustakas, *Loneliness.*

[77] Ibid., p. 82.

[78] R. R. Greenson, *Psychoanalytic Quarterly*, 18 (1949).

[79] H. D. Strassman, M. B. Thaler, and E. H. Schein, "A Prisoner of War Syndrome: Apathy as a Reaction to Severe Stress," *American Journal of Psychiatry*, 112 (1956).

[80] We should point out that this is true only when the ego strength of the narcissist

for most people and it is upon them that other people lean,[81] they are the ones that others seek to follow and emulate.[82] The narcissist does not lean on others; so the relationship which ensues is a "tilted" one, one without reciprocation, but interpersonal nevertheless. The interesting thing here is that most people simply will not leave the narcissist "alone," a point Slater makes with brilliant insistence.

2.   The main point of Slater's essay has to do with *social regression*, a form of interpersonal withdrawal which draws the social anxiety of the group because of its violations—real and fantasied—of group and societal norms. It is a form of libidinal contraction, a withdrawal in concert with someone else, which denies the existence of others and imperils the integrity of social institutions. An example of social regression might be a violation of the incest taboo where a brother and sister engage in sexual relations. What is important for us to note is the social and interpersonal aspects of this withdrawal and how the libidinal contraction tends to intensify the expression of interpersonal feelings of the withdrawing unit.[83]

3.   The last form of withdrawal I will mention here was covered by Bateson et al. in their brilliant analysis of communication difficulties.[84] Their theoretical framework identifies the kinds of communication patterns set up in families (although painfully noticeable in other social patterning, such as authority relations in organizations) which can lead to various forms of psychoses. This type of withdrawal can be referred to as the "double-bind," withdrawal caused by a complete inability to understand the mixed signals induced by ambivalence. So, when the mother tells her child to "go to bed," the child can interpret this message in various ways—such as "get the hell out of my sight!" or "Darling, you'd better get the proper amount of sleep." Or when the boss asks a subordinate if he or she is too autocratic, the subordinate may not understand whether to respond with submission or rebellion. And so on.

Our knowledge is however still meager; we know very little. Fromm-Reichmann says:

> . . . loneliness is one of the least satisfactory conceptualized psychological phenomena, not even mentioned in most psychiatric textbooks. Very little is known among scientists about its genetics and psychodynamics, and

---

is strong and adaptive. See Philip Slater's, "On Social Regression," *American Sociological Review*, June 1963, pp. 334–64.

[81] Freud, "On Narcissism."

[82] J. Adelson, "The Teacher as a Model," *American Scholar*, 30 (1961), pp. 383–406.

[83] In the Thomas Mann story, "The Blood of the Walsungs" (*Stories of Three Decades* [New York: Knopf, 1936], pp. 279–319), note that the dyadic withdrawal of the twins ended in sexual intercourse.

[84] Gregory Bateson, Don D. Jackson, Jay Haley, and John Weakland, "Toward a Theory of Schizophrenia," *Behavioral Science*, October 1956, pp. 251–64.

various different experiences which are descriptively and dynamically as different from one another as culturally determined loneliness, self-imposed aloneness, compulsory solitude, isolation, and real loneliness are all thrown into the one terminological basket called "loneliness."[85]

These words of Fromm-Reichmann could be applied to all three interpersonal styles examined in this essay: love, hate, *and* isolation. I am also left, alas, with a distinct feeling that my analysis of aggression was more convincing than my discussion of love. Who can say why? What I am left with now, at the close of this essay, is an awesome feeling that I have barely scratched the surface and that I must again turn for help outward to the poet and scientist and inward to myself.

---

[85] Fromm-Reichmann, "Loneliness."

5

Personal Change through Interpersonal Relationships[1]
by EDGAR H. SCHEIN

ORGANIZATION OF THIS ESSAY

In the previous essays, the process of interpersonal relations, the development of self, and interpersonal emotions have been considered. Interpersonal relationships also serve the function of inducing or facilitating change in one or both parties through a process of influence. The interpersonal events which occur in socialization, education, role training, persuasion, seduction, consultation, therapy, and the like will be my focus in the present essay.

Almost any change in behavior, beliefs, attitudes, and values is mediated by interpersonal relationships of one kind or another. The child learns the mores and values of society from parents and parent-surrogates; pupils learn from teachers; patients learn from therapists; salespeople influence their customers' buying behavior and product attitudes; friends and lovers induce subtle changes in each other; seductive persons influence the behavior and self-image of those prone to seduction. Some of the changes which result from interpersonal relationships are considered desirable by both parties and sanctioned by *society;* some are desirable but not sanctioned; some are desirable to only one party; and some are not desired by either the participants in the relationship or by *society.*

As we confront the bewildering array of types of change which result from interpersonal relationships, we face a number of issues which must be clarified and which will serve as the major foci for the organization of this essay. The questions I will try to deal with are:

1. Can the *types* of change processes be classified into some meaningful framework?

---

[1] This chapter is a revised version of the essay which appeared as the Introduction to Part III of *Interpersonal Dynamics,* editions 1, 2, and 3.

2. Can the *process* of change be conceptualized in terms of a model which will have meaning for the different types of change identified?
3. Can one begin to develop a theory of interpersonal influence by identifying some *mechanisms* which occur within the broader process of change?

I will attempt to develop tentative answers to these questions in terms of the following general scheme. For the first question I have used a frame of reference which starts not with the individual but with *society*. Thus, from a societal point of view, there are two basic dimensions which prove useful in identifying different types of change or influence: (1) the degree to which the process is *planned* by the individual or social group; and (2) the degree to which the process is *institutionalized*. By institutionalized influence I mean influence which results from *stable recognized patterns of interaction sanctioned by society* rather than accidental or unstable encounters. The four types of change or influence which result are shown in Figure 1 at the beginning of the next part.

For question *two*, the problem of the *process* of change, I have used a frame of reference which is anchored in a time dimension. Change is a process which occurs over time and must, therefore, be conceptualized in terms of *phases* or *stages*. I have found Kurt Lewin's conceptualization of the change process—a stage of *unfreezing*, a stage of *changing*, and a stage of *refreezing*—a convenient starting point and have elaborated some mechanisms within these stages.

For question *three*, I have used a heterogeneous, eclectic point of view which reflects several theoretical strands. The symbolic interactionist point of view highlights the kinds of interpersonal forces which make people stable. Unless such forces are altered, no personal change can occur. The process assumes that people's stability derives from the confirmations they receive from their network of significant others. In analyzing the mechanisms by which *changes* occur, I will rely more heavily on psychoanalytic and cognitive models of learning. In analyzing the stage of *refreezing*, once again I will lean on the symbolic interactionist point of view.

The Problem of Terminology

A central issue which must be confronted is the problem of what kinds of terms to choose when discussing interpersonal change processes. In using the words *change* or *influence* rather than *growth* or *learning*, I have attempted to buttress a desire to be morally neutral about the process by choosing terms which are as nonevaluative as possible. Though they are awkward, I will adopt the terms *change agent* and *change target* when referring to the parties in the relationships. When referring to what is changed or influenced, I will use primarily two terms—*behavior* and *atti-*

tudes. Behavior refers to *overt* acts which may or may not reflect covert mental processes or feelings. *Attitudes* blanket the whole range of *covert* responses from beliefs and values on one extreme, to feelings, impulses, and motives at the other extreme.

Two Other Issues

The first issue concerns the question of whether to include in the conceptual scheme problems of influence through the mass media of communication as in propaganda, advertising, or educational television. Because such influence is clearly a one-way process flowing from an impersonal source to a passive audience, I have chosen not to treat it here. The mass media do not involve *inter*personal dynamics as central mechanisms of change.

A second issue concerns the problem of the level of abstraction or generality to seek in any preliminary theoretical structuring of an area of human interaction. Do I seek the abstract generality of a social learning theory like Miller and Dollard's,[2] or do I settle for the descriptive uniqueness of a novel like Hulme's *The Nun's Story?*[3] Both deal with the problem of how people change in response to or in concert with other people. But, where Miller and Dollard seek generality through aggregating many processes under one very abstract mechanism, the principle of reinforcement, Hulme seeks understanding by fully describing the nuances of each instance of influence which she could identify in the process of becoming a nun. My position approximates Merton's[4] in seeking the interim solution of a "theory of the middle level," recognizing that in this quest, I risk losing both generality and intuitive understanding.

BASIC TYPES OF CHANGE PROCESSES

Figure 1 shows the classification of types of change processes in terms of whether the process is planned or unplanned, and in terms of whether it occurs through an institutionalized mechanism or not.

Planned institutionalized influence is exemplified in the socialization of the child, education, institutionalized rehabilitation and therapy, formal role training in organizations or professional training institutions like academies or medical schools, and brainwashing or other attempts to re-educate through formal institutional mechanisms. Society designates certain official positions, the occupants of which perform change agent roles

---

[2] N. E. Miller and John Dollard, *Social Learning and Imitation* (New Haven: Yale Univ. Press, 1941).

[3] K. Hulme, *The Nun's Story* (Boston: Little, Brown & Co., 1956).

[4] R. Merton, *Social Theory and Social Structure* (Glencoe, Ill.: The Free Press, 1949).

FIGURE 1
Classification of Types of Change Process

	Institutionalized	Not institutionalized
Planned	Formal socialization Education Formal role training Institutional therapy Rehabilitation Brainwashing	Persuasion Selling Seduction Therapy Coaching Consultation Human relations training
Unplanned	Unintended consequence of the above process	Emergent change

—parents, teachers, therapists, indoctrinators. The targets of influence—children, students, criminals, or patients—are also designated through official procedures or institutions.

The content or area in which influence is supposed to occur is circumscribed: children have to learn the basic culture and values of the society in which they live; students have to learn a designated curriculum; criminals have to learn certain social values and approved behavior patterns; and patients have to learn the behavior patterns, motives, attitudes, and values, defined as "normal" or "healthy" in the society in which they live. The nature of the change in the target person is generally defined as *basic* and is expected to be stable; it concerns the fundamental beliefs and values of the society. The influence is generally expected to flow in one direction only—from agent to target.[5]

Unplanned institutionalized influence is change which results through formal institutional mechanisms of influence but which is unintended and often undesired. In a way, each of the institutionalized forms of influence have their planned and unplanned outcomes. Thus, in the process of socialization, the child learns not only the parents' overt values and attitudes but also often acquires their conflicts and antisocial impulses. Parents sometimes communicate their fears and repressed impulses in the very attempt to teach their child not to have those same fears and impulses. In the same way, teachers, therapists, and bosses communicate attitudes which they seek to hide, through behavior inconsistent with their official position. Some of the more tragic aspects of socialization and role

---

[5] Those occasional cases in which children, criminals, or patients influence parents, teachers, or therapists provide the kind of dramatic exceptions which highlight the degree to which we tend to take the unidirectional flow of influence for granted in the settings of home, school, prison, or hospital.

training result when the change agents discover that they have been more successful in imparting undesired behavior and attitudes than those desired ones which their official position required them to impart.

The lack of integration within any society, organization, or group are exposed in the unintended consequences of socialization or role training. Lack of integration manifests itself when change agents disagree among themselves on what is to be taught or when they carry within themselves the personal counterpart of the cultural conflict. Perhaps it is the necessity to minimize such conflict which causes institutions to put so much emphasis on the proper selection of change agents. Change agents such as priests, teachers, and therapists must be minimally conflicted and highly congruent with the values of that institution. They must minimize unplanned uninstitutionalized outcomes.[6]

Planned uninstitutionalized influence occurs when one participant in an interpersonal relationship decides (for whatever reason) to influence another participant or to induce some change in that person. Examples of this kind of process fall into two general categories:

a.   Those where the change target is assumed to have some initial, conscious resistance to the change, as in persuasion, selling, or seduction; and

b.   Those where the change target is considered to be a willing accomplice to the change, as in informal role training, coaching, or consultation.[7]

In either of the above cases, change agents usually assume their roles voluntarily. They may or may not operate with formal, official sanctions to influence others. The status of change target is also accepted voluntarily; in the former case, as a result of being put into that position by the activities of the change agent; in the latter case, as a result of their own initiative.

The nature of the change may or may not be as basic as that defined by planned institutionalized influence processes, but, generally, we associate this type of influence with the more surface and less permanent aspects of the change target's personality. The agent of change in this type of process has fewer formal rewards and punishments available with which to control the target. Hence, the agent is more vulnerable to counterinfluence from the target if the latter chooses to define the situation as one in which he or she will change only if the agent also changes (through not neces-

---

[6] The fact that society has relatively less control over who becomes a parent introduces some interesting problems. Adolescent delinquency or schizophrenia can both be viewed as unintended features of the socialization process because of the lack of certain qualifications in the parents. On the other hand, Israeli experiments with the kibbutz illustrate an attempt by society to control socialization more closely.

[7] The change target is, of course, often *unconsciously* resistant to the change induction.

sarily in the same area). This type of influence is therefore more likely to be reciprocal than is institutionalized influence.[8]

Unplanned uninstitutionalized influence or *emergent change* is a spontaneous outcome of the relationship itself and may involve one or both parties in the relationship. It is often associated with relationships formed primarily for reasons *other* than influence; that is, influence is not a pivotal function of the relationship. Thus, lovers and friends induce a variety of changes in each other; the members of a work or athletic team influence each other in areas unrelated to their immediate work or play situations; and fleeting contacts between people in spontaneous situations often produce marked changes in one or both of them.

The statuses of change agent and change target are difficult, if not impossible, to identify because a mutual influence often occurs with the result that both people simultaneously occupy both statuses. The change may involve anything from relatively trivial behavior accommodations to major reorientations of values. As we will see, the actual change mechanisms which occur will vary by the type of change process which is involved because the options available both to the change agent and the change target differ according to whether or not the process is planned and whether or not the process involves institutionalized mechanisms or not.

THE PROCESS AND MECHANISMS OF CHANGE OR INFLUENCE

The conceptual scheme shown in Figure 2 was developed to encompass the kinds of changes in beliefs, attitudes, and values which I regard as fairly "central" or "deep"; changes which occur during socialization, therapy, and other processes involving the person's self or identity. The scheme also draws attention to a much neglected problem, that of having to *unlearn* something before something new can be learned. Most of the kinds of changes we are concerned with involve attitudes or behaviors which are integrated around the self, where change implies the giving up of something to which the person has previously become committed and which he or she values.

Any change in behavior or attitudes of this sort tends to be emotionally resisted because even the possibility of change implies that previous be-

---

[8] Certain cases, like the practice of private psychotherapy, are difficult to categorize in terms of our scheme. Society has institutionalized the role of the doctor and has created for the psychiatrist the mandate to change people who are defined as patients. But this very process of definition is highly fluid and unplanned. Similarly, there are a variety of change agents who have social sanction but who operate outside institutional structures without detailed planning either on their part or on the part of the change target. In our society, aunts, uncles, big sisters, big brothers, advisers, leaders, and charismatic personalities fall into this borderland between uninstitutionalized and institutionalized change.

FIGURE 2
The Process of Change or Influence

Stage 1.   *Unfreezing:* creating motivation to change
           Mechanisms: *a.* Lack of confirmation or disconfirmation
                       b. Induction of guilt-anxiety
                       c. Creation of psychological safety by reduc-
                            tion of threat or removal of barriers
Stage 2.   *Changing:* developing new responses based on new information
           and cognitive redefinition
           Mechanisms: *a.* Identification: information from a single
                            source
                       b. Scanning: information from multiple sources
Stage 3.   *Refreezing:* stabilizing and integrating the changes
           Mechanisms: *a.* Integrating new responses into the total per-
                            sonality
                       b. Integrating new responses into significant
                            ongoing relationships through reconfirma-
                            tion by significant others

havior and attitudes were somehow wrong or inadequate, a conclusion which the change target would be motivated to reject. If change is to occur, therefore, it must be preceded by an alteration of the present stable equilibrium which supports the present behavior and attitudes. It is this step, difficult to pin down precisely, which I believe Lewin correctly saw as akin to "unfreezing"—making something solid into a fluid state. Any viable conceptual scheme of the influence process must begin with the process of unfreezing and thereby take account of the inherent threat which change represents. For any change to occur, the defenses which tend to be aroused in the change target must be made less operative, circumvented, or used directly as change levers.

Once the change target's present equilibrium has been upset, once one has become motivated to change, one will seek information relevant to one's dilemma. That is, one will seek cues as to the kind of changes to make in one's behavior or attitudes which will reestablish a comfortable equilibrium. Such information may come from personal or impersonal sources, from a single other person or an array of others, from a single communication or a prolonged search. It is this process, the seeking out, processing, and utilization of information for the purpose of achieving new perceptions, attitudes, and behaviors, which I have called "changing" through cognitive redefinition.

There remains the problem of whether the new behavior and attitudes fit well with the person's other behavior and attitudes, and whether they will be acceptable to significant others. The process of integrating new responses into the ongoing personality and into key emotional relationships leads ultimately to changes which may be considered to be stable. If the new responses do not fit or are unacceptable to important others, a new process of unfreezing is initiated and a new cycle of influence is thereby set up. *Stable* change thus implies a reintegration or a stage of "refreezing," to continue with Lewin's terminology. Just as unfreezing is necessary for change to begin, refreezing is necessary for change to endure.

Let us next examine some of the key mechanisms which can be identified in each stage of the influence process.

Mechanisms of Unfreezing

Lack of Confirmation or Disconfirmation. The assumption which underlies a conceptual scheme such as the one proposed is that the change target's significant behavior, beliefs, attitudes, and values are organized around and supported by his or her self-image. It is further assumed that persons present themselves differently in different social situations. Therefore, it is their "operating self-image" which is relevant in any given situation. This operating self-image does not exist in isolation but is usually integrated with the person's definition of the situation and his or her image of the other people in the situation. For example, when a young man enters a classroom and adopts the appropriate self-image of "student," this image is integrated with his view of the larger situation as a school in which certain kinds of learning are supposed to take place, and with his image of others who are defined as teachers and fellow students.

Because of the interdependence of self-image, definition of the situation, and image of others in the situation, the process of unfreezing can begin by a failure of confirmation or actual disconfirmation in any one of the three aspects of the total situation.[9] The change target may then be confronted with the information: (1) that his or her self-image is out of line with what others and the situation will grant or be able to sustain; (2) that his or her definition of the situation is out of line with "reality" as defined by others in the situation; (3) that his or her image of the others is out of line with their image of themselves or of each other; and (4) that two or more of the above are operating in combination.

For example, the student entering the classroom may have seen himself as a passive listener only to discover suddenly that the teacher has called upon him; he may have defined the classroom as primarily a place to relax and meet girls, but discovers that the course is, in fact, "hard" and that the

---

[9] In the fairly common situation where information conflicts, where both confirming and disconfirming cues are available, the person probably tends to pay attention only to the confirming cues. As long as any confirmation occurs, therefore, there are no real unfreezing forces present.

instructor defines the classroom as a place for active participation by students; he may have perceived the instructor as a *laissez-faire* type of "good fellow," only to discover that the instructor sees himself as a tough taskmaster determined to make his classroom into a real learning environment. Each of these types of information can be thought of as *disconfirmatory* of some assumption which the student had made about himself, the situation, and/or the others in the situation.

By contrast, *lack of confirmation* occurs when relevant information is lacking. Thus, if the student placed high value on himself as a ladies' man and defined classrooms as places to meet girls, he would experience *lack* of confirmation if he discovered that there were no girls among his fellow students. Another example might be the case of two students who initially reinforce in each other a self-image of indifference to learning and engage in horseplay during class meetings. If the teachers asks them to sit far apart, and if little opportunity to interact outside of class exists, one could say that these aspects of their self-image would subsequently be lacking in confirmation. In a situation where aspects of the self fail to be confirmed, one may predict that a *gradual* atrophy or unlearning of those aspects will occur.[10] In a situation where aspects of the self are actually disconfirmed, the person confronts a more immediate disequilibrium which requires some immediate change or new learning.

The Induction of Guilt Anxiety.   The induction of guilt anxiety refers to the process wherein persons react to lack of confirmation or disconfirmation, not by rejecting the information or its source, but by feeling some sense of inadequacy or failure in themselves. The sense of inadequacy may (1) be felt in reference to a failure in living up to some ideal self-image; (2) result from a feeling of disappointing others whose reactions are valued; or (3) result from a failure to honor some obligation that has been assumed. Such feelings may be summarized by the concept of "guilt anxiety." Change will occur in the attempt to reduce or to *avoid* guilt anxiety.[11]

Guilt anxiety occurs sequentially after some disconfirming cues have been provided and apprehended by the change target. If the target fails to pay attention to the cues, or defends against them by denial, distortion, or some other perceptual defense mechanism, no unfreezing has occurred. In other words, the presence of disconfirming cues or the absence of confirm-

---

[10] The best examples of lack of confirmation occurred in Communist-controlled POW camps in which prisoners were systematically segregated from each other and their social structure undermined to such a degree that mutual mistrust led to virtually no meaningful communication. See E. H. Schein, "The Chinese Indoctrination Program for Prisoners of War," *Psychiatry*, 19 (1959), pp. 149–72; E. H. Schein with I. Schneier and C. H. Barker, *Coercive Persuasion* (New York: W. W. Norton & Co., Inc., 1961); and R. J. Lifton, " 'Thought Reform' of Western Civilians in Chinese Communist Prisons," *Psychiatry*, 19 (1956), pp. 173–95.

[11] See Schein, Schneier, and Barker, *Coercive Persuasion*.

ing cues from the target's immediate social environment is a necessary but not sufficient condition for unfreezing to occur. Only when such cues are perceived, and when some guilt or anxiety occurs because one realizes that one is not living up to some ideal, or has disappointed someone, or has violated one's own values in some way, can one say that unfreezing has occurred.

Because of the complexity of psychological defenses, it is possible that an individual experiences disconfirmation, denies the validity of the cues at the time they occurred, but, then, at some later time when more psychological safety is available, "remembers" by allowing the original disconfirming cues that had been forced into the unconscious to surface and then becomes unfrozen. For example, a common situation which occurs between parents and children is that the child may be told that he or she is "selfish" in connection with some behavior. If that cue is strongly inconsistent with the self-image and if there is enough threat and insecurity, the child will deny and fail to act on this feedback. Later, in adulthood, events may stimulate a memory of that event and the remembered feedback from the parent about selfishness may then operate as a powerful incentive for change. In other words, though the process of unfreezing is sequential with respect to disconfirmation and the induction of guilt anxiety, there is no implication that the two processes have to occur in close proximity to each other in order to have their motivational effect. In fact, most people have a storehouse of remembered but repressed disconfirming cues which they carry around but which do not produce motivation to change until enough psychological safety is present to permit real recognition and acceptance of the cues (something which may occur only years later).

Creation of Psychological Safety by Reduction of Threat or Removal of Barriers. Unfreezing has not occurred until the person has perceived the disconfirming cues and is experiencing some guilt or anxiety. As I have said above, in order for this perception to occur, in order to create a condition where the person does not have to defend against the anxiety or guilt, it is necessary to create a condition of psychological safety. This creation of psychological safety typically has to occur simultaneously with the presentation of disconfirming cues or the cues will not be attended to. On the other hand, as was pointed out above, one can identify situations where the disconfirming cues have been perceived, repressed, and, thereby, made inoperable until some later time when it becomes safe to let them into consciousness.

The presence of psychological safety is, therefore, a third necessary condition for unfreezing to occur. I can summarize the argument best by restating that unfreezing has occurred when the change target is experiencing some degree of guilt or anxiety as a result of some disconfirming cues, and is able to experience the discomfort because there is sufficient psychological safety present in the situation to make the discomfort tolerable. All the conditions are necessary because we have assumed that any change is inherently dangerous to the change target because it brings with it the unknown or else is perceived to have consequences which the person is unwilling or unable to contemplate.

How then is psychological safety produced? The change agent may deliberately set out to: (1) reassure the change target; (2) try to help the target to bear the anxiety or guilt by providing immediate support; and/or (3) attempt to convince the change target that the ultimate outcomes of changing are more palatable and desirable than the target may have assumed. Some of the most subtle tactical maneuvers of a change agent have to do with the production of psychological safety since it is not always possible to predict where the areas of insecurity in a person being influenced will be encountered.

Looking at the three unfreezing mechanisms together, it is clear that a change or influence process can only be started when there is some *optimum balance* of disconfirmation, guilt anxiety, and psychological safety. It is the achievement of this balance which makes the job of change agent so difficult and, at the same time, so creative.

If disconfirmation and/or guilt anxiety are too high, the change target will either leave the situation or, if this is not possible, will become defensive and more rigidly cling to the present equilibrium. He or she will deny the validity of, or fail to perceive, disconfirming cues, and will repress feelings of guilt anxiety. If psychological safety is also high, the target might risk being less defensive, but it is difficult to create conditions where disconfirmation and safety are both very high.

If psychological safety is low, even minimal disconfirmations will appear as threats, thus reducing the likelihood that the person will pay attention to them. On the other hand, if psychological safety is high, conditions may be set up where either small disconfirmations in the present situation start a change process, or where *remembered disconfirmation from past experiences* serves to start the process of change. Thus, when persons enter a very supportive therapeutic relationship, they may find that they can begin to explore disconfirmatory experiences which happened long ago but which, for the first time, they can allow themselves to plumb the real meaning of. In other words, it is not always necessary for the disconfirmation to occur in the psychological present. All of us have accumulated a history of disconfirmations which, however, never led to change because there was insufficient psychological safety to permit us to really pay attention to the cues. Once we are in a supportive safe relationship, these early cues can lead to significant change.[12]

---

[12] As Harris points out in his excellent discussion of transactional analysis, every person comes through childhood with many feelings of being "NOT OK" because of the multiple disconfirmations experienced. All of these experiences are recorded in the person and must, in adulthood, be worked through in order for the person to achieve a sense of "I'm OK." See T. A. Harris, *I'm OK—You're OK* (New York: Harper & Row, 1967).

Examples of the Unfreezing Process

To illustrate these ideas, let us consider some examples from each of the basic types of change cited above.

1. *Institutionalized* influence, *both planned and unplanned*, typically operates through routinized, often institutionalized, methods of *disconfirmation*. The child, the criminal, and the sick person are systematically punished for responses out of line with expected cultural norms. Deviant behavior is pointed out and sanctions are brought to bear if it continues.

Institutions devoted to producing a change in self-image such as rehabilitation centers, schools, military academies, and mental hospitals usually begin their influence process by dramatic disconfirmations which Goffman has called "mortifications of the self."[13] Thus, the entrants may be deprived of their clothes, their names, their personal possessions, their hair, and their status, all of which communicates to them, in as clear a fashion as possible, that their old identity will be minimally valued in the new setting. Even *voluntary* entrants into the institution may find that the change demanded of them is more than they bargained for, thus requiring them to unfreeze further before successful influence can occur. Stories of officer training procedures in a tough academy or in an officers candidate school and descriptions of the religious novitiate abound with examples of this type of unfreezing.[14]

Guilt anxiety is induced when (1) the change target perceives himself or herself as having failed to live up to the image which society expects as conveyed either implicitly or explicitly by parents, teachers, and significant others or (2) when one feels one has disappointed a change agent who has invested time and effort in changing one. The unfulfilled obligation theme is reflected in the parental message that children *owe* certain kinds of behavior to their parents because of the heavy investment the parents have made in the children. Other kinds of change agents, such as therapists, also use this process. By investing a great deal of time, effort, and emotional energy in their change targets, they may succeed in arousing a need to change in the target who sees this as a form of repayment for the efforts invested in him or her.

The best examples of *threat or barrier reduction* may be found in those educational efforts which view certain kinds of limited performance in children not as instances of limited capacity, but as instances of learning blocks. Only when such blocks are removed is the child able to operate at full capacity. Many forms of rehabilitation and therapy operate on the

---

[13] E. Goffman, "On the Characteristics of Total Institutions," *Proceedings of the Symposium on Preventive and Social Psychiatry* (Washington, D.C.: Walter Reed Army Institute of Research, 1957). See, also, Goffman's *Asylums* (New York: Anchor, 1961).

[14] For an excellent example see Hulme, *The Nun's Story*.

assumption that one cannot *induce* motives toward change, but can attempt to locate and unblock such motives in patients and delinquents. It is my assumption that both kinds of influence operate—that which takes advantage of motives already present in the person, and that which initiates the process by inducing motives through lack of confirmation or through actual disconfirmation.

2.   In *planned uninstitutionalized* forms of influence, we find the process of disconfirmation somewhat less organized but no less potent. For ex ample, a man invests in a get-rich-quick scheme, thinking of himself as a sharp operator, only to discover that not only has he failed to become rich but also has been defrauded by confidence men. The sudden discovery that what we claim to be and have committed ourself to is thoroughly discredited by others and external events serve to operate as powerful forces toward some new self-definition.

The major difference between the institutionalized and uninstitutionalized processes lies in the degree to which the potential change target can evade the situation in which unfreezing and changing is likely to occur. In most institutionalized change situations, both agent and target accept the fact that some change in the target is expected. In uninstitutionalized situations, by contrast, the influence agent may initially confront a potential target who will resist the role of target and refuse to define the situation as one in which influence is legitimate.

The salesperson must first convince the person to see himself or herself as a *potential* customer. Only then can he or she try to sell the particular product. The consultant is often in a situation where the person most in need of change is the one least likely to recognize this need. The consultation process may then involve a long period of unfreezing in which the major goal is to help the client define the situation as one in which he or she can accept help. Only then does the question shift to *what kind* of change is relevant for the client. But, even then, the potential customer or client can terminate the relationship at any time and thus evade any further influence attempts.[15]

The agent of uninstitutionalized influence cannot make use of coercive power or some of the more basic rewards and punishments which are available to parents, teachers, and doctors. As a result, he or she must rely more heavily on the manipulation of guilt anxiety or on unblocking already present motives to change by showing potential targets that they are not living up to some ideal which they themselves have stated or that the ideals have some flaw in them. Both processes presuppose that the influence agent has somehow captured the attention of the target and is able to present himself or herself in a believable and convincing manner.

---

[15] For a full discussion of this process see E. H. Schein, *Process Consultation* (Reading, Mass.: Addison-Wesley, 1969).

Having captured the potential customer's attention, the salesperson can (1) try to show how buying a certain product is essential to the upholding of a self-image which the salesperson presumes or knows that the customer holds; (2) try to build an ideal self-image which can be achieved primarily through purchase of the product; or (3) try to reduce whatever anxiety or barrier the customer is assumed to have about the purchase (for example, "You can buy it on the installment plan," or "It will only cost you pennies a week"). Dramatic instances of failure to influence may result when the change agent incorrectly diagnoses the nature of the target's anxieties or barriers.

The consultant similarly tries to influence a client by (1) pointing the way toward a desired state; (2) demonstrating that this state can only be achieved through certain changes which the consultant advocates; and (3) helping the client to overcome barriers to these changes. The coach uses the trainee's desire for some ideal performance as a lever for influence, though sometimes he or she also functions as the person who defines what the ideal should be. The ability of a coach to be reassuring and to deal with barriers, without compromising performance standards, may be one of the important characteristics which differentiates the good from the poor coach.

A strategy which the change agent may employ to unfreeze the target is to elicit, either by persuasion, seduction, or outright trickery, some behavior which is inconsistent with the image the person is trying to uphold or achieve. This type of disconfirmation produces immediate embarrassment and guilt, and thus serves to initiate the influence process. In the sales situation, this process would be exemplified by the seduction of the steadfast "noncustomer" into trying out some product. Once one has agreed to a trial, one has implicitly given up the self-image as a "noncustomer." One has opened the door to further sales efforts as well as to guilt feelings which may be based either on a sense of failure to live up to the "noncustomer" image or on the reluctance to disappoint the salesperson who has now invested more heavily in the situation.

The consultant often does not have to elicit behavior inconsistent with the client's self-image. Such behavior may already be present, but outside of the client's awareness. The consultant's problem then becomes one of how to point out the inconsistency so as to produce sufficient guilt to induce change without producing so much anxiety as to create defensiveness and thus block change.

3.   In the case of *emergent change*, the influence process also begins by lack of confirmation, disconfirmation, the induction of guilt anxiety, and the reduction of threat. However, the interpersonal messages which initiate the process are more spontaneous and may not be sent with the explicit aim of influencing the other party. Friends or lovers, in their desire to maximize mutual gratification in their relationship, will tend to be highly

sensitive to disconfirmatory messages or lack of confirmation. Such sensitivity may result from the fact that mutual confirmation is the basis for defining the closeness of the relationship in the first place. That is, the growth of intimacy can be conceived of as a series of successive experiments by the parties to the relationship. As each private area of the self is tentatively exposed, the response of the other party is carefully calibrated so as to determine the amount of acceptance or confirmation it implies. As given areas are confirmed, the person feels more and more "accepted" and he or she may be motivated to experiment with ever more private areas.

However, in any relationship, certain areas will, in fact, not be acceptable to the other party, thus necessitating either some change in one or both parties, or an agreement to avoid that area in the relationship. The relationship of friends or lovers is therefore characterized by a constant tension between the process of mutual influence and mutual acceptance. Depending on the actual personalities which the partners bring with them, there will be some areas in which mutual acceptance is high. No change will be required in either party because of an initial harmony of personalities and roles. There will be some areas where the presented self of one partner (A) is more central to him or her than whatever disconfirmatory feelings or reactions are aroused in the other partner (B). In this case, B will change. He or she will withhold reactions and gradually try to unlearn them. Finally, there will be some areas where the centrality of the disconfirmatory reactions in B is greater than the centrality of A's presented part of himself or herself. In this case, A will attempt to change that part of himself or herself so as not to arouse the painful reaction in B on future occasions.

Much of the emotional work of a close relationship is the complex dialogue which this difficult calculus of feelings makes necessary. Each partner must obtain valid information about the relative cost of changes in himself or herself and changes in the other in order to make those changes which seem mutually desirable by properly balancing disconfirmation, reassurance, and help.

From the point of view of the psychologist, a further complexity derives from that fact that many factors influence how a given person will react to disconfirming information, and how he or she will decide how central some part of the self is relative to some part of the partner. The person who feels more strongly about something and who is able to present himself or herself as totally *sincere* may induce change in another person even if the behavior is "sick," "antisocial," and ultimately destructive to the change target. The successful persuader may well be the person who can convince others that it would cost him or her more to change than it would cost them to accommodate.

4. In summary, I have argued that any interpersonal change or influence presupposes a process of unfreezing which, in turn, consists of

several other processes which must occur. These are: (1) a process of *disconfirmation* or *lack of confirmation* of some part of the change target's self; (2) the *induction of guilt anxiety;* and (3) the creation of psychological safety by *reduction of threat or removal of barriers to change* if some change motive is already present in the target person because of prior disconfirmation.

The process of unfreezing has been discussed in considerable detail because it is this stage of the influence process which is usually given least attention. Indeed, in the traditional social psychological literature on attitude change, the process is hardly considered at all. The present theoretical formulation makes unfreezing a critical and necessary step in any change process. Without unfreezing, no change will occur, no matter how much effort is put into selling, persuading, coercing, rewarding, or punishing. Or to put it another way, the reason why so many change efforts run into resistance or outright failure is usually directly traceable to their not providing for an effective unfreezing process before attempting a change induction. Or, to put it another way, no matter how much pressure is put on a person to change, no change will occur unless there is an optimal balance of disconfirming cues, guilt/anxiety feelings, and psychological safety which makes it possible for the person to pay attention to the cues and contemplate some new behavior and/or attitudes.

Mechanisms of Changing

Cognitive Redefinition. The learning of a *new* response or the changing of an attitude can be thought of as a process of seeking out *reliable* and *valid* information from the plethora of sources which may or may not be credible to the target. In making this assertion, I am limiting the learning or change situation to those situations which are governed by *social reality* as contrasted with *physical reality;*[16] that is, we are only considering situations in which validity is *consensually* judged in terms of the beliefs and attitudes of others.

How does the change target choose and make up his or her mind from the welter of sources available? In the typical, stable social situation, persons pay attention to those sources of information (other people) who confirm their present behavior and attitudes. If others fail to provide confirmation or actually disconfirm present attitudes, yet the person must continue to interact with them (for example, because the job demands it), we have a typical unfreezing situation with respect to those attitudes. The person knows something is wrong and that some kind of change is demanded, but does not automatically know what is wrong and how to correct the situation.

---

[16] L. Festinger, "Informal Social Communication," *Psychological Review,* 57 (1950), pp. 271–82.

In order to determine what is wrong or how to change one must first re-examine certain assumptions or beliefs one has about oneself, others, and one's definition of the situation. That person must then decide if these assumptions are unwarranted or inconsistent with feelings and evaluations which the others in the situation hold about themselves, oneself, and the situation. *The first step in the change process, then, is to develop alternate assumptions and beliefs through a process of cognitive redefinition of the situation.*

This process involves (1) *new definitions* of terms in the semantic sense, (2) a *broadening of perceptions* or expanded consciousness which changes the frame of reference from which objects are judged, and/or (3) *new standards of evaluation and judgment*. The new attitudes and behavior which are the eventual outcome of the influence process result from this intermediate step of cognitive redefinition.

From this perspective, the process of unfreezing can be viewed as *becoming open* to certain kinds of information which are actually or potentially available in the environment. The process of changing is the *actual assimilation* of new information resulting in cognitive redefinition and new personal constructs.[17] These, in turn, form the basis for new attitudes and new behavior.

The best examples of this process were provided to us by the Chinese Communists. The prisoner in a POW camp changed his attitudes only after a prolonged process of unfreezing, the end result of which was a readiness to pay attention to the cues which cell mates were providing all along. Once he was paying attention to this category of information, the prisoner discovered that his meanings for words such as "crime" were different from theirs, and his standards of judgment based on his frame of reference were different from their standards because of their different frame of reference. Once he had redefined his own semantics and attempted to view the world from the cell-mates' frame of reference by applying their standards, he could accept himself as a guilty criminal and make a sincere confession.[18]

In making cognitive redefinition pivotal to the change process, I have clearly allied myself with Gestalt theories of learning and have rejected reinforcement theories of learning. I would like to point out, however, that the reinforcement principle is very much relevant to the process of unfreezing and refreezing. The process of influence *begins* with the failure to obtain certain social reinforcements (lack of confirmation or disconfirmation); the process of influence *ends* with the reinforcement (confirmation) of new attitudes and behavior. The reinforcement principle

---

[17] We are using constructs here in the sense that G. A. Kelley, *The Psychology of Personal Constructs* (New York: W. W. Norton & Co., Inc., 1955), defined them as the beliefs, assumptions, and evaluations a person has about some object in his or her social world.

[18] Schein, Schneier, and Barker, *Coercive Persuasion.*

cannot conveniently explain the actual mechanisms by which new assumptions, beliefs, or constructs develop and in turn lead to new attitudes and behaviors. I reject the notion of blind trial and error learning in the realm of social reality, favoring instead a position which makes the assimilation of information from the social environment the central process. The person does experiment in the process of change, but each experiment is based on some new definition of self, others, and the situation and has, therefore, already been preceded by some cognitive redefinition.

The question arises whether this mechanism of change is always conscious or not. The answer is clearly negative. We have dramatic examples of cognitive redefinition in the realm of physical perceptions which occur entirely without awareness. There is no reason to doubt the existence of a similar process in the realm of social reality. The best examples come from psychophysical studies of judgments of weight or brightness. The entire frame of reference and pattern of judgments of the same stimuli can be altered simply by introducing an anchoring stimulus at either extreme of the scale.[19] The person does not realize that his or her judgments have changed, yet clearly, cognitive redefinition has taken place. In the realm of social perception and rumor transmission, we have similar effects. Once certain key stimuli are introduced as anchors (such as identifying a certain person in the story as black), the scale of judgment of other stimuli shifts though the person may be completely unaware of the process.[20]

Let us turn now to the next problem, that of the *source of information* which the person utilizes in redefining cognitions about self, others, and the situation. At one extreme, we have the acquisition of new information through a single source via some process of *identification*. The cues to which the person responds are those that come from a model to whom the person has chosen to relate emotionally. At the other extreme, we have the acquisition of new information through *scanning* a multiple array of sources, which may vary in salience and credibility but which do not elicit the kind of emotional focusing implied by identification. The sources are usually other people, but they do not need to be physically present to exert an influence. Their information may have just as much potency in written or broadcasted form.

I have labeled these two extreme forms of information acquisition by the terms *identification* and *scanning*, recognizing that there are many forms, like imitation, which fall in between. Let us now examine each of these processes in greater detail.[21]

---

[19] H. Helson, "Adaptation-Level as a Basis for a Quantitative Theory of Frames of Reference," *Psychological Review*, 55 (1948), pp. 297–313.

[20] G. W. Allport and L. Postman, *The Psychology of Rumor* (New York: Holt, 1947).

[21] This analysis has been influenced by Kelman's excellent work on mechanisms of attitude change (H. C. Kelman, "Compliance, Identification, and Internalization:

Cognitive Redefinition through Identification. We can distinguish two basically different kinds of identification which have major consequences for the kind of influence or change produced in a change target: *Type I* or *defensive* identification and *Type II* or *positive* identification. The conditions for, psychological process of, and outcomes of these two types are shown in Figure 3.[22]

Looking first at the *conditions* for identification, there is *defensive identification* which tends to occur in settings which the target has entered involuntarily and from which he or she cannot escape. One usually experiences a sense of helplessness, relative impotence, fear, and threat. The relationship to the change agent is an imbalanced one in that the agent has most of the power. The agent usually occupies a formal position supported by institutionalized sanctions. The target's role is to change or learn and not to ask too many questions. The prototype of this relation is the child vis-à-vis the powerful parent or the concentration camp prisoner vis-à-vis the captor.

Positive identification, by contrast, tends to occur in situations which the target has entered voluntarily and from which he or she feels free to leave. One experiences a sense of autonomy and feels one can make choices. Instead of fear and threat vis-à-vis the change agent, one experiences trust and faith. The power relationship is less tilted and is generally not supported by formal positions or institutional sanctions, though they may be present, as in the case of the psychotherapist. The prototype of this relationship is the mutual identification of husband and wife or close friends.

In terms of the *psychological processes* involved in the two types of identification, *defensive identification* generally implies a relationship in which the change agent operates as the primary source of unfreezing such as providing the bulk of the disconfirming cues. The target responds to this situation by becoming preoccupied with the change agent's position or status which is perceived to be the primary source of the change agent's power. The preoccupation with the position, in turn, implies a limited and often distorted view of the identification model. The change target tends to pay attention only to the power-relevant cues, tends to have little or no empathy for the person actually occupying the position, and tends to

Three Processes of Attitude Change" *Conflict Resolution,* 2 [1958], pp. 51–60). I have not used his concepts of *compliance, identification,* and *internalization* because of our emphasis on deeper levels of change than those he deals with in his experiments. Kelman's concepts have greatly aided, however, in achieving some conceptual clarity in this area.

[22] The analysis of identification follows closely Slater's analysis of personal and positional identification. My analysis, however, deals more with adult processes whereas his focuses on childhood socialization. For an excellent analysis see P. E. Slater, "Toward a Dualistic Theory of Identification" *Merrill-Palmer Quarterly of Behavior and Development,* 7, no. 2 (1961), pp. 113–26.

FIGURE 3
Analysis of Two Types of Identification

	Type I *Defensive Identification*	Type II *Positive Identification*
Conditions for the process ..	Target is captive in the change situation	Target is free to leave situation
	Target role nonvoluntarily acquired	Target takes role voluntarily
	Agent in formal change agent position	Agent does not necessarily occupy formal role
	Target feels helpless, impotent, fearful, and threatened	Target experiences autonomy, sense of power, and choice
	Target must change	Target experiences trust and faith in agent
		Target can terminate change process
Psychological processes involved	Agent is primary source of unfreezing	Agent is usually not the source of unfreezing
	Target becomes position oriented to acquire the agent's perceived power	Target becomes person oriented because agent's power is seen to reside in the personality, not the position
	Target has limited and distorted view of agent and lacks empathy for agent	Agent will be chosen on the basis of trust, clarity, and potency
	Target tends to imitate limited portions of agent's behavior	Target sees richness and complexity of agent as a person
		Target tends to assimilate what is learned from the model
Outcomes	New behavior in target is stilted, ritualized, restrictive, and narrowing	New behavior in target is enlarging, differentiated, spontaneous, and enabling of further growth
	New behavior is more likely to be acceptable to the influencing institution	New behavior is personally more meaningful but may be less acceptable to influencing institution

imitate blindly and often unconsciously only certain limited portions of the model's behavior. Or, to put it another way, if existing attitudes and parts of the target's self are chronically and consistently disconfirmed in a coercive way, one solution for the target is to abandon them completely and to substitute those attitudes and values perceived to be a property of the powerful disconfirmer.

Positive identification, by contrast, tends to be *person*—rather than *position*—oriented. The potential model is rarely the source of unfreezing and hence is less threatening. The model's power or salience is perceived to lie in some personal attributes rather than in some formal position. Because the change target feels free to leave the situation, he or she will use the criteria of trust and clarity to choose a model which, in turn, will lead to a fuller richer view of the personality of the model. He or she will tend to have empathy for the model and genuinely to assimilate the new information obtained from seeing the world through the model's eyes rather than directly imitating the behavior. Thus the target's new behavior and attitudes may not actually resemble the model's too closely. The whole process of identification will be more spontaneous, differentiated, and will enable further growth, rather than be compulsive and limiting.

Looking now at the *outcome, defensive identification* leads to a somewhat restricted, ritualized, and stilted set of responses and attitudes. On the other hand, *positive identification* leads to an enlarged, more differentiated, and fluid set of responses and attitudes. There is a greater likelihood of the latter process leading to psychological growth. However, the likelihood that the changes will be acceptable to the institution which has initiated the change process may be greater if defensive identification has taken place.

In both types of identification, the basic mechanism of change is the utilization of interpersonal cues which come from a change agent with whom the target identifies. These cues serve as the basis for redefining the cognitions the target holds about self, others, and the situations. But, it is obvious that a great deal of change occurs through processes other than these two types of identification. Even in the most coercive institutions, defensive identification may account for only a small portion of the total change in the target. To gain a more balanced picture of change mechanisms, we must look at the other end of the information acquisition scale, to the process we have called *scanning*.

Cognitive Redefinition through Scanning. The process of *scanning* can best be differentiated from the process of *identification* by the degree to which the change target or learner focuses on multiple models as contrasted with a single model in the social environment. Scanning thus involves a "cafeteria" approach to the utilization of the interpersonal information, and the absence of strong emotional relationships between the change target and his or her sources of relevant information. At the extreme, *scanning* implies attention to the *content* of the message regardless of the person, whereas *identification* implies attention to the *person* regardless of the content. In both cases, other people tend to be the primary source of information, but in scanning, others become salient only in terms of their perceived relevance or expertness in solving the particular problem which is bothering the change target.

The contrast between *scanning* and *identification* can best be exemplified in situations such as group therapy or in human relations training. Let us assume that each member of the group is unfrozen with respect to some areas and is seeking information which will permit redefinition of the situation so as to reach a more comfortable equilibrium. An example of *defensive identification* would be the case of the group member who, because of great fear of the authority of the therapist or staff member in the group, attempts to change by mimicking and imitating what he or she perceives to be the staff member's behavior and attitudes. An example of *positive identification* would be the case of the group member who establishes a close emotional relationship with another group member or the staff member, and attempts to view his or her problems from the perspective of this other person. An example of *scanning* would be the case of the group member who looks to any source in the group for reactions which bear upon the particular problem he or she perceives, and attempts to integrate *all* the reactions obtained. To reiterate, when one scans, one relates oneself primarily to the *information* one receives, *not* to the particular *source* from which the information comes.[23]

How does scanning compare with identification in the change outcome? In the case of scanning, one may have a more difficult time locating reliable and useful information, but the solution one eventually finds is likely to fit better into one's personality because of ones power to accept or reject information voluntarily. If the change goal is personal growth, the change agent should attempt to produce a setting conducive to scanning or positive identification, and avoid a setting conducive to defensive identification. If the change goal is the acceptance of a particular set of behaviors and attitudes, the change agent should attempt to produce a setting conducive to positive identification and provide the target with a good representative of the point of view to be learned. To achieve the latter change goal, defensive identification would be next best and scanning would appear to be least likely to succeed.

---

[23] Scanning could involve noninteractive processes such as reading, observing the reactions of others, conscious attempts at self-analysis and reorganization of one's own thoughts, listening to advice, and other similar processes. What limits such noninteractive processes as a basis for attitude and behavior change, however, is that the information obtained often turns out to be irrelevant or useless to the problems the target is working on. More useful information is likely to come from the individuals with whom the target is interacting in that he or she can at least infer their reactions and their way of looking at things.

Attributes of Potential Positive Identification Models

It is my assumption that scanning is the primary process by which people change, and that it would always occur in the absence of certain salient, threatening, or seductive people in the social environment. Once certain people become salient, identification becomes more probable. I would further assume that role relationships which are institutionalized, thus making certain people salient through their position, tend to elicit primarily a defensive type of identification. Parents, teachers, and bosses are good examples of such roles. An intriguing question is, in the absence of such preordained role relationships, what factors make people salient as potential identification models, particularly for positive identification? The following discussion outlines two typologies which appear to be relevant to this problem. They concern the kinds of attributes which make people more or less likely to be chosen as positive identification models.

Typology A: Attributes which Recreate Family Relationships. In any given interpersonal situation, the relative age, status, experience, and formal position of the potential model *vis-à-vis* the change target will determine whether the relationship will tend to be structured in terms of a parent-child, older sibling-child, or peer-group relationship. Potential models can therefore be thought of as surrogates of parents, older sibling, or peers and their attributes can be analyzed in terms of the likelihood that they will represent one or another of such types for the change target. For purposes of this discussion, I label such potential models as:

1. *Parent* figures
2. *Older sibling* ("big brother or sister")
3. *Peer* figures
4. *Transitional* types, i.e., from peer to older sibling or sibling to parent.

The likelihood that a given person in the change target's environment will be perceived and treated as a parent, older sibling, peer, or person in transition will depend on that person's actual formal status relative to the target, the degree of perceived similarity to such figures from the target's earlier life, and the target's self-presentation (conscious or unconscious) as a parent, older sibling, or peer.

The type of emotional relationship which is recreated has implications for the *trustworthiness, clarity,* and actual *content* of what can be transmitted to the change target. Specifically, I would hypothesize that other things being equal, peer figures are more likely to be trusted than parents. I would also hypothesize that peer figures are more understandable and clearer than older siblings, who are, in turn, more understandable and clearer than parent figures. Therefore, the likelihood of positive identification is greatest with peer figures and least with parent figures.

These hypotheses are based on two underlying theoretical assumptions. One is that the more powerful we perceive potential models to be and the more dependent we are upon them, the less likely we are to trust them in the sense of perceiving their goals and motives to be similar to our own. The second assumption is that the more similarity we perceive between potential models' experiences and our own, the more likely we are to be able to understand them and trust them. In the paradigm of child-parent relationships, the child is less likely to trust and understand the parent than the older sibling because the parent is perceived to be powerful, independent, and impossible to influence. The child sees the parent as living in a different world and as having had experiences which are perceived to be so dissimilar that he or she cannot help but question whether the parent can understand the child and therefore whether he or she can be trusted.

In stating these hypotheses I am speaking probabilistically. There are, of course, many situations where parent figures do elicit trust and do serve as clear models. There are equally as many situations where the competition between siblings or peers destroys trust, however clear the sibling model may be. Consequently, siblings and peers *may* elicit *defensive* identification, but generally speaking, parents would tend to do so more often. It is likewise true that parents *may* elicit *positive* identification, but older siblings and peers would tend to do so more often.

The kinds of influences which can be and generally are exerted by peers and older siblings often lead to behavior, attitudes, and values in the change target which run counter to those desired by the formal change institutions such as the family or school. Thus, while peer culture is a powerful instrument of influence, its values often run counter to those of the society in which the peer culture exists, setting the "parental" and peer culture into conflict with each other. *If* positive identification with parent figures can be achieved, the change target can learn the key norms, values, and behavior patterns of the society or organization to which he or she belongs. The dilemma of socialization, therefore, is how to balance the greater power of potentially countercultural change agents against the more functional learning to be obtained from change agents who have less chance of becoming influential.

Some Applications of Typology A. The relevance of this typology to the process of childhood *socialization* is obvious. Somewhat less obvious is the fact that we tend to *recreate* these kinds of relationships in *adult* change or influence situations. An understanding of the change outcomes of such situations may then depend upon our ability to understand correctly the nature of the relationship which exists between change agent and target. For example, we rarely analyze the ubiquitous superior-subordinate relationship of modern organizational life in terms of whether the superior functions essentially as a parent, older sibling, or peer. Yet, we may not be able to understand why some superiors are able to influence the values of their subordinates more than others unless we stop to consider the role of such relationships.

Many business organizations, for example, have found that apprenticing a new member to an older, senior, high-ranking individual in the firm results in relatively little constructive learning in the new person. On the other hand, a productive and influential relationship results when the new person is assigned to a person only slightly older and one or two levels higher. Similarly, it is probably not accidental that so many induction programs, whether in military or civilian organizations, build in a "buddy" or "big brother" system. The function of these systems is to communicate the *informal* culture of the organization to the inductee, a task which would be difficult for the immediate superior to fulfill because of the likelihood that he or she would be viewed as a parent figure and, therefore, as a symbol of only *formal* organizational values and norms.

The role of peer group influence can be seen clearly in prisons and certain mental hospitals where the inmates or patients band together to form a culture of their own in order to resist the formal authority of the institution. As new members join the organization, they learn the peer culture far more rapidly than the official value system. In industry, the counterpart of this phenomenon is "restriction of output," where such restriction is based on peer group norms of a "fair day's work for a fair day's pay." Once such norms have become established, incentive systems based on individual performance are relatively powerless to combat peer group pressures. Because the peer group relationship is such a powerful one, it has great potential for the transmission of organizational norms and values. The problem, from the point of view of the change agent, is how to insure the *congruence between peer group norms and organizational values*. Induction programs, such as those conducted by the Marines or by certain corporations which involve the peer group in "around the clock" organizational activities and which function primarily in terms of *group* incentives, appear to be able to achieve this goal. Perhaps the most notable industrial example is the Scanlon Plan, where even in unionized companies, workers and management organize into teams to fulfill the common aim of improving total organization performance.[24]

A few comments must be made on the role of the "person in transition," because this type of person is potentially the most powerful model of all. Persons in transition still belong to the peer group, but their movement out of the group implies that they are embracing some values other than those of the group. If the group trusts them enough, and if it seems clear that these new values are being rewarded by the organization and are rewarding to the transitional persons, it is possible that the entire group will change with them in the direction of these new values.[25]

---

[24] F. G. Lesieur, *The Scanlon Plan* (New York: John Wiley and Sons, 1958).

[25] The dynamics of this process are complicated because alongside the trust and faith may exist feelings of jealousy and having been betrayed. The whole problem of sibling rivalry versus learning from a sibling requires further analysis.

In industry, there is a clear dictum that one way to get ahead is to learn to be like those who are already on the move. Many social service organizations established for the purpose of rehabilitating others, such as Alcoholics Anonymous, use former "patients" as the key change agents in the process of influencing new patients. Perhaps the clearest example of this type of influence comes from Chinese Communist coercive persuasion attempts. Prisoners who were already *partly* reeducated were assigned to the same cell as the lone newcomer to the prison and proved to be powerful agents of influence.

The power of persons in transition depends very much on whether they are perceived to be "still one of *us*" or are perceived to "have gone over to *them*," particularly in those instances where the peer group is defensively arrayed against the authority. Thus, in the prison, the trusty's influence over inmates is negligible because the trusty has gone too far, has defected. In the treatment of juvenile delinquent gangs, some therapeutic gains may be achieved if the leader or some respected member of the gang can be induced to accept the psychiatrist. But if this person accepts therapeutic goals to too great an extent, the others may handle the situation by rejecting the leader or reducing his or her status rather than allowing themselves to be influenced.

Typology B: Attributes Which Reflect Personal Qualities. The second typology is built on the personal qualities of the potential model and the manner of self-presentation. I am concerned here with the kinds of qualities which are sometimes referred to as *charisma,* and with the kinds of people who seem to inspire, be magnetic, and have a "powerful personality." These qualities may be stable personality characteristics, as in the case of the dedicated leader who trades on sincerity, conviction, and zeal; or they may be skills learned for the purpose of managing interpersonal relationships, as in the case of the skilled salesperson, persuader, or seducer.

Adelson has adapted a typology of primitive healers or witch doctors in his discussion of the kinds of teacher-student relationships which occur in classrooms.[26] The categories he describes can be usefully applied to any potential identification model or change agent. Thus, the change agent can present himself or herself to the change target as a shaman, magician, naturalist, mystic healer, or priest.

Shamans communicate to the target a sense of personal power, conviction, autonomy, faith-in-self, and narcissism. They demand allegiance and acceptance of their personal influence on the basis of their power and faith in themselves. They stimulate the "fatal fascination" which others have for the narcissist.

---

[26] J. Adelson, "The Teacher as a Model," *The American Scholar*, 30 (1961), pp. 383–406.

Magicians, by contrast, purport to produce changes in the target through the manipulation of secret rites and materials to which they have sole access. They elicit trust on the basis of the actual miracles they are able to produce through their magic.

Naturalists, too, claim power on the basis of some knowledge they possess rather than on some innate personality trait. They differ from magicians in that their knowledge is scientifically verifiable and not secret. Their function is to translate natural principles into practical considerations. While presenting a façade of indifference to the change target, they nevertheless are able to communicate that anyone who does not take advantage of the scientific knowledge offered is a fool.

Mystic healers function as catalysts of the change process. They communicate the assumption that the potential for change is already present in the target and offer the needed help to get the process started. In a sense, they demand change because of their investments in and altruistic concern for the target.

Priests present themselves as gatekeepers, persons who have the official power to control entry into some desired group or desired status. Because they are invested with power from a high source, they are able to specify what the target must learn to achieve membership or status in the desired profession, group, or organization.

Adelson makes an analogy between these types and different kinds of teachers. Equally instructive might be a consideration of psychotherapists in these terms—the powerful personality (shaman) who achieves results through molding patients in his or her own image; the magician who may use hypnosis, electroshock, and other devices to impress patients; the naturalist who uses a method such as psychoanalysis because he or she believes that if the method is followed correctly, the patient will be cured regardless of the particular personality of the therapist; the mystic who relies heavily on concern and regard for the patient as the primary lever of influence and change; the priest who dispassionately lays out the requirements for entering the community of the "healthy."

Some Applications of Typology B: Mentoring.   A common phenomenon in organizational life is what has come to be called "mentoring," a situation where someone more senior or more experienced forms a kind of emotional relationship with a younger member in order to educate, teach, coach, or help the younger person to get ahead.[27] Though the relationship is most often analyzed in terms of the family model, seeing the mentor in the parent or older sibling (or possible a kindly uncle or aunt or grandparent) role, it may be more instructive to apply typology B based on

---

[27] On mentoring, see D. J. Levinson, *Seasons of a Man's Life* (New York: Alfred A. Knopf, 1978) and G. W. Dalton, P. H. Thompson, and R. Price, "Career Stages: A Model of Professional Careers in Organizations, *Organization Dynamics,* Summer, 1977, pp. 19–42.

personal self-presentation to this phenomenon. For example, mentors are sometimes direct supervisors who exchange their wisdom and know-how for the allegiance and admiration of the subordinate, playing primarily the role of shaman, magician, or naturalist. Some mentors, on the other hand, function as gatekeepers and standards setters, exchanging their wisdom and support for the direct support and loyalty of the "mentee." Finally, some mentors, those typically identified as "good developers of people," function more like mystics, producing their influence by having great faith in and commitment to the person being developed. In the latter case, the mentor may be organizationally on the same level or even lower than the mentee, or may be a supervisor whose own career has levelled off but who continues to contribute to the organization by "developing others." In each of the above cases, the change produced in the change target is a function of a close personal relationship, typically characterized by positive identification.

To conclude this section, let me state several hypotheses about the relative impact of the different change mechanisms relative to the salience of the potential identification model. Naturalists are most likely to arouse scanning because they minimize their own salience and encourage the target to learn the truth from the environment around them. They encourage the learner to acquire data wherever it can be found. Priests and magicians are most likely to arouse defensive identification because of their power positions relative to the target. Mystic healers are most likely to arouse positive identification because of their nonthreatening altruistic concern for the target. Shamans are most likely to arouse some kind of identification because of their very salient positions and their narcissistic drawing of attention to themselves, but whether or not the identification will be positive or defensive will depend upon the particular approach they take, that is, whether they arouse in the target primarily trust or primarily fear.

Examples of the Changing Mechanisms

1. Most *institutionalized* influence processes operate through defensive or positive identification and leave little room for scanning. Change targets are not expected to discover their own cultural solutions to problems but are expected to benefit from the experience of their elders. If they cannot use symbolic models as guides (those ideal characters they hear about from parents and teachers or those they read about), they can always resort to identification with those models who happen to be physically available in the environment.

2. *Planned uninstitutionalized* influence is more difficult to characterize. If we are dealing with situations which involve primarily behavior change, as in the salesperson-customer relationship, scanning is not apt to

be prevalent, but whatever identification does take place is likely to be only with symbolic models. That is, the salesperson may find that his or her best appeal is to discover who the customer's important identification model is and to link the product with that model (as most advertising attempts to do). For many reasons, the salesperson himself or herself is not likely to become a model.

The consultant often is in a situation where, having unfrozen the client, he or she would like to engage in scanning to find a solution which best fits the client's needs. The target, however, may be too uncomfortable to search for a solution, preferring instead to seek out the nearest available identification model for emulation. Under some conditions, the consultant may be an adequate model and thus facilitate the influence process; but, under other conditions, this process may produce an uncomfortable situation where the consultant is unable to come up with the ready solution expected by the target, resulting in a weakening of his or her position as an agent of effective unfreezing. All of us have witnessed cases where consultants were dismissed psychologically on the grounds that they could not handle the client's situation any better themselves. All of us have heard of therapists who were dismissed on the ground that they had "worse" problems than some of their patients or were "unable to bring up their own children."

The change target evidently is very disappointed if he or she discovers that the change agent is not an adequate positive identification model. Once unfrozen, the target often sees identification as the easiest, even if it is not always the healthiest, influence mechanism. One reason why so many members of the "helping professions" emphasize that the greatest part of their job is to help the client recognize what his or her problem is, may be the recognition, on their part, that they play a more important role in unfreezing the client than they are able to or want to play in the actual induction of change. At any rate, this remains an important area for further study and conceptual analysis.

3.   In the case of *emergent change,* we are least likely to get defensive identification and most likely to get positive identification. Scanning appears to be less probable because friends and lovers often serve as ideal identification models for each other. One may expect scanning to occur, however, in the case where disconfirmation is so severe that the relationship itself is severed. Unless the disconfirmed party can retrospectively discount the disconfirmation, he or she remains in an unfrozen condition without an immediately relevant identification model. In this instance, one may seek new attitudes and self-perceptions in a wider social network by a systematic search for relevant information about oneself.

This example raises the whole issue of whether or not a separation of the unfreezing and changing phases should be built into an effective change strategy for maximum personal growth. The agent of unfreezing inevitably becomes salient in the relationship yet may be a poor role model. The agent's dilemma is how to keep the change process going without becoming too influential as an identification model.

Mechanisms of Refreezing

Personal and Interpersonal Reintegration. Once the target has made a change or been influenced, there still remains the problem of how well the new response fits in with other parts of the personality and whether or not it will be accepted and confirmed by significant others. One can cite many examples from training programs or psychotherapy of changes which satisfied the trainee or patient but which were rejected by friends, relatives, and co-workers. One can find examples where, particularly through a process of identification, a person acquired beliefs, attitudes, and values which he or she later discovered did not fit well with other parts of the person. For any change to become a stable part of the person, it must, at some level, become integrated with other parts of the personality acceptable to those whose opinions and reactions are valued.

In situations of *planned institutionalized* influence, such as socialization and education, refreezing forces are automatically built into the situation, since the responses which the change target is expected to learn are those which the society or group which is doing the influencing defines as basic to its purposes. Thus, any successful change is automatically rewarded by the social environment as well as by the change agent. To the extent that the areas of learning or influence are defined as basic, the person is expected to accommodate other parts of himself or herself to them. In the case of adult socialization, if the new values and attitudes really do not fit, the person has only one alternative—to give up membership in the group or society into which he or she is being socialized (unless, of course, he or she can tolerate the dissonance or incongruity).

Refreezing forces are also potentially built into *emergent change* situations. The change agent and/or identification model is usually also a significant other who can confirm whatever changes are induced. It is also possible, however, that the changes which a person makes in response to one significant other may give rise to a disconfirmatory response in other relevant people, thus creating further problems for the change target. We often see this exemplified in cases where one member of a family comes under the influence of a doctor, confidant, or other change agent outside the family and begins to change in a direction which threatens the family and is thus rejected by it.

As long as communication channels remain open, the changes resulting from a relationship of lovers or friends are likely to be easily integrated into the personality of both members and into the relationship. There are, however, dramatic instances where changes made by one party produce a greater negative reaction than the original behavior which initiated the change process. A husband gives cues to his wife that her knowledge of politics and world affairs leaves something to be desired. She responds not only by becoming knowledgeable, but by actively participating in political groups with the result that she has little time left for the activities that she and her husband had previously valued. Or, to take another example, a wife disconfirms certain patterns of masculine aggression in her husband. He responds by becoming overly passive and overly solicitous (which she discovers she likes less than the aggression). If the relationship is secure enough, it will allow several cycles of unfreezing, changing, new unfreezing, new changing, and so on, until the new behavior is mutually satisfactory and can become refrozen. But problems can obviously arise when a change is satisfactory to the person making it but unsatisfactory to significant others. In such instances, an unanticipated outcome of the change process may be that the relationship itself is gradually undermined.

Planned uninstitutionalized influence is least predictable with respect to refreezing because the change agent who is involved in the unfreezing and changing stages is often unrelated to the significant others who must refreeze the change. An excellent example is the evangelist crusades, such as those of Billy Graham, where a high percentage of the people who are converted during the services give up the religion within a matter of days or weeks *unless they are immediately integrated into a local church in their own community.*

Industrial training programs in human relations often produce changes which may disappear and even arouse an adverse reaction in the trainee if fellow workers disconfirm the new attitudes and behavior learned during training.[28] A salesperson can obtain a promise of a purchase from a potential customer only to have the order turned down later because the person's family "talked him or her out of it."

If the change agent is really concerned about the direction and permanence of change, he or she must worry not only about providing identification models or other information which will communicate the desired direction of change, but must also make provisions for the adequate refreezing of those changes which do occur. What this means, in practice, is that the change agent must spend some time working on the significant others of the change target in order to get them ready for and convinced of the desirability of the change which is being induced in the target. Thus, the consultant may spend a great deal of time training the client's associates in the organization, even though the client is the prime change target. Therapists often discover that though their role as change agent is ade-

---

[28] E. A. Fleishman, "Leadership Climate, Human Relations Training and Supervisory Behavior," *Personnel Psychology,* 6 (1953), pp. 205–22. See also E. H. Schein, *Organizational Psychology* (Englewood Cliffs, N.J.: Prentice-Hall, Inc., 1970).

quately institutionalized, the changes they are able to produce do not receive institutionalized support. Thus, the family of a schizophrenic will provide treatment for the patient, but will be unprepared to reinforce and confirm the minor changes which initial treatment may make possible. The therapist, then, is often forced to work with the family and teach them to refreeze the changes which he or she has induced.

It should, of course, be noted that the mechanism by which the change is induced in the first place, has consequences for the ease or difficulty of refreezing. To the extent that scanning leads to self-selected solutions, it produces changes which are automatically integrated into the person's total personality. From the outset, such solutions have more stability and may, therefore, be more desirable in situations where the change agent has little control over the reactions of significant others. The therapist or consultant attempts to induce changes which fit the person's own needs in the hope that such changes will have a chance of surviving whatever negative reactions they may arouse in others.

Changes produced by positive identification, on the other hand, derive their stability from the stability of the relationship between the target and the model. If the model reinforces the changes and continues to be available to the target, the changes can be long lasting and stable. However, they may not necessarily be integrated into other parts of the target's self, and they may not be accepted by people other than the model.

The problem for the change agent, then, is to assess whether or not the changes which might be induced by identification, will, in fact, fit the person's needs and be reinforced by others. For example, consultants often observe that clients tend to emulate them and identify with them and they must decide whether to encourage or discourage this process in terms of the above criterion. Similarly, the coach or therapist must decide how much identification to encourage. Of course, if the influence models are also the significant others with whom the target will have a continuous, long-run relationship, then positive identification is a highly functional mechanism of change, and one which will lead readily to refreezing. Thus, when one can, one puts change targets into groups in which all the members set a correct example so that identification with any one of them will produce desired changes which will be reinforced.

SUMMARY AND CONCLUSIONS

An attempt has been made in this essay to identify some important dimensions of influence or change induced by interpersonal relationships. I have not dealt with all possible cases of influence or change, but rather have tried to focus on the kinds of changes which are generally associated with interpersonal relationships, namely changes in beliefs, attitudes, and values. The kind of conceptual scheme or model which has been presented is primarily geared toward attitudinal learning and relearning, and contributes little to an understanding of short-run behavioral compliance or reactions and impulses which arise in momentary encounters between people.

The conceptual scheme is organized around the notion that change or influence must be thought of as three separate though overlapping processes—unfreezing, changing, and refreezing. *Unfreezing* involves several basic mechanisms: (1) disconfirmation or lack of confirmation; (2) the induction of guilt anxiety; and (3) the removal of threat or barriers to change. *Changing* can occur through one of two basic mechanisms— identification or scanning. Both are mediated by a process of cognitive redefinition which makes the ultimate attitudinal change possible. *Refreezing* involves the integration of any new responses (attitudes) into the rest of the person's personality and into his or her significant ongoing relationships.

Several conclusions can be derived from an examination of the change process in terms of this model. *First,* it is apparent that the conceptual definition of *change agent* depends on the phase of the change process under discussion. Some persons may function as disconfirmers, others as inducers of change motives, and others as removers of barriers. Whatever their function, they all facilitate unfreezing. They may not necessarily serve as identification models or make the decisions as to what kinds of models will be available and whether identification or scanning should be encouraged, insofar as any control over the change mechanism can be exerted. Furthermore, the unfreezers and changers are not necessarily the refreezers. Because each phase of the change process is different from the other phases, it is difficult to pinpoint a single set of attributes for the effective change agent which will be suitable for all cases. I have tried to show that the attributes of the effective unfreezer are not the same as those of the effective changer, which in turn, are not the same as those of the effective refreezer.

Second, it should be apparent that a stable change of attitudes or values results from a particular *combination* of several sets of circumstances, *all of which have to be present.* Change is not possible if there is no motivation for change and the induction of such motivation is often a complex process; no change is possible if the person cannot locate solutions by scanning his or her social field or by finding identification models; and change will not persist unless it is integrated into the personality and into all relationships in which the target is involved. To define influence as just one of these phases is an oversimplification which can only result in conceptual confusion.

Third, within the total range of interpersonal change situations I selected out four types which have different goals, different outcomes, and involve different combinations of unfreezing, changing, and refreezing mechanisms. These types were labeled *planned* and *unplanned institutionalized influence,* as exemplified by formal and informal socialization, education, and rehabilitation; *planned uninstitutionalized influence,* as exemplified by persuasion, consultation, and coaching; and *emergent change,* as exemplified by those changes which are the unintended by-products of the relationship of lovers, friends, and co-workers. One of the advantages of this conceptual scheme is that it enables us to think about the similarities and differences between these types of change situations.

Fourth, in thinking about actual mechanisms of change, it is important to differentiate two types of identification, one resulting from the change target's need to defend against coercive forces from which one cannot escape, and the other based on the target's recognition that the attitudes and responses of certain available models in the environment could offer solutions to the problems one experiences as a result of having been unfrozen. Certain personal characteristics of potential influence models are associated with the latter kind of identification. Two typologies of models were presented—one based on the kind of family situation which the relationship recreates (whether the model is seen as a parent, older sibling, peer, or person in transition), and one based upon an analysis of primitive healers which deals with the more personal attributes of the change agent. Certain hypotheses were stated about the relative likelihood of identification with the different types of models and the kind of influence each of these types could exert in a relationship.

Finally, the process of refreezing was analyzed. Depending on the goals of the change effort and the means available to the change agent, it makes a considerable difference for the change outcome whether the situation is set up to be one which encourages identification or encourages scanning. I also pointed out the increasing importance of the change agent as an agent of refreezing through work with the target's "back home" situation in an effort to insure that induced change will be reinforced.

In conclusion, I would like to underscore my conviction that interpersonal influence is an extremely complex process which has not as yet yielded to definitive theoretical analysis. Whether we take reinforcement theory or Gestalt theory from the psychology of learning, or balance theory from the psychology of attitude change, or some theory of growth and change derived from clinical work with patients, we will continue to find examples and processes which somehow are not adequately dealt with by these models. We must face this complexity directly and tolerate some of the ambiguity which a more complex conceptual scheme inevitability brings with it.

6

The Instrumental Relationship[1]
by FRED I. STEELE

INTRODUCTION

In this essay, I will consider a type of relationship which is central to our lives—the instrumental or work relationship. While it is true that men and women do not live by bread alone, it is equally true that bread (or some other product) is vital to life; and often that bread is obtained through a process of interaction with other people. An "instrumental relationship" may be defined as any relationship of two or more persons which has as its ultimate function the performance of a task.

The main portion of this essay will be concerned with some of the issues relevant to the *work* relationship. In the closing part, a special case will be considered: that of the "creative relationship," where the desired output is some sort of new, innovative product such as a creative solution to a problem or an artistic work.

BACKGROUND

Until the early 1940s, most of the attention in studying work life was centered on its more technical and formalistic aspects. Problems of the work setting, the proper rules structure, the nature of the technical operations required, and so on, received the major focus of attention. In other words, work was generally conceived as being something which an isolated individual or single person performed. Only recently has there been a shift of emphasis toward recognition of the fact that work itself usually involves a relationship between people.

We may mark the Hawthorne Studies of Elton Mayo and his associates[2] as the beginning of a shift of interest toward the interpersonal aspects of

---

[1] This chapter is a revised version of the essay which appeared as the Introduction to Part IV of *Interpersonal Dynamics,* editions 1, 2, and 3.

[2] F. J. Roethlisberger and W. J. Dickson, *Management and the Worker* (Cambridge, Mass.: Harvard University Press, 1939).

the work process and a movement toward adding more flesh to mankind's skeletal conception of task interaction. From these studies to the present there has been a continual increase in the amount of research effort and interest directed toward this area, especially toward such phenomena as group norms and their growth, problems in communication between individuals and groups,[3] and resistances to change in work and interaction routines.[4]

THE BASIS FOR INSTRUMENTAL RELATIONSHIPS

I now turn to a simple but fundamental question, the answer to which should provide us with a clearer image of our topic. Why is an instrumental relationship necessary, desirable, or useful in a given task situation? There are several rather basic answers to this question.

1. For a number of reasons, one person may not be able to do the work alone. There may be too much to do, too much time pressure, or some other constraint, so help from another person is needed to complete the task. Or there may be a set of complementary skills required for completion, such as in certain kinds of problem-solving situations which require members to have varied bits of knowledge or different skills. Or, there may be too many activities required simultaneously to permit their performance by one individual, even if he or she does have the requisite abilities. Too much to do, too little time, too many skills required, too many things to do at once. These factors may be summarized as follows: People need the help of others when their activities or instrumental goals become so large or complex that they prohibit obtaining them alone. This is clearly one major source of work organizations, and of most other organizations that have some sort of output as a goal.[5]

---

[3] A. Bavelas, "Communication Patterns in Task-Oriented Groups," in *The Policy Sciences*, ed. D. Lerner and H. D. Lasswell (Stanford, Calif: Stanford University Press, 1951), pp. 193–202; also H. Guetzkow and H. A. Simon, "The Impact of Certain Communication Nets upon Organization and Performance in Task-Oriented Groups," *Management Science*, 1 (1955), pp. 233–50.

[4] L. Coch and J. R. P. French, "Overcoming Resistance to Change," *Human Relations*, 1 (1947), pp. 512–32.

[5] Much of the research and thinking done on the work process today may also be considered under the field of "organization theory." For extensive bibliographies specifically related to this field, see C. Argyris, *Personality and Organization* (New York: Harper Brothers, 1957); P. Blau and W. R. Scott, *Formal Organizations: A Comparative Approach* (San Francisco: Chandler Publishing Co., 1962); J. G. March and H. A. Simon, *Organizations* (New York: John Wiley & Sons, 1958). For collections of articles, see M. Haire, ed., *Modern Organization Theory* (New York: John Wiley & Sons, 1959); J. C. March, ed., *Handbook of Organizations* (Chicago: Rand McNally and Co., 1963); James D. Thompson, ed., *Approaches to Organizational Design* (Pittsburgh: University of Pittsburgh Press, 1966), and H. Coffey, A. Athos, and P. Reynolds, *Behavior in Organizations: A Multidimensional View* (Englewood Cliffs, N.J.: Prentice-Hall, Inc., 1975).

2.   Those who perform a service for others generally must enter into a relationship with the recipients of the service, even though that relationship may be quite "fleeting" and only minimally cooperative.

3.   The relationship may be of value as an end in itself—it may simply be more satisfying to work with others than to work alone. There appear to be wide individual variations in the degree of importance placed on satisfaction of relational needs.[6] As Rosenberg[7] found, some people hold as one of their major criteria for choice of work the opportunity to perform their work in relationships with others, while others expressed little or no specific interest in this aspect of different occupations.

In the 1960s and 1970s, an increasingly large percentage of the new entrants into the work force have seemed to have reversed the order of traditional American work values, so that relationships are primary to them, and the work itself is secondary.

4.   A work relationship may also be formed in order to reduce competition which, if continued, could be harmful to both parties. When two news agents on the same corner decide to work together at rush hour, with one handing out papers and the other collecting money, this decision may come in part from a belief that together they will sell more than they would separately. It may also be motivated by anxiety stemming from each's fear that he or she may be completely driven out of business by the other. The actual danger of this happening may be real or fantasied, but the force toward getting together can act in either case.

5.   The example just cited implies an ultimately cooperative relationship. The relationship may also be formed *in order to compete.* This was evidently the case with Lee and Yang, the Nobel Prize winning physicists,[8] who helped to keep their interest high by racing each other to different kinds of solutions. Even in this type of competitive relationship, however, there is an implicit agreement to cooperate in the competition.[9]

6.   Finally, an instrumental relationship may result when the distribution of power between the partners is so uneven that one can control the others and keep them in the relationship for the controller's own ends. The prototype of this is, of course, the master-slave relationship, which has mostly lost its importance in the United States but still exists in some other cultures.

---

[6] For a systematic measuring of these needs see William Schutz, *FIRO–B: A Three-Dimensional Theory of Interpersonal Behavior* (New York: Rinehart & Winston, 1958).

[7] M. Rosenberg. *Occupations and Values* (Glencoe, Ill.: The Free Press, 1957).

[8] "Profiles, A Question of Parity," *New Yorker Magazine,* May 12, 1962, pp. 49–104.

[9] The mere fact of remaining together in the relationship may not *always* indicate an agreement to cooperate. There may be other forces keeping the parties together. An interesting case of this is the small-group experimental setting where the subjects' decisions to participate in the experiment create a commitment to remain in the group even though the task demands continued competition.

To summarize, I have presented six bases for the formation of an instrumental relationship: (1) to *break down* a task that is too large, complex, and so on, to be performed alone; (2) to have someone for whom to perform a *service*; (3) for the satisfaction of *interacting* with another person; to either (4) *avoid* the costs or (5) *gain* the benefits of *competition*; and (6) because one who *holds power* over another wishes to accomplish certain goals through the other. Two final comments are needed to clarify this list. First, a specific relationship may be initiated for any one or for a *mixture* of these reasons. Second, a relationship may be formed for one reason but may become important for other reasons as it changes over time.

TYPES OF INSTRUMENTAL RELATIONSHIPS

Having considered the reasons for the formation of instrumental relationships, let me move on to the question of how we might classify relationships. Two basic dimensions will be used here to illustrate how we can make distinctions.[10] Both dimensions relate to the personal orientation of the parties in the relationship. The first is concerned with the trust orientation of the parties toward each other. For simplicity, the two alternatives will be called *friendly* and *antagonistic*. In the friendly orientation, the dominant assumptions people hold toward each other are positive. On the whole, person A trusts the other person, B, and does not fear that B will strive to fulfill some vested interest of his or her own at A's expense. Conversely, in the antagonist orientation there is a negative set and a sense of mistrust—that A must be alert lest B use an opening to some personal advantage that A considers inappropriate and harmful.

The second dimension is concerned with whether ends to be obtained in the relationship will be joint or individual. The two possibilities here are a *cooperative* orientation, where the effort of each member is seen as collaborative and useful to the other, and a *competitive* orientation, where attainment of goals by one member is seen as a threat to the goal attainment of the other.[11]

These two dimensions, then, provide us with four logical types of instrumental relationship: (*a*) friendly cooperation; (*b*) antagonistic competition; (*c*) friendly competition; (*d*) antagonistic cooperation. Each of these will be briefly described in turn.

a. Friendly Cooperation. In this type of instrumental relationship the

---

[10] These are, of course, only two out of many different dimensions that might be used to develop typologies of instrumental relationships.

[11] This dimension is basically the same as Deutsch's "orientation" variable based on what he calls "promotive interdependence" in cooperative situations. " 'Promotive interdependence' specifies a condition in which individuals are so linked together that there is a positive correlation between their goal attainments," (M. Deutsch, "Cooperation and Trust: Some Theoretical Notes," *Nebraska Symposium on Motivation* [Lincoln: University of Nebraska Press, 1962], pp. 275–319).

general orientation of the parties is one of generally positive feelings toward one other and help is given and received in the process of moving toward what is usually a common goal. One example of this type might be two mechanical engineers trying to solve a heat transfer problem.

b. Antagonistic Competition. This is the opposite of friendly cooperation and might be considered by many not to be a relationship at all. I consider it to be such by using "relationship" to mean that one person's actions must be recognized and responded to by the other, and vice versa. In this type, the personal orientations of the participants are generally negative, including disrespect, mistrust, and often hostility. The individual efforts are not seen as contributing toward any common end. An interesting example of this type is the relationship between a dance musician and the audience, where the competition is for a curious mixture of power, self-esteem, enjoyment, and artistic taste.[12] Some office relationships fall into this category when the climate encourages mistrust, competition, and noncooperation.

c. Friendly Competition. This is a mixed case, where the parties have a basically positive personal orientation toward one another, even though at some level they are using their individual efforts to compete with one another. An example already cited earlier is quite appropriate here: the case of Lee and Yang, who raced each other to problem solutions. Another would be professional athletes opposing each other in a tournament where they are essentially competing for victories and often still feel quite close and trusting toward one another, playing under an elaborate system of implicit courtesies and norms. The existence of such agreement is made more visible when the balance breaks down, as in the case of the fight between Kermit Washington and Rudy Tomjanovich in a 1978 National Basketball Association game.

d. Antagonistic Cooperation.[13] This is the other mixed case, where there is a negative personal orientation of the parties toward each other, even though there is also some need for cooperation or pooling of efforts in pursuit of a group goal. A good example of this type of relationship is that of a student discussion group trying to arrive at solutions to assigned cases. In some of these groups, the participants cooperate in a generally polite manner, but they may be actually holding back their best ideas for individual use at a later date.[14]

---

[12] Howard Becker, "The Professional Dance Musician," *American Journal of Sociology*, September 1951, pp. 136–44. Becker also raises the question of *which* relationship is chosen for analysis of instrumental activities like services—the relationship between performer and client, or the one between performer and colleagues. It would appear that in most cases of antagonistic-competitive performer-client relationships the performer also has simultaneously a more supportive relationship with his or her own colleagues.

[13] This term was originally suggested by David Riesman.

[14] Robert Ardrey provides a fascinating chapter describing the antagonistic-cooperative orientation in certain groups of animals and people—the society of inward

FIGURE 1
Orientation to Contributions

		Cooperative	Competitive
Orientation to other party	*Friendly*	(*a*) Friendly Cooperation	(*c*) Friendly Competition
	Antagonistic	(*d*) Antagonistic Cooperation	(*b*) Antagonistic Competition

Figure 1 presents these basic dimensions. Once again it should be noted that instrumental relationships do not necessarily occur in these "pure" types. Any given relationship may have elements of any or all of these types in it, in varying strengths.

By way of illustrating the possible implication of this typology, I will consider the six bases of a work relationship presented above and ask whether relationships formed for different reasons would tend to be found consistently in specific cells of Figure 1.

1. *Relationship formed to reduce complexity.* We would expect the majority of these relationships to be found in cell (*a*), Friendly Cooperation, since they are generally formed voluntarily to accomplish some sort of joint goal that cannot be obtained singly. There will also be some cases of (*d*) Antagonistic Cooperation, as when the task demands that people work together who would ordinarily not choose to associate; and cases of (*c*) Friendly Competition, as in the Yang-Lee case noted above, where the participants compete within a limited framework while agreeing to pool their output in the end.

2. *Service relationship.* This may fall into any one of the four cells, depending on the nature of the roles involved. Important here would be such elements as the expectations of each party for the other and the type and length of contact between the parties.

3. *Relationship formed for interaction.* This relationship would generally fall in cell (*a*), Friendly Cooperation, and secondarily in cell (*c*), Friendly Competition. The very nature of its formation indicates that when it ceased to have a friendly and trusting orientation it would not satisfy its original function and would tend to break down.

4. *Relationship to avoid competition.* This type will by definition fall into the two cooperative cells. It may result in Friendly Cooperation, but there is also a good chance for an orientation of Antagonistic Cooperation, especially if feelings of mistrust, hostility, and the like that were built up

---

antagonism which he calls "the noyan." In fact, these groups reverse the axes of our typology and are really "cooperatively antagonistic," where the antagonism is the output and they need one another to continue the process. See Robert Ardrey, *The Territorial Imperative* (New York: Atheneum, 1966), chap. v.

during the competitive phase were not adequately worked through when the switch was made from competition to cooperation.

5. *Relationship to gain effects of competition.* The predominant orientation here would be cell (*c*), Friendly Competition, especially since there has usually been a Friendly Cooperative orientation prior to the decision to compete. If the orientation changed over time to an antagonistic one, we could assume that the basis for the relationship had also changed.

6. *Relationship formed because of the power one holds over another.* This would result in a generally Antagonistic orientation, in cells (*d*) or (*b*). This orientation is caused on the one hand by the controller's feelings that power *must* be used to obtain desired performance from the controlled person, and, on the other hand, by the controlled's feelings of hostility for being controlled by someone who does not share common interests. This relationship is probably most often found to be a mixture of Antagonistic Cooperation and Competition, as in the case of construction laborers who both produce some work and sabotage their foremen by explicitly following some directives which they know from experience to be incorrect.

PROBLEMS IN THE RELATIONSHIP AND THEIR SOLUTION

Now that I have considered formation of the instrumental relationship and one possible typology, let me move on to the kinds of problems that must be solved if the relationship is to continue once it has been formed.

My basic assumption, following several different authors,[15] is that there are two fundamental problem areas which must be dealt with in an instrumental relationship: (*a*) problems concerning the *task* involved and operations for its performance, and (*b*) problems concerning the *maintenance* of the relationship or control of its "socioemotional" state.[16] In making this assumption I am also more generally asserting that a system has two

---

[15] The "Task" and "Socioemotional" distinction has been closely associated with Bales and his associates; these are similar to the leadership functions of "initiating structure" and "consideration" associated with the Ohio State studies. See E. A. Fleishman, "Leadership Climate, Human Relations Training, and Supervisory Behavior," *Personnel Psychology*, 6 (1953), pp. 205–22; and A. W. Halpin and B. J. Winer, "A Factorial Study of the Leader Behavior Descriptions," in *Leader Behavior: Its Description and Measurement*, Bureau of Business Research Monog. 88, ed. R. M. Stogdill and W. M. Coons (Columbus: Ohio State University, 1957). This section is also influenced by the formulations of the National Training Laboratories concerning task and maintenance functions in a group. See L. P. Bradford, J. R. Gibb, and K. D. Benne, *T-Group Theory and Laboratory Method* (New York: John Wiley and Sons, 1964).

[16] Another way of making the division would be (1) technical or content aspects of the job itself; (2) the area of structure—division of labor, who does which parts of (1); (3) the socioemotional problems listed as (*b*) above. However, for simplification of the considerations which follow, my purposes are best served by combining (1) and (2) under the general heading of "task problems."

needs, both of which must be met to some minimum degree and balanced with each other if the system is to continue. Members must therefore enact roles during the life of the group which carry out these functions or meet these needs.[17]

Task issues, generally, are concerned with how to proceed in performing the task—what goals are to be set for the relationship; how influence and control are to be distributed for decision making; which strategies, division of labor, and the like are to be used; what actual operations are to be used and how they will be carried out; and feedback on past performance. Note that these task areas are more relevant for shared communication in some types of instrumental relationships than they are in others. For instance, they would be of prime consideration in most relationships formed specifically to get help in doing a certain job. On the other hand, for a relationship that was formed for the relational value itself, task problems may at times be suppressed to a great extent. Intermediate between these two would be the service relationship, which would have certain task areas defined as being the responsibility of the service person and *not* appropriate for sharing with the client.

Maintenance issues, on the other hand, are oriented more specifically toward the relationship itself and its continuance; that is, these issues most often have to do with tensions that result from either just being together or from trying to do a task. They can be characterized by such questions as: How close or distant are the partners with each other, and how do they want to be? How do members *feel* about each other? How shall hostility and other *disruptive feelings* be handled in the relationship? What effect will *transference* phenomena (reacting to the partner in terms of people in earlier relationships) have on the relationship? How will *evaluations* of one another be handled?[18]

For each of these two sets of problems the basic process for solution is usually some sort of *information transaction* between the parties. Task and maintenance functions are accomplished through a *feedback* process where information is exchanged concerning the state of the task, the relationship, or the individuals involved.[19] This exchange serves both to change the states and to trigger other kinds of action which change the system. For instance, if one partner in a relationship tells the other that he or she dislikes having to do all the detail work, this might then create a

---

[17] For an enumeration of the forms which these roles may take, see K. D. Benne and P. Sheats, "Functional Roles of Group members," *Journal of Social Issues,* 4 (1948), pp. 41–60.

[18] For a view of this area which is not limited to the instrumental relationship, see Henry C. Smith, *Sensitivity to People* (New York: McGraw-Hill Book Company, 1966).

[19] For a fuller description of this feedback process and one author's view of the effect that it can have on an instrumental relationship, see Chris Argyris, *Interpersonal Competence and Organizational Effectiveness* (Homewood, Ill.: Richard D. Irwin Co., 1962), especially pp. 38–54.

situation where the distribution of work may be rearranged to be more satisfactory to both parties or more realistic in terms of abilities. Task performance might improve as a result of this process. Then information must be exchanged again, and the general process is repeated.[20]

These transactions may be verbal, such as the sharing of ideas or personal feelings at a particular moment, or they may be nonverbal, such as actual physical action that is taken. The transactions may also be *intended*, as when one party to the relationship tells the other that they might be able to accomplish more if they divided up the work, or they may be *unintended*, as when the same statement about work division is made and the listener gets two other messages that the sender is unaware of transmitting—(a) that the sender does not trust the listener in certain work areas and (b) does not feel able to discuss it openly with the listener, for whatever reasons.

A number of more structured processes have also been developed to help work groups deal directly with task and maintenance problems. One is *Transactional Analysis* (TA), based on Dr. Eric Berne's theories concerning the ritualized games which people tend to develop with one another over time. TA at work attempts to help people analyze their games and improve the consequences.[21] *Role Negotiation* was developed by Dr. Roger Harrison as a technique for partners to sort out their mutual expectations of one another and to make clearer "contracts" about who will be doing what for whom.[22] *Norms Analysis* is a technique designed by Steele and Jenks to be used by a group in creating a more conscious and useful set of norms about both task and expressive behaviors.[23] These are just three examples among many schemes that now exist for helping in the analysis of relational work problems.

RELATIONSHIP BETWEEN TASK AND MAINTENANCE PROBLEMS

There are many ways in which task operations affect maintenance of the relationship. *First*, decisions and arrangements concerning the power

---

[20] Related to this feedback process, but more general, is the function of *reality testing* which may be performed by these information transactions between parties to a relationship.

[21] See Eric Berne, *Transactional Analysis in Psychotherapy* (New York: Grove Press, 1961), and Thomas Harris, *I'm OK—You're OK* (New York: Harper and Row, 1967).

[22] Roger Harrison, "Role Negotiation: A Tough-Minded Approach to Team Development," in *Interpersonal Dynamics*, 3d ed., ed. Bennis, Berlew, Schein, and Steele (Homewood, Ill.: The Dorsey Press, 1973).

[23] Fritz Steele and Steven Jenks, *The Feel of the Work Place: Understanding and Improving Organizational Climate* (Reading, Mass.: Addison-Wesley Publishing Co., 1977), chaps. 5 and 6.

distribution may strongly affect both parties if (*a*) the one with less power feels hostile toward the one with more power, or (*b*) if either has less commitment because of the unequal distribution, or (*c*) if it is equally distributed and one party feels ambivalent about this because of previous relationships, which have all been unbalanced.[24] *Second,* decisions, ideas, plans, and so forth, and the process by which they are produced will affect the participants' evaluations of one another, and these impressions will affect each's feelings about the other and his or her own feelings about and perception of himself or herself in the situation.[25]

Third, just general interaction and contact in performance of a task may tend to increase the participants' feelings for one another as a result of a continuing increase in information held about each other.[26] *Fourth,* the giving or receiving of help on a particular task may affect one's sense of self-esteem, the status that one confers on the other, and one's desire to continue in the relationship. *Finally,* the general trustworthiness which one exhibits in working on the task may have a strong effect on the other's perception of him or her as trustworthy in other areas of the relationship.[27]

There may be points where task and maintenance considerations come into conflict. It may be necessary because of time limitations to overemphasize completion of the task, even to the detriment of the relationship itself. This is especially likely if the relationship must meet some external standard such as showing a profit.[28] Or it may be necessary to discuss maintenance in order to break out of a situation which has become locked on one task element which will remain unproductive, as when an argument over appropriate meeting times must be considered in terms of the influ-

---

[24] It should be pointed out here that although the question of power and influence distribution is not emphasized in this essay, it is a major concern of many writers who have developed normative theories of organization. See such writers as C. Argyris, *Integrating the Individual and the Organization* (New York: John Wiley and Sons, 1964); R. Likert, *New Patterns of Management* (New York: McGraw-Hill Book Co., 1961); *The Human Organization* (New York: McGraw-Hill Book Co., 1967); D. McGregor, *The Human Side of Enterprise* (New York: McGraw-Hill Book Co., 1960); the synthesizing article by W. G. Bennis, "Leadership Theory and Administrative Behavior: The Problem of Authority," *Administrative Science Quarterly,* 4 (1959), pp. 260–301; Barry Oshry, *Notes on the Power and Systems Perspective* (Boston: PST Inc., 1977); and David C. McClelland, *Power: The Inner Experience* (New York:

[25] For a broader perspective on this view, see the classics by C. H. Cooley, *Human Nature and the Social Order* (New York: Scribner's, 1922) and G. H. Mead, *Mind, Self and Society* (Chicago: University of Chicago Press, 1934).

[26] G. C. Homans, *The Human Group* (New York: Harcourt, Brace & World, 1950).

[27] For an experimental analysis of trust as a variable in the relationship, see M. Deutsch, "Cooperation and Trust," *Nebraska Symposium on Motivation, 1962* (Lincoln, Neb.: Univ. of Nebraska Press), pp. 275–319.

[28] There is a trap here, however. The relationship may be ignored in order to meet some external standard in the short run, and the resulting deterioration in the state of the relationship may then cause failure of task performance in the long run. See Likert's (*New Patterns*) analysis of the differences in how this problem is handled by effective and ineffective leaders of work groups.

ence or control each party is exerting before a final decision can be made. In this case a maintenance problem is blocking progress and must be dealt with, even if it is an apparent digression from work on the schedule.

In the other direction, as well as helping loosen a persistent problem situation, discussion of the relationship may drive out all task considerations and contribute to anxiety-motivated flight from the task at hand.[29] This would be exemplified by the case of a partnership that spent all its time talking about the effects the partners had on one another, thereby preventing them from making any decisions or producing anything. The motive here would generally be an avoidance of the possibility of making mistakes or failing in some task situation.

In the 1960s, proponents of the "countercultural" established various kinds of communes that generally had a higher value placed on relating than on task work. Many of these communal experiments dissolved fairly quickly due to a lack of accomplishment of needed tasks, forcing members to go elsewhere to survive.

Implied but not explicitly stated above is the notion that the conflict between task and maintenance may be reduced by a higher-order maintenance element: a commitment or climate in the relationship which allows a free and open interchange about the *state* of a relationship and how the task and maintenance functions themselves are being performed. This climate allows the relationship and its parties to learn from their experience and grow toward more effective attainment of their goals since this type of information transaction determines in part the effectiveness of transactions in both of the basic problem areas.

Although it is easy to state that an open interchange about relational problems will help in solving problems, the usual interpersonal work climate has many blocks to this openness. Low disclosure is the more usual pattern, and it takes conscious work to develop more consistent disclosure, especially in reducing peoples' feelings of risk in disclosing what is really happening to them in the relationship.[30]

DEALING WITH TASK AND MAINTENANCE PROBLEMS IN THE DIFFERENT TYPES OF RELATIONSHIPS

In this section, I would like to make some predictions about tendencies toward effective information sharing about task and maintenance issues in the four types of relationships described above. These tendencies would be

---

[29] M. S. Olmstead, "Orientation and Role in the Small Group," *American Sociological Review*, December 1954, pp. 741–51.

[30] For an indepth examination of disclosure patterns in work organizations and their costs and gains, see Fritz Steele, *The Open Organization* (Reading, Mass.: Addison-Wesley Publishing Co., 1975).

a factor in whether the relationship would be productive and/or would continue.

a. Friendly Cooperation. The tendency here would be toward being able to deal with both task and maintenance issues as they are appropriate. The friendly (high trust) orientation would promote the taking of risk as far as raising embarrassing or difficult issues is concerned, and the cooperative orientation would provide a basic motivation—wanting to do better as a team—which could be related in the partners' minds to a striving and sharing together (about the task) rather than separately.

b. Antagonistic Competition. In this case, the tendency would be toward low willingness to deal with both maintenance and task issues. The low trust level would make risk taking more difficult, and the open competition would orient the persons toward not dealing with task issues, since any information shared might help the other and consequently hurt one's self. Information that is shared is often calculated to mislead or distort, thus pushing the two persons (or groups, or nations) further apart.

c. Friendly Competition. In this instance, the basically positive orientation toward one another would promote dealing with maintenance issues. However, talking about the task would be more questionable, since the competitive situation again means that information sharing might mean a lost advantage. Individuals would probably experience some conflict over how to proceed on the task and would be drawn toward seeking out "safe" moments when the task can be talked about without hurting one's own position—such as professional football players on opposing teams discussing crucial plays *after* the game or at the *end* of a season. The competitive element makes it hard for them to examine what they are doing *in process.*

d. Antagonistic Cooperation. In this other mixed case, dealing with maintenance would tend to be low, owing to negative feelings and mistrust (poor climate for risk taking), and dealing with the task would probably be moderate. There is a pull toward task discussions because of the partners' interdependence, but this pull could "run down" over time as untended maintenance problems build up. Motivation toward the task goal could become less potent than desires to get out of the relationship or to protect one's self from the other person. Unsatisfactory superior-subordinate relationships often fit this pattern.

By way of summarizing these predictions, I should note one striking pattern: There is a clear trend toward "the rich get richer and the poor get poorer."[31] In Friendly Cooperation, where tensions and difficulties would tend to be lower than the other three, the tendencies are toward freer discussion of both task and maintenance. Conversely, in Antagonistic Coop-

---

[31] This point was clarified through a discussion with Tim Hall.

eration a good deal of tension is generated by the process of working together, and the situation is loaded against dealing with it, thus allowing the problems to build, making it still more difficult to share information, and so on.

From this view, one can see why in recent years a good deal of interest has been generated in the process of helping a relationship through a third party (consultant, counselor, and so forth).[32] An "outsider" can often observe patterns and can communicate information that is too risky for the partners to raise. This sharing may provide them with a view of reality that they can use to break out of their downward spiral.

In recent years, a different approach has been taken to the study of interpersonal work relationships: identifying special problems caused by the combinations of different types of people who are working together, such as race relations or male-female relations. Although beyond the scope of this chapter, these approaches assume that there are special features of these mixed relationships which are not explained by general theories such as those discussed in this chapter.[33]

THE ORGANIZATION DEVELOPMENT PROCESS

In the last 12 years, a growth in concern for more systematic integration of task and maintenance work in organizations has led to the birth of a new area in the applied behavioral sciences: organization development, or OD, as it is now called. The fundamental assumption behind OD is that organizations need a regular, natural process of self-correction and self-renewal in order to promote an effective use of internal resources and an adaptive relationship with the surrounding environment.

Although OD is often discussed in programmatic terms, it is first and foremost a *process*—a process of planned change whose emphasis varies as situations and problems change, but whose major purpose remains the promotion of changes which help the system's members use their resources more fully. The process of improvement is a continuous one, and it implies a more positive direction of growth than does the term *maintenance* which I used above (although I do intend for this term to imply the development of the potential of a relationship, not just a holding to a particular level of competence or intimacy).

---

[32] See R. Beckhard, "The Confrontation Meeting," *Harvard Business Review*, March–April 1967; R. R. Blake, Jane S. Mouton, and R. L. Sloma, "The Union-Management Intergroup Laboratory," *Journal of Applied Behavioral Science*, Spring 1965; F. I. Steele, "Consultants and Detectives," *Journal of Applied Behavioral Science*, 5, no. 2 (1969); R. W. Walton, *Third-Party Consultation* (Reading, Mass.: Addison-Wesley Publishing Co., 1969).

[33] For example, see Rosabeth Moss Kanter, *Men and Women of the Corporation* (New York: Basic Books, 1977).

The roots of the OD process are deep in the behavioral sciences.[34] Many of the early OD practitioners (Richard Beckhard, Edgar Schein, Robert Blake and Jane Mouton, Warner Burke, and Sheldon Davis) were involved in the laboratory method of experienced-based education. Although OD still retains laboratory training methods for many activities (such as, team-building sessions or problem-confrontation meetings), the process has expanded far beyond the interpersonal sphere. It now includes such change targets as authority structures, sociotechnical systems, physical settings, and relations between a system and its environment.[35]

Even with this expansion, however, interpersonal work relationships are a central focus in OD work today, both as a tool for change and as an outcome of the OD process. Building better work relationships permits more disclosure and freer problem solving in an atmosphere of trust. This freedom of action facilitates more systematic handling of such organizational issues as the need for more responsive decision structures. In the other direction, changes in structure, technology, or physical settings can result in improved working relationships with less energy being drained off in unnecessary stress from conflicting expectations and demands.

This two-way influence process illustrates the most important lesson to be learned from the OD process: interpersonal relationships in organizations are one subsystem of the total set of factors that, taken together, result in work experiences that range from efficient and satisfying to inefficient and frustrating. Attempts to change work relationships without attention being paid to supporting variables, such as structure or reward systems, are likely to be neutralized by the system. Conversely, attempts to change structural variables without accompanying development of the relational skills needed by members to carry out the changes are likely to falter through incomplete applications and half-trials. An effective OD process works at a number of levels, and tries to build continuous processes which integrate interpersonal experiences with the settings in which they take place.

THE CREATIVE RELATIONSHIP

Let me now consider a special case—that of the *creative* relationship. By a creative relationship I mean a relationship whose main product is some new, unusual, original combination of elements that is found to be

---

[34] A good overview on OD and its varieties in practice can be obtained from the Addison-Wesley Publishing Company (Reading, Mass.), which has published 11 books in its "Series in Organization Development" since 1969.

[35] For a quick survey of these approaches, see Harvey Hornstein, Barbara B. Bunker, W. Warner Burke, Marion Gindes, and Roy Lewicki, eds., *Social Intervention: A Behavioral Science Approach* (New York: The Free Press, 1971).

useful by some group at some time.[36] The output can involve music, drama, painting, sculpture, and other visual art forms; architectural products combining form and function; ingenious solutions to business-related problems; new experience in an affective relationship; new solutions to pressing problems of international cooperation; and interaction advances in scientific knowledge, theory, organizations of concepts, and so on.

From this list it can be seen that type of relationship really cuts across many of the categories found in this book and may exist simultaneously in any of them at a given time. The reason for its inclusion in this part is that there is a *product* of some sort involved. It is, however, the *creative* aspect of this product that is of importance at this point. At the same time I do not mean to deny the fact that the instrumental aspects of a relationship may have a marked effect on the creative output of the relationship. This effect is interestingly demonstrated in an artcle by Becker,[37] who analyzes the role of the professional dance musician. In it he illustrates vividly the tensions of dance musicians, who resent the fact that they are forced to satisfy the requirements of an instrumental relationship with their audience because the audience response determines the economic criterion of success or failure. The musicians feel that the need to satisfy an audience prevents development of a creative relationship with that audience and severely handicaps them in their efforts to be creative, spontaneous artists with expressional integrity.

Background

By and large, the interpersonal aspects of creativity have been neglected in social science[38] and even in the humanities. Even for those who have been students of this area, the issue that has preoccupied most of them has been group versus individual problem solving, with no clear-cut evidence emerging that would be of general application to different kinds of groups and situations.[39]

The same formulation of this issue has pervaded areas other than the academic. The technique of "brainstorming" grew up in the American

---

[36] M. I. Stein, "Creativity and Culture," *Journal of Psychology*, 36 (1953), pp. 311–22.

[37] Becker, "The Professional Dance Musician," in *Outsiders: Studies in the Sociology of Deviance* (Glencoe, Ill.: The Free Press, 1963).

[38] For an illustration of the scope of work in the general area of creativity, see the bibliographic collection by M. I. Stein and S. J. Heinze, *Creativity and the Individual* (Chicago: Graduate School of Business, University of Chicago; and Glencoe, Ill.: The Free Press, 1960).

[39] I. Lorge, D. Fox, J. Davitz, and M. Brenner, "A Survey of Studies Contrasting the Quality of Group Performance and Individual Performance," *Psych. Bulletin*, 55, no. 5 (1958), p. 337.

business world as an effort to stimulate creativity, especially in the pursuit of advertising themes. Then Taylor and his associates did their well-known experiment on brainstorming versus individual idea production. Some real doubt was cast upon the efficacy of the group-creation process with the finding that *ad hoc* groups of individuals whose ideas were pooled *after the fact* did better than the real groups whose members interacted with one another.[40]

In general, this result confirms the belief of those whose basic orientation toward creativity is that it must be an individual phenomenon. For example, C. P. Snow, in summing up his point of view on science and its values in *The Search*, has Fane say, with regard to the proposed concept of a *team* to do the research in a new institute, that "I'm inclined to think we want more individuals in research, not less . . . I don't believe very much in these teams of yours for solving problems . . . and even if I did, I think I'd prefer that a few things in life were left to the individual man."[41]

With a few exceptions, psychoanalysts have also tended to ignore the interpersonal aspects of creativity. Ernest Schachtel is one of the exceptions, but he, too, emphasizes the inhibitory side of interpersonal relations. He illuminates quite effectively what he feels are the interpersonal sources of people's blocks to experiencing in actual terms that which happens to and around them.[42] His thesis is that as people grow and are socialized into the ways of their society, they begin to experience phenomena in terms of the categories which they are taught. Subsequently they do not necessarily experience phenomena in ways which are most appropriate for the reality itself. Schachtel sees this socialization as a source of stereotyped or rigidly structured cognitions denying the experiential process. This leads to an attenuation of fresh ideas, phenomena, and concepts available to people.

His most striking point is a description of how people experience events in categories or terms which they anticipate will best serve to describe the event or experience to others and in terms which are most appropriate for themselves in the actual situation.

Even when Schachtel mentions the relationship with the psychoanalyst as one way to break down certain of the systematized schemata that have been built up by people to view their world, he merely mentions it in passing but does not deal with the actual aspects of the relationship that might help in this process.

In a *New Yorker* profile[43] the reporter wrote about Yang and Lee, the

---

[40] D. W. Taylor, P. C. Berry, and C. H. Block, "Does Group Participation When Using Brainstorming Facilitate or Inhibit Creative Thinking?" *Administrative Science Quarterly*, 3 (1958), pp. 23–47.

[41] C. P. Snow, *The Search* (New York: Charles Scribner's and Sons, 1958), p. 226.

[42] E. G. Schachtel, "On Memory and Childhood Amnesia," in *A Study of Interpersonal Relations*, ed. P. Mullahy (New York: Hermitage Press, 1949).

[43] "Profiles," *New Yorker Magazine*, May 12, 1962.

two Nobel Prize winning physicists who have produced some good results while working as a team. Yet in the article no investigation was made into the elements or factors which made this relationship a creative one. The author's only note on the relationship itself was that it was "unusual" for two physicists to work closely together and to produce results such as theirs.

One gets the general feeling in this example, as in many others that could be presented, that creativity is viewed as being of necessity an individual process, and, therefore, a relationship has no relevance to it; or if it does, it is one of inhibition only. An essay by Gardner Murphy[44] is one counter to this orientation—although in very general terms. It is his thesis that not only is a relationship not necessarily antithetical to the creative process, but that it may be vital to creativity, given the nature of our rapidly changing society. From this he concludes that people's real task may be to deal with the reality of the existence of interpersonal relationships rather than to reject or deny that they have any part in the creative process.

Henry Murray, in an article entitled "Unprecedented Evolutions,"[45] also calls for a new look at the possibilities for creative relationships, especially with respect to the kinds of international problems which threaten the very continuation of life itself on this planet. It is his view that the solutions to these kinds of problems may in fact be the result of creative "synthesism" or combination of diverse points of view in relationships.

What Is the Creative Process Itself?

For the moment, let us consider one model of the creative process, that presented by Murray.[46] He distinguishes what he considers to be the four necessary conditions for creativity: (a) the circulation of combinable entities; (b) permeable boundaries between categories, spheres of interest, the conscious and the unconscious, and so on; (c) periodic decompositions —de-differentiations and disintegrations (or reexaminations of what has already been done—and discarding if necessary); and (d) favorable conditions for new combinations.

In general, the process seems to be that of "mixing it up," or of having as wide as possible a conception on the part of those involved of the alternatives available or potentially available, plus favorable conditions

---

[44] Gardner Murphy, "Creativeness in Our Own Era," *Human Potentialities* (New York: Basic Books, 1958), chap. x.

[45] Henry Murray, "Unprecedented Evolutions," *Daedalus*, 90, no. 3 (1961).

[46] H. Murray, "Vicissitudes of Creativity," in *Creativity and Its Cultivation*, Interdisciplinary Symposia of Creativity, Michigan State University, 1957–58, ed. H. H. Anderson (New York: Harper & Bros.; 1959), pp. 110–18.

for becoming aware of new "paths," even after having traveled part way down one that originally appeared to be fruitful.

Effects of Interpersonal Relationships on the Creative Process

The kinds of processes that I have described above as being most relevant to creativity include experimentation, innovation, regeneration, risk taking, starting over, questioning of assumptions, relief from anxiety, and so forth. What is the relationship between these processes and interpersonal phenomena? In general, most of these processes would seem to vary with the strength of *perceived threat* in different situations. More specifically, creative processes would be undermined in situations where anxiety is aroused concerning loss of one's status, inclusion in the relationship, or basic self-worth and sense of self-esteem. When these kinds of threats are perceived, then internally or externally produced alternatives (relating to a particular problem or to a more general style of operation) are reduced, often with no awareness on the part of the individual that this limiting has taken place.

For the relationship to facilitate creativity, therefore, a climate must be created which reduces perceived threat and makes creativity the norm.[47] However, when creativity becomes the only acceptable product, new anxiety will be generated in the participants over their relative status or sense of self-worth if they are not able to be creative 100 percent of the time. This new anxiety may again limit alternatives. To avoid this new anxiety the relationship must develop a climate of mutual support and reduced competitiveness.

Thus, the two necessary elements of a creative relationship appear to be (a) appropriate norms toward creativity and innovation *plus* (b) a shared feeling of acceptance of the individual as an individual in the relationship.[48] This acceptance should include a willingness to allow and help one to be oneself in the relationship, to grow as a result of it, and to make the most of one's experiences. There is good evidence that for most creative people, such a Darwin or Freud, there is a small but strong reference group supporting them, even in the face of much larger opposition from the total society.

These are not the only variables relevant to a creative relationship. The interpersonal competence of the individual members may allow a broader spectrum of thought and action to come into play in combination than

---

[47] See W. J. J. Gordon, *Synectics: The Development of Creative Capacity* (New York: Harper & Bros., 1961).

[48] Carl Rogers, "The Characteristics of a Helping Relationship," in *On Becoming a Person* (Boston: Houghton-Mifflin Co., 1961).

either member had alone. Individual differences are also important in determining the extent to which this kind of climate effectively releases these potential abilities. An individual who is immobilized by the mere presence of others, regardless of the immediate atmosphere that a partner attempts to foster, may be quite inappropriate for collaborative creative endeavors, and should be recognized as such. This does not rule out the possibility of the relationship serving as a change environment in which such people can express themselves more freely, thereby allowing a more creative output, which in turn may further free them from former inhibitions. The question of how this circular process can be initiated is beyond the scope of this paper, but satisfactions coming from relating per se early in the relationship may be a crucial element here.

After thinking about all these variables, one fact still remains: some relationships have a certain magic or spark which leads to extremely innovative, high-quality products. Other sets of four popular musicians may have been more talented individually than the Beatles, but none has clicked in the way they did in producing an output that changed popular music in the 1960s and 1970s. Similarly in the field of comedy, some very special combinations of people led to the crazy exuberance and trail breaking of the Goons on British radio in the 50s and of Monty Python's Flying Circus on British television in the 70s. These mixes of talent, process, and energy don't happen very often, but when they do the products of the relationship are truly special.

Toward Better Interpersonal Relationships[1]

by WARREN BENNIS

> This is our pad
> we all have a ball here
> we don't have much bread but
> bread is really not very important
> when you have good relationships
>
> From SUZUKI BEANE

Social scientists, more often than not, are reluctant to expose their own value systems. To make matters worse, the idea of a "good" *relationship* is slightly foreign, even distasteful, to many students of human behavior who can regard only individual skin boundaries as "real." I will have to forego both of these biases in what follows.

Covered here are two important aspects of interpersonal relationships. The first has to do with the word *better* in my title; *better* implies improvement, and improvement implies a desired state, that is, a "good" state. So I will be dealing here with the normative side of interpersonal relationships, with notions about "good and bad," "healthy and sick." The aim is to make explicit the values that govern our own choices and styles of interpersonal relationships.

Secondly, if one can envision a good relationship, then one must ask: "What kinds of personal competencies and what kinds of environmental conditions are conducive to the development and maintenance of these relationships?"

In short, this essay is concerned with (1) a vision of ideal interpersonal relations, and (2) the most effective way to reach that state. Let me start with the normative question: What is a *good* relationship?

---

[1] This chapter is a revised version of the essay which appeared as the Introduction to Part V of *Interpersonal Dynamics*, editions 1, 2, and 3.

NORMATIVE ASPECTS OF INTERPERSONAL RELATIONSHIPS

A Framework for Evaluating Interpersonal Relationships

Can we establish a single criterion of goodness or badness which would be relevant for all interpersonal relationships? Consider the following: customer-salesperson, psychiatrist-patient, husband-wife, manager-foreman, guard-inmate, lover-mistress, nurse-doctor. Or take the following kinds of relationships; puppy love, friendship, a crush, an affair; rivals, enemies, boyfriends, fraternity brothers, colleagues, cousins, siblings, or conditions like enforced, contractual, clandestine, accidental, "stuffy," informal, creative, chronic, stable. Or take the following settings: bureaucracy, sorority, family, board of education, classroom. Does goodness mean the same thing for all of these? Obviously not.

We have to ask: "good for what?" As a starting analytic point, all interpersonal relationships are oriented toward some *primary goal*, that is, some goal or function whose presence is necessary for the relationship to exist and whose absence would seriously undermine it. For example, if two friends stop satisfying each others' affiliative needs, the relationship would end. If two research collaborators can no longer do good research together, they will drift to more productive partners or work on their own. When the pupil can no longer learn from the teacher or the teacher thinks he or she can no longer impart new knowledge, the relationship will draw to a close. Thus, the *raison d'être* of the relationship, the salient reason for its formation, serves as a framework for evaluation.

On this basis four distinct types of relationships can be characterized: *Type A,* a relationship formed for the purpose of fulfilling *itself,* such as love, marriage, friendship. The main transaction in the relationship is "feelings," and, for that reason I will refer to Type A as *expressive-emotional.*[2]

A *Type B* relationship exists in order to establish "reality," but of two distinct kinds. The content of the interpersonal transaction for one kind of Type B (1) is information about the "self" or about the relationship. This could include interpersonal "feedback" or reflected appraisals. The content of the interpersonal transaction for the other kind of Type B (2) encompasses information about the environment or a "definition of the situation." The former kind (1) exists in order to understand the relationship and the "self;" the latter (2) exists in order to construct social realities. An example of (1) might be a pair of friends who help each other find their identities. The other (2) can often be observed in social groups, say a fraternity, where the norms of the group establish certain social realities:

---

[2] Essentially, a good part of this book is organized around the four types of relationships discussed here. For example, the "expressive-emotional" is treated in Chapter 4.

for example, "what courses or professors are best," "what kind of girls are the best 'dates,' " and so forth. In either case (1) or (2) I refer to Type B as *confirmatory*.[3]

A *Type C* relationship is formed for the purpose of *change* or *influence*. Thus one or both parties to the relationship come together to create a change in each other or the relationship. The change may entail anything from acquiring new behaviors to attitude change. The main transaction between the change-agent and change-target is information about the desired state to be achieved and feedback on how the target is doing. Examples of change are psychiatrist-patient, teacher-student, parent-child, and so forth.[4]

A *Type D* relationship is formed in order to achieve some goal or task. A conductor and the violin section or a foreman and the workers or collaborators on a research project are all examples of Type D. I will call this type *instrumental*; the main coin of interpersonal exchange is information *about the task*.[5]

Before continuing this analysis, it should be mentioned that these four types can rarely, if ever, be observed in "pure" form; the purpose of a relationship cannot be so simple or monolithic. A couple, for example, may marry not only for the relationship itself (Type A) but for some instrumental purpose as well (Type D). For example, I know of two anthropologists whose marriage was based on "love" and the need to work together. And I know also of many co-workers, engaged in instrumental activities who permit—even desire—the relationship itself to take priority over the task. Conversely, there are partners in business, often brothers, whose relationship has become increasingly contractual rather than familial. And Type B, confirmatory relationships, are, of course, a category of the more general types, as are Type C, change relationships. In any case, I have never seen a purely "confirmatory" relationship. So we are not dealing here with mutually exclusive types, but with overlapping categories with multiple functions. Despite this qualification, I do want to stress for analytical purposes that every relationship is formed—indeed, is caused—in order to realize one primary function.

Now let me return to the question raised earlier on what is a good relationship. Consider Figure 1. This diagram shows the four types of relationships ordered down the vertical axis. In column (1) the content of the interpersonal transactions is listed. In column (2) the various criteria for a good relationship are listed. This is based on my main assertion, only implied until now, that a relationship is considered good to the extent that it fulfills its primary function. Thus, to determine whether a Type A re-

---

[3] See Chapter 3 for a complete treatment of these types of relationships.

[4] See Chapter 5 for a complete treatment of these types of relationships.

[5] See Chapter 6 for a detailed treatment of Type D.

FIGURE 1
Multiple Criteria Framework for Evaluating Interpersonal Relationships

	(1) The Content of the Interpersonal Transaction	(2) Criteria for Good Relationships	(3) Outcomes of Good Relationships	(4) Outcomes of Bad Relationships
Type A: Emotional-Expressive	Feelings	Mutual satisfaction	"Solidarity"	Alienation Ambivalence Hostility
Type B: Confirmatory	Information about self: 1) Interpersonal feedback; reflected appraisals	1) Confirmation	1) Integrated identity Self-actualization Consensus about reality	1) Disconfirmation
	Information about environment: 2) Definitions of the situation	2) Consensus	2) Cognitive mastery Consensus about reality	2) Anomie
Type C: Change-Influence	Information about desired goal and progress toward achieving goal	Desired change	Growth Termination Internalization	Resistance Interminable dependence
Type D: Instrumental	Information about task	Productivity Creativity	Competence Output	Inadequate Low output

lationship is good, we have to estimate if it is mutually *satisfying* to the participants; that is, do they have the desired relationship? For Type B there are two kinds of criteria depending on whether or not the exchange concerns the establishing of an interpersonal or self-reality or whether or not the relationship was used to apprehend external reality. If (1), then we observe confirmation, some agreement about the relationship. If (2), then we observe consensus, some agreement about the definition of the situation. For Type C, the desired change is the main criterion; for Type D, productivity (or creativity) is the key. *Satisfaction, confirmation* (and *consensus*), *desired change,* and *productivity* are the terms which can be applied to the goodness of a relationship, depending upon its unique function.

Outcomes of Good and Bad Relationships

If the primary function of a relationship is fulfilled—what I have been calling a *good* relationship—we can expect a positive outcome; if not, then a negative one. What are the outcomes of good and bad relationships? Columns (3) and (4) list these.

A. For Type A, solidarity is the indicator of a good relationship, and *ambivalence, alienation,* or *chronic hostility* are the indicators of a bad relationship. Let me say a word or two more about *solidarity,* a term which has had the recent misfortune of connoting "togetherness." What I have in mind is closer to Murray's Dionysian couple:

> . . . engaged now and again in unpremeditated, serious yet playful, dramatic outbursts of feeling, wild imagination, and vehement interaction, in which one of them—sometimes Adam, sometimes Eve—gave vent to whatever was pressing for expression. Walpurgis was the name they gave to episodes of this insurgent nature . . . each of the two psyches, through numberless repetitions, discharged its residual as well as emergent and beneficient dispositions, until nearly every form of sexuality and nearly every possible complementation of dyadic roles had been dramatically enacted . . . and all within the compass of an ever mounting trust in the solidarity of their love, evidenced in the Walpurgis episodes by an apparently limitless mutual tolerance of novelty and emotional extravagance.[6]

From this view, then, solidarity encompasses a wide range of complex emotions as well as the capacity for the individuals to risk the confrontation of their emotional vicissitudes; at the same time they must remain together despite and because of their own anxieties and appetites.

B. It might be useful to state with greater clarity than before the two classes of relationships grouped in Type B. Both have to do with construct-

---

[6] H. A. Murray, "Vicissitudes of Creativity," in *Creativity and Its Cultivation,* Interdisciplinary Symposia on Creativity, Michigan State University, 1957–58, ed. H. H. Anderson (New York: Harper & Bros., 1959), pp. 110–18.

ing reality, one an *interpersonal* reality that develops from the interactions between the participants and serves to define the boundaries of self-hood and of the interpersonal relationship. The "self" is born in the communicative acts and, according to this symbolic-interactionist position, "we begin to see each other as others see us" and begin to "take the role of the other." Thus, the formation, definition, and evaluation of the self emerge from the successive interactions we have with significant others.[7]

The other class of Type B has to do with apprehending some element in the environment, an item "x," let us say, for which we require interpersonal support in order to "understand" it. This is identical to Festinger's idea concerning the attainment of "social reality."[8] He asserts that opinions, attitudes, and beliefs—as differentiated from physical realities, which could be proved or disproved by physical means—need anchorage in a socially valued group. Thus, one powerful motive for people to come together in interpersonal relationships is to "make sense," to order, to develop cognitive mastery over the outside world. As Festinger says: "An opinion, a belief, an attitude is correct, valid, and proper to the extent that it is anchored in a group of people with similar beliefs, opinions, and attitudes."[9]

To this extent we are all "conformists;" that is, all of us need interpersonal evidence to attain cognitive control over our environments.

Let me come back now to the possible outcomes of good and bad Type B relationships. If we consider the interpersonal class (1), then in a good relationship, an integrated "personal identity" or self-actualization and self-enhancement would emerge as well as a realistic relationship; in the external case, (2) cognitive mastery over some salient aspect of the environment would emerge. In either case *the outcomes of goodness in Type B is the consensus and confirmation regarding the perception of reality.*

This increased perception of reality that comes through consensus or confirmation—regardless of its *validity*—has a tremendous liberating effect leading to a self-expansiveness and self-acceptance in (1) and a high degree of morale and confidence in (2).

A bad Type B (1) would consist of chronic refutation and dissonance and therefore probably not last. Farber[10] writes movingly of his experience with a patient who refused to confirm him (Farber)—by simply not getting "well;" that is, by not acting like a patient should. We have all

---

[7] For a recent discussion stemming from this tradition of Mead and Cooley see H. D. Duncan, *Communication and the Social Order* (New York: Bedminister Press, 1962). See Essay 2 for a review of this treatment.

[8] L. Festinger, "Informal Social Communication," *Psychological Review*, 57 (1950), pp. 271–82.

[9] Ibid., p. 273.

[10] L. Farber, "Therapeutic Despair," *Psychiatry*, 21 (February 1958), pp. 7–20.

experienced and witnessed situations like this where a group or person has denied self or role confirmation to another, consciously or not: students who won't learn, children who won't obey, audiences who won't approve, followers who won't be influenced, and friends who won't share or confirm our delusions about self, and in fact, stubbornly transmit cues counter to our own self-image.[11]

A bad type B (2) exists when the parties to a relationship cannot agree on or make sense about external realities. It is most graphically described in the words of Kafka where even the reader gets fooled into thinking that the Kafkaesque world *is* more eerie and ambiguous than "real life." The fact of the matter is that the *world* is no more or less complicated but *people* cannot arrive at any agreement about it. So it is a world without "norms," without clear-cut references—evolved out of a shared frame of reference—necessary to establish consensus about "reality." The ability to predict future events, the need to reduce uncertainty—all these matters we call "cognitive mastery"—are essential for mankind's security. It is one of the main reasons (and costs) for interpersonal relationships, for without it, relationships devolve into *anomie*, a disoriented, ambiguous, uncertain world.

There is a special case of a bad outcome for a Type B that bears some attention. Imagine a situation where two or more people come together and confirm their own relationship but seriously distort some aspect of "social reality." Let me again take an example from literature. In Thomas Mann's story, "The Blood of the Walsungs,"[12] the twin brother and sister seriously misperceive (but agree on) the outside world and withdraw further and further into the nest of their own distortions. The fact that they hold a unique and different view from most people tends to further intensify their alienation, for the only support they can find is restricted. This form of social withdrawal has been observed, for example, among apocalyptic messianic groups.[13]

This distortion of and rejection by the outside world—always linked with libidinal contraction and intensification—leads to a state of affairs Slater calls "social regression."[14]

---

[11] Some evidence has been gathered which shows the effects of role confirmation and refutation on a group of nurses. (J. E. Berkowitz and N. H. Berkowitz, "Nursing Education and Role Conception," *Nursing Research*, 9 [1960], "briefs"). It was felt that the patients who responded to treatment were confirming the nurses' role and those patients who did not respond to treatment were refuting the nurses' role. The hypothesis, supported by the data, was: patients who were disconfirmers would not be liked or treated as well by the nursing staff as those patients who were role confirmers.

[12] Thomas Mann, *Stories of Three Decades* (New York: Alfred A. Knopf, 1936), pp. 279–319.

[13] L. Festinger, H. W. Riecken, Jr., and S. Schachter, *When Prophecy Fails* (Minneapolis: University of Minnesota, 1956); also J. A. Hardyck and M. Braden, "Prophecy Fails Again: A Report of a Failure to Replicate," *J. of Abn. Psychol.*, 65 (1962), pp. 136–41.

[14] P. Slater, "On Social Regression," *American Soc. Review*, 28 (1963), pp. 339–64.

The tandem alcoholism of the married couple in the movie, "Days of Wine and Roses," as well as the bizarre and autistic games played by George and Martha in Albee's play, *"Who's Afraid of Virginia Woolf?*[15] are both good examples of this phenomenon. Sometimes this type of relationship resembles "solidarity," like the Walsungis experiences reported above, but they are always different by nature. "Social regression" flourishes only in a social vacuum and when there is a powerful motive to *distort external reality.* Solidarity can last only if there is some *realistic* connection with the outside world.

C.   A Type C relationship is defined by its pivotal concern with the acquisition or modification of behavior or attitudes, as imparted by a change-agent (A) to some change-target (B). It is true that changes occur in the other types of relationship discussed, but only spontaneously and adventitiously. Type C encompasses primarily the class of change-inductions that are planned; for example, it would include primarily relationships resulting in changes due to formal course work (teacher-student or work partner in "lab"), and only incidentally the informal or unplanned kinds of relationships such as those which occur in "bull-session" groups. Type C covers a wide range of relationships, from parent-child to psychiatrist-patient, from coach-pupil to warden-inmate.[16]

In addition to this emphasis on *change, growth,* and *learning,* an analysis of Type C further reveals two unique characteristics. First, these relationships are almost always oriented toward termination (graduation, parole, or death). An "interminable" psychoanalysis is considered deplorable, while an "interminable" marriage is considered honorable. Second, Type C reveals a special kind of relationship between the change-agent (A) and the target (B) which I refer to as "tilted." In other words, we expect A to influence B, to "give to" B, to teach B more—than the other way around. As a rule, students learn from teachers, patients from psychiatrists, pupils from coaches.[17] Thus the interpersonal exchange is slanted and less reciprocal, by definition, than other types. With these preliminary considerations out of the way, let me turn to the indicators of a good and bad Type C relationship.

A good Type C leads to three distinct, but related, outcomes. First, there is consensus between A and B that the desired growth or change or influence has been attained. Second, the relationship has reached a state

---

[15] E. Albee, *Who's Afraid of Virginia Woolf?* (New York: Atheneum Publishers, 1963).

[16] The reader is referred back to Essay 4 where change relationships are treated in detail.

[17] I have omitted those exceptional, but highly interesting, cases where B can influence A more than A can influence B. More often than not, these are perverse, given this definition of Type C. Teachers may indeed learn from students, but this is different from exploitation and "stealing ideas." Analysts may "use" countertransference productively for the patient's ultimate health, but this is different than cashing in on stock tips or sexual exploitation.

wherein its continuation, while possibly helpful, will not lead to significant advances. It must end. Third, the client must have internalized the learning process, such that the process of learning begun in the relationship can continue. Thus *growth*, *termination*, and *internalization* are the indicators of a good Type C relationship.

The reverse of these criteria serve to signify badness. Dissatisfaction with B's rate of progress on the part of either A or B is a common indicator. The frequently heard remark: "I must change my teacher-therapist-coach-trainer; we're not getting anywhere" is an example. Second, the relationship cannot be extended indefinitely. That is, there must be some point at which the hoped-for changes will occur. Without this explicit termination point, both A and B can possibly get trapped in a false dream where the original and primary purpose of the relationship gets sidetracked.[18] Third, the target must be able to use the knowledge learned in an autonomous fashion; that is, without undue dependence on the change-agent. Patients who are forever returning to their therapists are not "cured"; acting students who suffer immobilizing stage fright unless their coach is watching from the wings are not "trained." I do not mean to imply that in a good Type C relationship the client has nothing more to learn and never returns for further training; I do mean, however, that the client is relatively free of dependence and has learned how to continue the process on his or her own.

D.   Instrumental relationships, Type D, are formed in order to produce or create: a song, an idea, a car, a formula, a dress. It encompasses the range of relationships involved in those activities which function in order to produce a "good or service."[19] It is ordinarily what people "do for a living"; it is certainly what most people do to earn enough for other types of relationships. As the need for interdependence and collaboration increases—that is to say, as specialization increases—this form of relationship will grow in importance and will call for more searching examination. It may be already the most ubiquitous form of interpersonal relationship in an industrialized society such as ours.

---

[18] What often happens in these cases is that both partners in the relationship shift consciously or unconsciously to another type of relationship; the ski-instructor who marries the student, for example, is a switch from C to A. I will return to this point later.

[19] Unaccounted for here are those instrumental relationships associated with the service industries, such as some customer-salesperson relationships, cabbie-passenger, receptionist-customer. I have ignored this class of relationships for two reasons: first, because this type of relationship rarely involves more than a brief encounter in a transient setting; second, because there is a peculiar lack of reciprocity. The waitress is instrumentally involved with the diner, but he or she is not involved instrumentally with her—and typically he or she has only a "service" relationship to her. This is a difficult class of problems for an analytic scheme to handle. Temporary relationships, such as games, vacation trips, and so forth, are examined brilliantly in a recent essay by M. Miles, "On Temporary Systems," manuscript (New York: Columbia University, 1963); see, also, A. R. Anderson and O. K. Moore, *Autotelic Folk-Models* (New Haven: Sociology Department, Yale University, 1959).

These are two main indicators of a good instrumental relationship, *competence* and *output*. The latter is objectively measured, usually in the form of a productivity rate: stories sold *per* year, pages typed *per* day, articles published *per* year, bolts attached *per* minute, profits earned *per* quarter, and so forth. Because of the relative ease of measuring output, instrumental relationships are often easier to judge as good or bad.

Less objective than output, but equally important from this point of view, is the way participants engaged in an instrumental relationship manage their work. Decision making, problem solving, coordination, quality of collaboration, energy expenditure: these are some of the elements in the complex factor I refer to as *competence*.[20]

A bad instrumental relationship exists, then, if either competence or output is unsatisfactory relative to certain norms. One would expect that these two factors would be positively correlated, but there is inadequate evidence to make this assertion.[21]

Aberrations, Anomalies, and Confusions in Interpersonal Relationships

Before going on to part two of this essay, where the personal and environmental conditions for attaining good interpersonal relations are discussed, it might be useful to pause briefly to pursue some suggestive leads which the foregoing analysis provides. These have to do with those relationships which seem "special" or irregular, relationships which capture the imagination, which attract the public eye, which fascinate.[22] Often they are puffed-up beyond all recognition by the popular press; at times they seem bizarre and/or perverse. In any case, they seem to be the stuff of romance, tragedy, farce and dreams—of fiction and plays—rather than "real life." In fact, they seem to represent a class of problems, latent in all interpersonal relationships: *problems arising out of (a) transformations, (b) conflicts and ambiguities, and (c) deceit regarding the goal of*

---

[20] Time and space considerations do not allow for a complete discussion of these issues. They go far beyond the purposes of this essay. The so-called "criterion problem" has perplexed industrial psychologists and students of organizational behavior for some time and I do not aim to settle any issues with this inadequate discussion. For a fuller statement, see W. G. Bennis, "Towards a 'Truly' Scientific Management: The Concept of Organization Health," *General Systems Yearbook* (Ann Arbor, Mich.: Mental Health Research Institute, 1962).

[21] C. Argyris, *Interpersonal Competence and Organizational Effectiveness* (Homewood, Ill.: Irwin-Dorsey Press, 1962); R. Likert, *New Patterns of Management* (New York: McGraw-Hill Book Co., 1961).

[22] Again, I am constrained here by a lack of concepts appropriate to describe a relationship. One can talk of a charismatic person; how about a charismatic "interperson"? or bizarre "interperson"? Don't married couples and types of relationships have "character" at least as much as a person does? Don't couples have a "presentation of a unit" as much as an individual has a "presentation of self"? A primitive start on such a language was made by Shepard and Bennis ("A Theory of Training by Group Methods," *Human Relations*, 9 [1956], pp. 403–44).

the relationship. The multiple criteria framework (Figure 1) can provide the necessary analytic framework for this analysis.

a. Collusive Transformations. In the musical comedy, "How to Succeed in Business without Really Trying," a chorus of secretaries cries out in shock and anger at one of their number who, on the verge of marrying her boss, decides to break the engagement. Their disappointment, and the audience's, is clear: the girl is about to destroy their constant dream, a cherished image they all hold and which partly keeps them at work. This fascination for secretaries who marry bosses, teachers who marry students, actresses who marry their leading men, analysts who marry their patients, we usually think of as "romantic" or morbid, depending on our orientation. In fact, it represents a joint decision—not necessarily conscious—where a relationship shifts from one modality to another. I call this "collusive transformation."

One of the most interesting examples of this can be seen in Shaw's "Pygmalion." Henry Higgins and Eliza Doolittle enter into a Type C relationship in order to alter her manners and "character," but end up with an incipient Type A relationship. Every bit of drama and comedy is derived from this shift: whether or not Eliza will return to Higgins, how Colonel Pickering, Mr. Doolittle, and Higgins' mother perceive the relationship,[23] how the Type A emphasis becomes more pivotal without awareness on the part of Eliza or Higgins and so forth. Another interesting example of the same shift (Type C to Type A) can be seen in the Rodgers and Hammerstein musical, "The King and I." The tension and drama of the play evolved from a collusive shift from a change (Type C) to an expressive-emotional (Type A) relationship. Romance, according to my analysis, can always be reduced to a collusive transformation, shifting from any type, to Type A.

An interesting example of another style of collusive transformation (Type A to B) can be seen in the play and movie, "Tea and Sympathy." A friendly relationship develops between the wife of an instructor and his student. The student becomes increasingly morose concerning doubts about his masculinity. The wife of the instructor, toward the end of the drama, decides to shift her relationship with the boy in order to *confirm* his manhood. The play ends as she removes her blouse in preparation for the rites of passage.

Other styles of collusive transformations can be observed, though possibly with less frequency than the shift to Type A. A shift from Type A to any other type is perhaps the rarest, though Danny Kaye and Sylvia Fine, his ex-wife, still collaborate on his musical numbers (going from A to D).

b. Conflict or Unclarity. There is a class of relationships which can

---

[23] For a discussion of class or hierachy as a determining feature in interpersonal relationships, see Duncan, *Communication and the Social Order.*

end only in one of two ways, depending upon one's orientation: if one is observing, then absurdity; if one is participating, then despair. It must end because the relationship is construed and entered into for different reasons. Turgenev's "A Month in the Country" provides an example. A young tutor falls madly in love with the mother of his charges—because she is a "lady." She in turn loves him because his love rejuvenates her. To the audience this is the absurd love of age and youth.

A more striking example comes from the novella, *One Hundred Dollar Misunderstanding*.[24] A young white college boy—middle-class and pompous—propositions and goes to bed with a fourteen-year-old black prostitute. He refuses to pay her her $100 fee because he näively thinks she went to bed with him because she "found him attractive." The entire book is based on this misperception of the relationship.

One other case, also from fiction, comes from James Baldwin's *Another Country*.[25] A young man enters into a relationship with a married woman in order to assert or confront his masculinity (Type B); she gets involved for love (Type A). The relationship was constructed on conflicting purposes and shortly dissolved. Baldwin writes: "But it was only love which could accomplish the miracle of making a life bearable—only love, and love itself mostly failed; and he had never loved her. He had used her to find out something about himself. And even this was not true. He had used her in the hope of avoiding a confrontation with himself. . . ."[26]

c. *Deceit.* The prostitute in the *One Hundred Dollar Misunderstanding* example was not dissembling; she was not "conning" the boy like a B-girl at the bar of some café who insinuates unimaginable sexual adventures awaiting the "unsuspecting" victim if he only continues to buy her more *ersatz* whiskey. The girl made it perfectly clear to the boy that she was a "pro" and that she was interested in him only as a client.[27] But in the case of the B-girl or the con-man or in any relationship of an exploitative kind, the relationship is jointly and publicly formed for one reason, but privately formed for another reason by one of the parties to the relationship: the teacher who makes "friends" with the ninth-grade girl because

---

[24] R. Gover, *One Hundred Dollar Misunderstanding* (New York: Grove Press, 1961).

[25] J. Baldwin, *Another Country* (New York: Dell, 1963).

[26] Ibid., p. 340.

[27] It's difficult to know who's dissembling to whom in such cases, and for what reasons. It's perfectly obvious, in most situations, that B-girls are using sex as a come-on, as a inducement. It is perfectly obvious to the reader in *One Hundred Dollar Misunderstanding* that the girl is a prostitute. It is hard to believe that the "mark" is oblivious to these cues or that he is unconscious of them. Most likely, he simply doesn't tell himself what is really going on because this doesn't conform to his self-image, at least his *ideal* self-image. It's a bit like cheating at solitaire; one knows one is acting not altogether "proper" but at the same time, one doesn't have to admit it fully.

she was told that the youngster is a "problem"; the opportunistic starlet who manages to "fall in love" with every director; the young executive who marries the boss's daughter for power; the psychologist who asks the college sophomore to do some work but, in fact, is using the student as an experimental subject; and so on. All these are basically exploitative, the basis of the "con-game."

To sharpen the focus on the exploitative relationship, one finds that it is always characterized by its *double meaning* to one, and only one, participant. So I am not talking about *joint mystification* where both parties enter into it for a professed reason, while each conceals a more basic, identical one. Comedy movies of the 1930s were made of this stuff: Girl meets Boy in fancy hotel on the Riviera; each pretends gigantic wealth and amorous interest in the other; each intends to use the other instrumentally. The movies usually end, after successively hilarious misunderstandings, in a collusive (and explosive) transformation to Type A.

Nor am I talking about *unconscious exploitation,* either of a collusive nature where both parties are involved in it or where only one participant is unconsciously involved. The boss's daughter marries the young executive because she unconsciously wants her father replaced; the man marries the daughter because he also unconsciously wants the father replaced. They are "in love," but under false pretenses; that is, unconsciously for other reasons.

Finally, exploitative relationships must be distinguished from *conscious collusion,* wherein A and B come together for a professed type of relationship which both know to be other than their real purpose. A middle-aged woman goes to a dance instructor for the expressed purpose of learning new dance steps. In fact, the woman knows she continues her lessons for other reasons, of an expressive-emotional kind, while he continues to see her for instrumental, not change, reasons. They both know that the other knows his or her reasons for their relationship. Thus, it continues, each of them satisfying a different pivotal goal than the other.

There are other classes of irregularities and anomalies which this approach cannot account for and others that it can. I have demonstrated, however, that if attention is focused on the primary function of a relationship and relates this to transformation, clarity, conflict, and deceit, it is possible to illuminate some relationships which we ordinarily consider bizarre or perverse, or at least, "irregular."

Before turning to part two, let me summarize this approach and propose some conclusions. The approach to the normative issue—of good and bad —is a *functional* one. If a relationship satisfies its functions, then it is good; if not, then it is bad. Inasmuch as there are *four* primary functions for relationships, this approach has been based on *multiple criteria.* Evidence is adduced for goodness (or health) by certain outcomes presented in

FIGURE 2

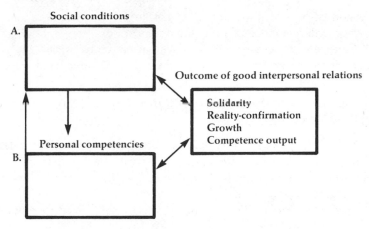

Figure 1. Irregularities and anomalies can be derived by analyzing confusions, transformations, conflicts, and deceit with regard to primary functions.

The final point I want to make, by way of conclusion, has to do with the outcomes of goodness presented in Figure 1: solidarity, confirmation and reality, growth, and competence. They cannot be, or should they be, restricted so neatly to their "own" type of relationship as portrayed. An instrumental relationship, devoid of change or solidarity, would be arid. A change relationship, devoid of competence or confirmation, would become stagnant. And so on. *All* of the outcomes must be involved, to some degree, in all relationships.

Figure 2 reveals the substance of the remainder of the essay. I start from the assumption that the fabric of our social environment and the personal competencies of the individuals involved determine the success of the interpersonal relationship. I hope to articulate these conditions in the most general way so that they encompass *any social milieu* where interpersonal dynamics occur.

All relationships exist in some social context—a group, an organization, a community, an institution. Whatever we call it—environment or society —it provides a texture within which our relationships are embedded and by which they are governed. To some degree the goodness and badness of interpersonal relationships are dependent on the conditions of the social setting. In any case, relationships do not exist in a vacuum. I intend now to explore the *social conditions* upon which our relationships are based. I shall also examine the *personal conditions* that determine the quality of relationships.

The Social Conditions

My vision of a "social architecture" conducive to forming and maintaining good interpersonal relationships consists of three sets of "blueprints." One set has to do with (1) "system-characteristics," the social processes which govern behavior. The others are (2) values and (3) goals.

SOCIAL AND PERSONAL CONDITIONS OF GOOD INTERPERSONAL RELATIONS

System Characteristics. A system is simply a set of mutually dependent elements or parts in interaction. Good interpersonal relationships can only occur in certain kinds of systems, specifically ones which have the following characteristics:

a. The System Should Be "Open." Allport has pieced together four criteria of open systems:

> (1) There is intake and output of both matter and energy. (2) There is the achievement and maintenance of steady (homeostatic) states, so that the intrusion of outer energy will not seriously disrupt internal form and order. (3) There is generally an increase of order over time, owing to an increase in complexity of and differentiation of parts. (4) Finally, at least at the human level, there is more than mere intake and output of matter and energy; *there is extensive transactional commerce with the environment.*[28]

The importance of the open system is its emphasis on the transactions between system and environment. A closed system, on the other hand, is defined as one which is isolated and self-contained: "Like a decaying bridge," Allport says, "it sinks into thermodynamic decay."[29]

Because an open system negotiates, merges, connects with its environments it contains a number of unique potentialities. Because it confronts unexpected stimuli, it can learn from external inputs; this allows for varied inputs and experiences, incongruities and surprises. These exogenous infusions, as well as providing productive energy and inputs, also work to challenge the system. If the system can "adapt" and cope with these external stresses, it can continually develop new patterns, possibilities and shapes—like a kaleidoscope with an infinite variety of designs. But these environmental transactions may also create insurmountable problems to the open system. New inputs may occur, for example, which are ignored by the system or inadequately managed. If the system fails to adjust to the environment it loses its integrity or it collapses and decays.[30]

---

[28] Gordon Allport, *Personality and Social Encounter* (Boston: Beacon Press, 1960), p. 43. Emphasis added.

[29] Ibid., p. 42.

[30] There are many ways for an open system to regress or decay: through com-

The cost of closed and open systems should be clear. In one case, we have a system which *contacts* the environment. In the closed-system case, there is practically no contact. Thus the closed system is adjustive, preservative, programmed, but insulative. We are opting for the strains of the open system: adaptive, restorative, unprogrammed, permeable, but stressful.

b. The Influence Structure Should Be Balanced and Characterized by Interdependence. Influence encompasses the ways in which people exert power and express subordination. In social systems this governs an important part of the interactions. People are made to do things by fiat, order, and command; or by fear, intimidation, and coercion; or by persuasion, reward, and attraction. And people respond to these forces by surrender, rebellion, "apeing," consent, agreement, consensus, avoiding, denying, dissembling, complying, and obeying. Whatever system we observe, there is some structure of influence.

One of the main problems in most influence structures is *hierarchy:* a formal or informal arrangement whereby some person—a boss, teacher, a police officer—tells other people what to do. When the subordinates do what they are told and do it well, they are rewarded; when they do not do it or do it poorly, the rewards are withheld or punishment is applied. This world view is partly based on this simple Law of Effect.[31] Party leaders, managers, teachers, parents, dictators, ministers all employ it.

Influence of this simple reward-and-punishment type is ubiquitous, tending more often than not to be dysfunctional. For example, one of its problems is that subordinates spend an awesome amount of time in an attempt to divine what they think the influencing agent, the authority, wants. Whether or not the subordinates guess correctly and act appropriately is problematical, what is not problematical is the fruitless complexity of the search. As one student put it: "We seem to spend about 75 percent of our time solving the professor, and 25 percent, the problem."[32]

Another problem with the traditional form of influence has to do with the assumptions bosses hold about subordinates. If one assumes that people are lazy, dumb, dishonest, passive, and simple hedonists—as the more

---

placency, poor reality-testing, and internal strains which reduce external commerce. The "casual texture of the enviroment" is another crucial variable which F. E. Emery and E. L. Trist ("The Causal Texture of Organizational Environments," *Human Relations*, 18 [1965], pp. 21–32) have analyzed.

[31] The Law of Effect can be summarized by saying that people tend to repeat behaviors which are rewarded and stop behaviors which are punished: "Spare the rod and spoil the child."

[32] The reader must be warned of our oversimplified discussion of this issue. We are compressing, but not, we hope, distorting the problem. For a thorough treatment, see W. G. Bennis, "Leadership Theory and Administrative Behavior: The Problem of Authority," *Administrative Science Quarterly*, 4 (1959), pp. 259–301; and D. McGregor, *The Human Side of Enterprise* (New York: McGraw-Hill Book Co., 1960).

traditional theories of hierarchical influence imply—then directive and co-ercive controls are probably necessary. Of course, the coercive controls produce the very behavior they assume, and thus we have a classic example of a self-fulfilling prophecy. An additional irony is that even people who are inadequate, passive, and inert rarely respond positively to uni-lateral subordination.

A number of behavioral scientists have been concerned with influence structures in a variety of settings: classroom, work place, research lab, family, office. Their recommendations are phrased in different ways but all point toward a more balanced and interdependent influence structure; from "informational-interdependent"[33] to "internalization";[34] from "Theory Y"[35] to "autotelic folk-models."[36] But the moral and practical impact is the same: influence is appropriate to the degree (1) that there is a col-laborative—not authoritarian—relationship; (2) that people act on "credible" information; and (3) that self-determination plays a crucial role in the influence structure.

These three factors define what I mean by *interdependence*. The concept can be further elaborated and summarized this way: Influence, of an interdependent type, involves a joint effort toward reaching some mutually determined goal which requires complementary skills and information. This collaborative interaction evolves from the press of task demands and personnel resources, not from formal status, personal tyranny, or bureaucratic code. Interdependence involves an integration between authority and the subordinate—not freedom from either. Freedom and autonomy are limited only by credible information, task requirements, and self-impositions. Restrictions to freedom are certainly never due to extrinsic rewards in the social system we are envisaging, but only to internal rationalizations. Finally, interdependence does not imply *permissiveness* or *protectiveness*; such terms indicate only the shallow indulgencies of a pseudodemocratic system.

   c.   Decisions Should Be Made by Consensus.   One can distinguish influence from decision making in an arbitrary fashion. The former was defined exclusively in terms of hierarchy, the power dimension. Decision making, on the other hand, encompasses two sets of activities: (1) procedures for conflict resolution and (2) procedures for choosing and evaluating alternatives. The criterion for these two activities can be briefly summarized as the *principle of consensus*.

Consensus is a *portmanteau* term which tends to mean all things to all

---

[33] O. J. Harvey, D. E. Hunt, and H. M. Schroder, *Conceptual Systems and Personality Organization* (New York: John Wiley and Sons, 1961).

[34] H. C. Kelman, "Compliance, Identification, and Internalization: Three Processes of Attitude Change," *Journal of Conflict Resolution*, 2 (1958), pp. 51–60.

[35] McGregor, *The Human Side.*

[36] Anderson and Moore, *Autotelic Folk-Models.*

people. To the "true-believer," consensus is democracy, if not truth. To the skeptic it is an uninformed majority and a cowed minority. To the innocent, it is a "unanimous vote." The problem is not only a conceptual one, though consensus *is* a protean and elastic idea. The fact is that it also bootlegs in an emotional and moral cargo, difficult to untangle from conceptual fuzziness.[37]

Consensus is a procedure for deciding among alternatives in interpersonal (or group) situations. This procedure must fulfill the following conditions: (1) It must include only those items which are salient to the membership and for which the membership has evidenced a distinctive competence. (2) If there is a conflict or difference, it must be resolved by valid and credible data, publicly shared and communicated; differences are never resolved by impersonal orders, rank, or personal vicissitudes. (3) If differences exist, they are always to be faced and dealt with, rather than avoided or denied. (4) There should be as much involvement and participation in the decision making process as salience and competence permits.

These are stringent criteria for consensus and only possible, perhaps, under unique conditions. But they are guidelines and may hold genuine promise.

d. The Communication Structure Should Maximize Clarity. Every system requires some mechanism for transmitting, receiving, and storing information. The ideal communication structure must function to maintain clarity, economy, and relevance. Three conditions should be realized for this: (1) Information must be transmitted in the most unambiguous fashion possible in order to insure cognitive clarity. (2) Information should be transmitted only to the relevant parts of the system. (3) Information must not be filtered or distorted because of status anxieties or threat to the organization.

This last point is probably the most crucial and vexing of the three. How does a system guarantee valid (undistorted) upward communication if the information may displease or contradict the boss or teacher? A story circulating about Samuel Goldwyn takes its humor from this theme. Apparently Goldwyn called his staff together and was reported to have said, "Now, look: I want each and every one of you to tell me what's wrong with our operation here—even if it means losing your job!"[38]

---

[37] It should be remembered that consensus is a moral as well as practical issue. The fact that I favor it morally (and ultimately for pragmatic reasons—under certain conditions) is not related to its empirical validation—which is problematical. There are many conditional qualifiers to be made for the effective operation of consensus or any kind of group decision making. The interested reader should consult Krech, Crutchfield, and Ballachey, *Individual in Society* (New York: McGraw-Hill Book Co., 1962), chap. 13.

[38] A more serious example of this same phenomenon can be inferred from research by E. P. Torrance, "Some Consequences of Power Differences on Decision Making in Permanent and Temporary Three-Man Groups," *Research Studies, State College of*

And how does a system guarantee valid information and feedback from its environment when these threaten the system's existence? Emery and Trist[39] have observed such cases where organizations misperceive or ignore environmental cues. This leads inexorably to an organizational demise, either by suicide or annihilation. Surely organizations, like individuals, have ways of distorting reality—or "selective inattention"—for who would dare to forecast doom, death, struggle, or any profound change when it's easier to deny, delay, or distort the truth?

e. The System Must Have Adequate Reality-Testing Mechanisms. These problems cannot be settled satisfactorily by providing only an adequate communication structure, whose main function is clarity and relevance. We need an additional mechanism, some way to guarantee adequate determinations of the internal state of the system as well as the boundaries relevant to the system and what is going on outside the boundaries. In short, every system requires some formal mechanism for establishing "truth" about its internal and external relationships and functioning. Most systems possess mechanisms that are either inadequate and convenient, or adequate and inconvenient. An example of the former is the (useless and illusory) bookkeeping statistics kept by some business firms. The latter can be seen when a system finds itself imperiled, too late to effect a "comeback." Emery and Trist, for example, tell of a case in which a canning company—going ahead in a major expansion—failed to recognize certain trends (frozen foods, Common Market, and so forth) and continued to fail to recognize them until it was too late. "The managing director and indeed most of the other senior people were removed."[40]

What is most needed is some formal agency to ascertain and measure the relevant values connected with the system, not only for the present but for the changing future.

Open-system, interdependence, consensus, clarity, and reality: These are the idealized set of system characteristics. There is a final one, only implied: that there be a "principle of appropriateness" which essentially determines the validity of the action. For example, it is not at all certain that interdependence and consensus are always appropriate. Some people and some situations, require different styles. Even "clarity" is not always desirable; sometimes a boss may have to employ "ambiguity" as a weapon or tool, and so on. We encourage these system-characteristics to be employed, but they should be used appropriately—not with a dogmatic or

---

Washington, 22 (1954), pp. 130–40. Here we see how subordinates in the military not only censored the communication of the right answer when they had it, but also allowed the authority to answer incorrectly when they, the subordinates, knew the correct answer. What permits a situation to develop where subordinates let superiors make mistakes when they know better and for superiors to assume that they, and never subordinates, have the key to intelligent action?

[39] Emery and Trist, "The Causal Texture."

[40] Ibid., p. 25.

Utopian vengeance. Let us now turn to the second set of conditions of our social architecture.

Values.   Values are those standards or directives upon which we base our decisions and to which we are committed. They are inherent in all systems for they govern to a great extent, the way people interact. They help to shape how "close" people get, how power and influence are enforced, how work gets accomplished, how truth is revealed, and so on. Values permit or preclude certain system characteristics; values stress and understress certain dimensions of institutional life. (If the system characteristics and the value systems are discordant, one must be modified or the system will fragment.) Values make possible the "identity" of a system, the possibilities and limitations of its actions. It follows that values are important, not just "academic."[41]

There are at least five values that affirm the system characteristics described in the previous section. The first is *openness* in interpersonal expression; to "speak what we feel, not what we ought to say." This openness implies the free expression of observations, feelings, ideas, associations, opinions, evaluations; free expression of thoughts and feelings *without*, however, threatening or limiting others. Obviously, there are precautions and choices which must be taken,[42] openness can be destructive, too. The important thing to register here, even with these qualifications, is that the system should encourage expression of feelings, rather than their suppression.

Closely related to openness is the value of *experimentalism*, the willingness to expose new ideas and to translate ideas into action. Experimentalism implies risk taking, uncertainty, "sticking one's neck out," as distinguished from "playing it safe," conservatism, and so on.

In order for openness and experimentalism to exist, another value must accompany them. This can be called *threat-reduction*, to signify values which can be characterized by a climate which allows mistakes readily, tolerates failures without retaliation or renunciation, encourages a sense of responsible risk taking without fear.

A number of writers have identified a similar, if not identical, value in discussions of the social conditions for learning or creativity: Carl Rogers' "psychological safety"[43] or Harold Lasswell's "warmly indulgent relation."[44] And Anderson and Moore[45] suggest that a good learning environ-

---

[41] For a penetrating analysis of the role of value in institutions, see P. Selznick, *Leadership in Administration* (Evanston, Ill.: Row Peterson, 1957).

[42] Uninhibited expression of feelings may be as dysfunctional and as phony as the uninhibited suppression of them. There is no easy formula for the right balance. It depends on the legitimacy of feelings, and the personalities, skills, insights of the participants.

[43] Carl Rogers, "Toward a Theory of Creativity," in *Creativity and Cultivation.*

[44] Harold Lasswell, "The Social Setting of Creativity," in Ibid., pp. 203–21.

[45] Anderson and Moore, *Autotelic Folk-Models.*

ment must be "cut off" from the more serious aspects of society's activities. They mean that a person should be allowed to make mistakes without dire consequences either to self or society.

The fourth value of this idealized system is *integration* or fusion between one's emotional needs and the system's rational goals. What is required is the understanding that people are not only heads and hands, but also hearts. The value system must encourage reciprocation between the emotions of the participants and the intellective press of the environment.[46]

The fifth and final value has to do with a *spirit of inquiry,* or unflinching curiosity to look at the way things are, a boldness with which to look at the processes which govern the behavior of the system. This value provides the security for the preservation of all other values for it insures the continual scrutiny of so-called "givens," and questions the legitimacy of "received notions" and the hallowed, but hobbling, "past." This process "or spirit of inquiry" provides the impulse for appropriate choices and adaptability.

Characteristics of Goal. The final consideration in this analysis of the social conditions required for good interpersonal relations is the *goal.* I want to stress only one aspect here. The goal should be *intrinsically* rewarding and should contain its *own sources of motivation.* In other words, the goal should contain enough valence or reward for the individual so that exogenous rewards are unnecessary.[47]

Figure 3 summarizes the social conditions for good interpersonal relations. However, before going on, I should note these remarks on social architecture deserve more elaboration and qualification than I provide. But, whatever unqualified exaggerations still exist can be blamed on the very nature of social Utopias.

The Personal Competencies

Assume that we are dealing with a population of mature adults reasonably motivated for interaction. What are the competencies that would lead to good interpersonal relationships? My bias here is toward those competencies that tend to deepen and widen the *emotional interchange* as well as *increase understanding:*

1. *Competence to Receive and Send Information and Feelings Reliably.* This not only includes the ability to *listen* and *perceive* accurately and fully, but other qualities as well. For example, it includes *sensitivity,* meaning a lowered threshold or heightened alertness to salient interpersonal

---

[46] See, for example, C. Argyris, *Personality and Organization* (New York: Harper & Bros., 1957).

[47] McGregor, *The Human Side.*

FIGURE 3

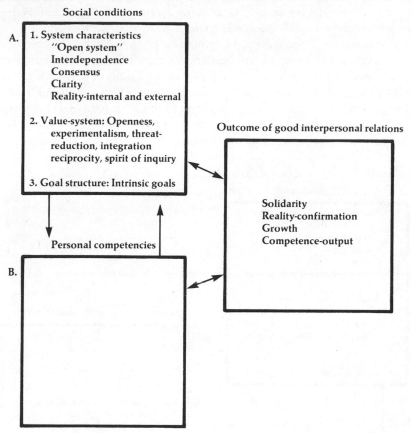

Social conditions

A.
1. System characteristics
   "Open system"
   Interdependence
   Consensus
   Clarity
   Reality-internal and external

2. Value-system: Openness,
   experimentalism, threat-
   reduction, integration
   reciprocity, spirit of inquiry

3. Goal structure: Intrinsic goals

Personal competencies

B.

Outcome of good interpersonal relations

Solidarity
Reality-confirmation
Growth
Competence-output

events, that is, an active and creative awareness, not simply a passive absorption.

2. *Competence to Evoke the Expression of Feelings.* Most anybody can listen passively to someone; the kind of listening that makes a difference is where the other is unafraid to express a thought, a belief, a feeling ordinarily reserved for autistic reveries or denied to the self. Just as we *maintain* a certain threshold to human experience, we also communicate our threshold, and quite often "stop" or inhibit the other.[48]

3. *Competence to Process Information and Feelings Reliably and Creatively.* This means that we can conceptualize and order our interpersonal

---

[48] An unexplored, but important, area for research is the role of the *listener* in interpersonal relations. There are "charismatic listeners" and "dull listeners"; there are listeners who evoke deep, meaningful human encounters and others who foreclose them. Why? We should know more about this.

experience, that we can obstract and play with various combinations of interpersonal exchanges and arrive at some diagnosis. Points 1 and 2 have to do with *sensitivity*, this point has to do with adequate *diagnosis*.

4. *Competence to Implement a Course of Action.* A diagnosis may indicate a certain behavior; say the girl really requires more dominance or the boy needs to be included more but doesn't know how to ask for it. What is required are *action*-skills. Diagnostic sensitivity without remedial action may be no more disastrous than action without diagnosis, but it is often sadder. *Behavioral flexibility plus* diagnostic sensitivity raises the prospects for better interpersonal relations.

FIGURE 4[49]

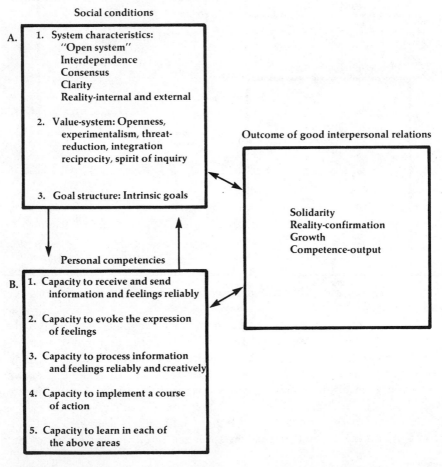

Social conditions

A.
1. System characteristics:
   "Open system"
   Interdependence
   Consensus
   Clarity
   Reality-internal and external

2. Value-system: Openness,
   experimentalism, threat-
   reduction, integration
   reciprocity, spirit of inquiry

3. Goal structure: Intrinsic goals

Personal competencies

B.
1. Capacity to receive and send
   information and feelings reliably

2. Capacity to evoke the expression
   of feelings

3. Capacity to process information
   and feelings reliably and creatively

4. Capacity to implement a course
   of action

5. Capacity to learn in each of
   the above areas

Outcome of good interpersonal relations

Solidarity
Reality-confirmation
Growth
Competence-output

---

[49] Figure 4 represents a summary of this essay. It was my intention to derive a set of criteria to represent good interpersonal relations and to speculate on the social conditions and personal competencies which lead in that direction.

5. *Competence to Learn in Each of the Above Areas.* It is far easier to talk of the *blocks* to learning—and "learning how to learn" in the interpersonal area—than to suggest some positive steps. Nevertheless, let me try. First, the individual must attempt to develop an attitude of "observant participation," that is, a frame of mind that permits and encourages a constant analysis and interpretation of interpersonal experiences. People simply do not learn from experience alone; it is experience observed, processed, analyzed, interpreted, and verified that we learn from. This constant scrutiny of one's own and others' behavior causes some stiltedness at first and may interfere with spontaneity, but gaining any new skill causes this initial uneasiness.

This constant review and reflection is difficult, for it asks the individual to consider data that may be not only "new" (that is, unnoticed until now) but also contradictory to the way the person ordinarily likes to see himself or herself. Socrates once said that "the unexamined life isn't worth living." Modern psychiatry would tell him that the examined life is no fun either.

In any case, learning is simply not possible without continual surveillance and appraisal. And this examination is not possible without the possibility of gaining validating (or disconfirming) data from one's personal environment.

How these competencies are developed; how individuals learn "empathy," or learn to "identify" or learn to listen and perceive more realistically; how individuals learn to make connections, to induce trust, to permit other people to understand them and vice-versa, to develop an observant-participating orientation; how human beings can become more sensitive: these are all questions that deserve better answers than we now have.

We are, all of us, in the dark about these matters. This essay, alas, also fails to do more than scratch the surface. Learning about interpersonal relations by *reading* about them is almost a contradiction of terms. One learns by doing and examining. But even this last sentence is hollow for this is hard work.